God in Paul's Letters

God in Paul's Letters

Edited by
Timothy Milinovich, Normand Bonneau,
and Robert F. O'Toole

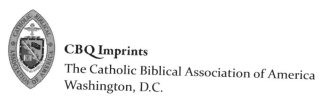

CBQ Imprints
The Catholic Biblical Association of America
Washington, D.C.

CASCADE *Books* • Eugene, Oregon

GOD IN PAUL'S LETTERS

Pickwick Publications
An Imprint of Wipf and Stock Publishers
199 W. 8th Ave., Suite 3
Eugene, OR 97401

www.wipfandstock.com

PAPERBACK ISBN: 978-1-6667-8128-1
HARDCOVER ISBN: 978-1-6667-8129-8
EBOOK ISBN: 978-1-6667-8130-4

Library of Congress Cataloging-in-Publication Data

Names: Milinovich, Timothy, editor. | Bonneau, Normand, 1948- editor. | O'Toole, Robert F., editor.
Title: God in Paul's letters / edited by Timothy Milinovich, Normand Bonneau, and Robert F. O'Toole.
Description: Washington, D.C. : The Catholic Biblical Association of America, [2023] | Series: Catholic Biblical quarterly imprints ; no. 4 | Includes bibliographical references and index. | Summary: "While the figure of Christ or the church have been mainstays in Pauline studies, the topic of God's characteristics and how God operates and oversees the narrative of salvation remains underappreciated. This book engages the question of God in Paul's letters in two ways: first, in seven chapters that cover God's actions and portrayal in each of the undisputed letters of Paul; and second, in three studies that cover topics regarding the gentiles, new creation, and the knowledge of God across multiple letters"—Provided by publisher.
Identifiers: LCCN 2023013620 | ISBN 9780915170623 (paperback) | ISBN 9780915170630 (ebook)
Subjects: LCSH: Bible. Epistles of Paul—Criticism, interpretation, etc. | God (Christianity)—Attributes. | Paul, the Apostle, Saint.
Classification: LCC BS2650.52 .G63 2023 | DDC 227/.06—dc23/eng/20230522
LC record available at https://lccn.loc.gov/2023013620

In Memory of
THOMAS D. STEGMAN, S.J.
In gratitude for his scholarship and
faithful witness to the gospel

Contents

Abbreviations

AB	Anchor Bible
AnBib	Analecta Biblica
AYB	Anchor Yale Bible
BECNT	Baker Exegetical Commentary on the New Testament
BETL	Bibliotheca Ephemeridum Theologicarum Lovaniensium
Bib	*Biblica*
BNTC	Black's New Testament Commentaries
BSCBAA	Biblical Studies from the Catholic Biblical Association of America
BTB	*Biblical Theology Bulletin*
BZNW	Beihefte zur Zeitschrift für die neutestamentliche Wissenschaft
CBQ	*Catholic Biblical Quarterly*
CBQMS	Catholic Biblical Quarterly Monograph Series
CurBR	*Currents in Biblical Research*
DPL	*Dictionary of Paul and His Letters* (ed. Gerald F. Hawthorne, Ralph P. Martin, and Daniel G. Reid; Black Dictionaries on the Bible; Downers Grove, IL: InterVarsity, 1993).
DSS	Dead Sea Scrolls
EKKNT	Evangelisch-katholischer Kommentar zum Neuen Testament
GNT⁵	*The Greek New Testament* (5th rev. ed.; ed. Barbara Aland et al.; Stuttgart: Deutsche Bibelgesellschaft, 2014).
HNTC	Harper's New Testament Commentaries
HTS	Harvard Theological Studies
ICC	International Critical Commentary
JBL	*Journal of Biblical Literature*
JMT	*Journal of Moral Theology*
JSNT	*Journal for the Study of the New Testament*
JSNTSup	Journal for the Study of the New Testament: Supplement Series
LNTS	Library of New Testament Studies
LXX	Septuagint
MNTC	Moffatt New Testament Commentary
MT	Masoretic Text

NABRE	New American Bible Revised Edition (2013)
NCB	New Century Bible
NCBC	New Cambridge Bible Commentary
NEB	New English Bible
NET	New English Translation
NICNT	New International Commentary on the New Testament
NIGTC	New International Greek Testament Commentary
NIV	New International Version
NJB	New Jerusalem Bible
NRSV	New Revised Standard Version
NT	New Testament
NTL	New Testament Library
NTS	*New Testament Studies*
OT	Old Testament
RB	*Revue Biblique*
ResQ	*Restoration Quarterly*
SacPag	Sacra Pagina
SBL	Society of Biblical Literature
SJT	*Scottish Journal of Theology*
SNTSMS	Society for New Testament Studies Monograph Series
TANZ	Texte und Arbeiten zum neutestamentlichen Zeitalter
TDNT	*Theological Dictionary of the New Testament* (ed. Gerhard Kittel and Gerhard Friedrich; trans. Geoffrey W. Bromiley; 10 vols.; Grand Rapids: Eerdmans, 1964–1976)
TS	*Theological Studies*
WBC	Word Biblical Commentary
WUNT	Wissenschaftliche Untersuchungen zum Neuen Testament

Ancient Manuscripts and Writings

D[2]	Western (D) tradition, second corrector, ca. ninth century
M [sy[p], sa[mss]]	M = Majority text; sy[p] = Peshitta; sa[mss] signals that two or more witnesses from Sahidic MSS support a particular reading
Ψ 044	New Testament Uncial Athous Lavrensis, ca. ninth–tenth century

Cicero	
De or.	*De oratore*
Part. or.	*Partitiones oratoriae*
Quintilian	
Inst.	*Institutio oratoria*

Contributors

AYODELE AYENI, C.S.SP.
Visiting Lecturer
Newman Theological College
Edmonton, Alberta, Canada

MARY T. BRIEN
Sacred Scripture Department, TRS
Mary Immaculate College
University of Limerick
Limerick, Ireland

NORMAND BONNEAU, OMI
Retired Professor of New Testament Studies
St. Paul University
Ottawa, Ontario, Canada

JOHN GILLMAN
Lecturer in Religious Studies
San Diego State University
San Diego, California

MARK J. GOODWIN
Associate Professor of Theology
University of Dallas
Irving, Texas

NAJEEB T. HADDAD
Chair and Assistant Professor of Religious Studies
Notre Dame of Maryland University
Baltimore, Maryland

ELLIOTT C. MALONEY, OSB
Professor of New Testament Studies and Biblical Languages
Saint Vincent Seminary
Latrobe, Pennsylvania

FRANK J. MATERA
Professor Emeritus of Biblical Studies
Catholic University of America
Washington, D.C.

TIMOTHY MILINOVICH
Associate Professor of Theology
Dominican University
River Forest, Illinois

FERDINAND OKORIE
Assistant Professor of New Testament
Catholic Theological Union
Chicago, Illinois

ROBERT F. O'TOOLE
Rev. Prof. (Emeritus) Biblical Faculty
Pontifical Biblical Institute
Rome, Italy
Assistant to the Division, Office of Admissions
St. Louis University
St. Louis, Missouri

MARIA PASCUZZI, CSJ
Sisters of Saint Joseph
Brentwood, New York

RONALD D. WITHERUP, P.S.S.
Superior General of the Priests of Saint Sulpice
Sulpician Generalate
Paris, France

Introduction: The Centrality of God in Paul's Thought

FRANK J. MATERA

The centrality of God for New Testament theology ought to be self-evident. It is God, after all, who creates, redeems, and sanctifies. It is God who is the beginning and the end of all things. It is God who orders the economy of salvation. And yet, the centrality of God for New Testament theology is sometimes overlooked.

Old Testament theology is less prone to overlooking the centrality of God since God (*Yhwh*) plays such an overt role in the drama of Israel's creation and election. God speaks to Abraham, Isaac, and Jacob. God gives Israel the gift of the law in a powerful theophany at Sinai, conversing with Moses and then with the prophets. In the New Testament, however, apart from a few episodes such as the baptism and transfiguration of Jesus, God seems to withdraw from the scene, giving the impression of inactivity. Instead, we hear the voice of Jesus, who reveals what he has heard in God's presence. Consequently, whereas topics such as christology, soteriology, ecclesiology, ethics, and eschatology are front and center in most theologies of the New Testament, the subject of God is often in the background.

In the subfield of Pauline theology, however, the subject of God has begun to play a more central role. For example, James D. G. Dunn begins his theology of Paul with a chapter devoted to God and humankind. He writes, "A systematic study of Paul's theology has to begin with his belief in God." The reason for this is that "God is the fundamental presupposition of Paul's theology, the starting point of his theologizing, the primary subtext of all his writing."[1] Consequently, even though Paul does not

---

1. James D. G. Dunn, *The Theology of Paul the Apostle* (Grand Rapids: Eerdmans, 1998) 28.

explicitly develop a theology of God in the same way that he lays out his teaching on justification by faith, his understanding of God is the presupposition for all that has happened in Christ.

Udo Schnelle makes a similar statement in his Pauline theology. Like Dunn, he dedicates a specific chapter to God. He writes, "The reality of God is the axiom of all Pauline theology, the all-determining point beyond which one cannot think or inquire, the point of departure for its all-encompassing world view."[2] He goes on to note, "At the same time, Christology effects a basic change in Paul's *theology*, for Paul proclaims a christological monotheism."[3]

The Pauline theologies of Thomas R. Schreiner and N. T. Wright take a different tack. Whereas Dunn and Schnelle dedicate specific chapters to Paul's understanding of God and then proceed to treat traditional topics such as anthropology, christology, soteriology, ecclesiology, and ethics, Schreiner and Wright develop the implications of Paul's thought about God throughout their works. Schreiner, for example, seeks to show how every aspect of Paul's theology (his proclamation of the gospel, his mission, his suffering, the law, the person of Jesus Christ, God's saving righteousness, ethics, the church) draws attention to God's glory in Christ. He affirms, "The passion of Paul's life, the foundation and capstone of his vision, and the animating motive of his mission was *the supremacy of God in and through the Lord Jesus Christ*."[4]

The centrality of God is also front and center in N. T. Wright's theology of Paul. He writes, "The central claim of this chapter, and in a measure of this whole book, is that Paul clearly, solidly, skillfully, and dramatically reworked exactly this 'monotheism' around Jesus the Messiah and also around the spirit."[5] Thus, while Paul reaffirmed Jewish monotheism, he also revised it in the light of his understanding of Jesus and the Spirit by which the one God of Israel was made known afresh. I have concluded my own Pauline theology with an extensive chapter on God as revealed in all the canonical Pauline letters, concluding that God is known in the saving grace of Jesus Christ.[6]

2. Udo Schnelle, *Apostle Paul: His Life and Theology* (trans. M. Eugene Boring; Grand Rapids: Baker Academic, 2003) 392.

3. Ibid., 392–93.

4. Thomas R. Schreiner, *Paul, Apostle of God's Glory: A Pauline Theology* (Downers Grove, IL: InterVarsity, 2001) 35 (emphasis added).

5. N. T. Wright, *Paul and the Faithfulness of God* (Christian Origins and the Question of God 4; Minneapolis: Fortress, 2013) 634.

6. Frank J. Matera, *God's Saving Grace: A Pauline Theology* (Grand Rapids: Eerdmans, 2012) 215–49.

The essays in this volume build on this renewed interest in Paul's understanding of God in contemporary Pauline studies. Their origin goes back to a CBA Continuing Seminar on Paul that Normand Bonneau organized several years ago, and that Robert O'Toole and Thomas Stegman later chaired. In the early years of that seminar, participants discussed a wide range of Pauline issues. But as the seminar developed it became apparent there was need for a more defined topic. The topic that emerged was Paul's understanding of God. Accordingly, the CBA Pauline Seminar became a CBA Task Force, co-chaired by Timothy Milinovich and Robert O'Toole, whose members committed themselves to investigating Paul's understanding of God.

The decision to study what Paul says about God makes eminent sense, since Paul's theology begins and ends with God. On the one hand, it begins with God whose Son was revealed to Paul (Gal 1:15–16), thereby transforming his understanding of how God was at work in the history of Israel and the gentiles. On the other hand, God's self-revelation in Christ taught Paul that the goal of God's salvific plan, inaugurated with the election of Israel, is the restoration of all things in Christ so that God will be all in all (1 Cor 15:25–28).

But how should we approach Paul's understanding of God given the contingent nature of his letters and his preoccupation with the diverse topics raised by the communities to whom he wrote? Rudolf Bultmann, in his magisterial *Theology of the New Testament*, broached the subject in this way. Noting that Pauline theology is not a speculative system, he wrote, "It deals with God not as He is in Himself but only with God as He is significant for man, for man's responsibility and man's salvation. . . . Every assertion about God is simultaneously an assertion about man and vice versa. For this reason and in this sense, Paul's theology is, at the same time, anthropology."[7]

While I agree with Bultmann that Paul was not a speculative theologian, I am not so confident about the correlation Bultmann establishes between theology and anthropology. My reading of Paul and the essays in this volume suggest that the better correlation is between Paul's theology and his christology. Accordingly, I would amend Bultmann's insight in this way: *Every assertion about Christ is simultaneously an assertion about God, and vice versa.* Paul's theology is his christology, and his christology is his theology; for what he affirms about God is intimately related to

---

7. Rudolf Bultmann, *Theology of the New Testament* (2 vols.; New York: Charles Scribner's Sons, 1951, 1955; repr., Waco, TX: Baylor University Press, 2007) 1:190–91.

what he believes about Christ, and what he believes about Christ is at the root of his understanding of God.

By affirming that christology and theology are intimately related to each other in Pauline thought, I am not suggesting that Paul, a convinced monotheist, broke with his former understanding of God in Judaism. Paul the apostle of Jesus Christ was and remained Paul the Jew. The words that Luke attributes to Paul when he defends himself before the Roman governor Felix are apropos: "I worship the God of our ancestors and I believe everything that is in accordance with the law and written in the prophets. I have the same hope in God as they themselves have that there will be a resurrection of the righteous and the unrighteous" (Acts 24:14–15). Paul the Christian continued to believe in the God of Abraham, Isaac, and Jacob. His new faith did not mean the end of his faith in the God who was revealed to Abraham, Moses, and the prophets. One thing, however, had changed, and it was this that made all the difference. Paul the Pharisee believed that the long-awaited resurrection of the dead had begun in one man, Jesus the Christ, God's Son.

Because the end-time had begun in the resurrection of God's Son, there was both continuity and disruption in Paul's understanding of God. God remained the same; God did not change. God did not make a midpoint correction in the economy of salvation. But Paul did change; he had to change. He came to a new understanding of how God had acted in Christ and was now acting in Israel's history. Thus, Paul's understanding of the law and its place in the economy of salvation altered as he grew in his knowledge of how the God of Abraham and Moses was revealed in the death and resurrection of Jesus Christ.

The authors of these essays are deeply aware of the issues and challenges outlined above. They understand the centrality of God in Paul's thought and the need to affirm the preeminent role of God in his theology for our generation, lest Pauline studies overlook the One without whom all else falls into nothingness. But how should the topic be approached, and what can we expect from such an investigation given the contingent nature of Paul's correspondence? Should the project proceed letter by letter, in the order in which they were written, with a grand synthesis at the end? Or should we look at the entire Pauline corpus and try to bring it into some kind of synthesis? The manner in which this volume is structured reveals this tension.

On the one hand, there are seven essays that deal with the seven undisputed Pauline letters arranged as they appear in the canon, each essay seeking to explore Paul's understanding of God in a particular letter. In addition to these essays, there are three others that investigate certain aspects of Paul's thought that occur throughout his letters, thereby highlighting the overall unity of his theology of God. What can we say about these two approaches?

Every investigation needs to begin with data. Rather than impose a theology of God on Paul, exegetes must sift through the data of his letters and learn what he says or supposes about God. While it is important to study those texts where Paul speaks explicitly about God, it is crucial not to overlook those where his understanding of God determines what he means, even if he does not explicitly mention God. For example, God remains the subject of Paul's thought when he speaks about the church or the moral life of believers, even when there is no explicit mention of God. Paul is just as likely, then, to speak about God when he does not mention God as he is when he explicitly names God.

But this is not the end of the task. After exegetes have sifted through the material, they must draw up a preliminary synthesis that states what a particular writing says about God. As they do this, they must keep in mind what occasioned the letter and how that situation impinged on what Paul writes. For example, Paul's discussion about God in the opening chapters of Romans is different from his discussion of God in the opening chapters of 1 Corinthians because he is addressing different issues in both letters. Whereas in 1 Corinthians he must show how God's power and wisdom are revealed in the weakness and folly of the cross, in Romans he shows how God's power is revealed in the saving righteousness of the gospel.

Once the work of sifting through the data is completed, there remains the daunting task of finding how it coheres. I have purposely chosen the verb "cohere" rather than "synthesize" to describe this task. For while it may be tempting to synthesize the data into a system, the resulting synthesis is apt to be artificial, imposed upon the material rather than drawn out of it. Given the contingent nature of Paul's writings, a better approach would be to ask how the material in Paul's letters coheres; that is, how are the different facets of his theology related to each other? For example, how does Paul's theology of *God who elects*, which is developed in 1 Thessalonians, cohere with his theology of *God who justifies*, which is the subject of Galatians and Romans? How does his theology of *God manifested in weakness*, as found in the Corinthian letters cohere with his theology of *God whose wrath is revealed*, as developed in Romans? The challenge is to determine how these various aspects of Paul's theology about God cohere and are related to each other.

While this volume deals with the Pauline letters whose authorship is not disputed there remain other letters that claim to be from Paul but whose authorship is contested (Colossians, Ephesians, 2 Thessalonians, 1 and 2 Timothy, and Titus). And even if they were written by others in Paul's name (as many contemporary scholars argue), they claim Paul as their author. That being the case, it would be surprising if their theology of God did not, in some sense, "cohere" with the theology of the one whose name they appropriate.

Given the centrality of God as revealed in Jesus Christ in Paul's thought, it is crucial that we do not overlook Paul's understanding of God. That is why these essays are so important. They remind us why we still read and study Paul's letters centuries after his death. But as significant as these essays are, they have not and cannot say the final word about the One who is hidden and beyond human understanding, and they leave many contemporary hermeneutical questions unresolved. For example, how should we speak about God today? What do we mean when we address God as Father? What do we understand when we say that God is All-Powerful? These are the kinds of questions that arise when we become more sensitive to the power of language and the abuse of power. Since this is a descriptive work of exegesis, hermeneutical questions such as these are generally not the focal point of these essays. Nevertheless, inasmuch as they present a clear and reliable description of Paul's understanding of God as revealed in Jesus Christ, the essays provide us with a good starting point to address these and other hermeneutical issues.

■ INTRODUCING THE ESSAYS OF THIS VOLUME

Romans is not a theological tract, but it is Paul's most complete statement of the gospel he preaches. To get at Paul's understanding of God, TIMOTHY MILINOVICH teases out the implied story of God that Paul presupposes in this letter. The story begins before creation with God's election of the justified in Christ, and it unfolds in God's dealings with Moses, Abraham, Israel, and the Christian community. In the light of this narrative, Milinovich identifies four traits of God as revealed in Romans' story of God: God's love, God's sovereignty, God's justice, and God's faithfulness. By approaching Romans in this way, Milinovich presents Paul as an evangelist called to tell the story of God, which is the framework for his proclamation of the gospel. This use of narrative criticism reminds us that our understanding of God is rooted in the story of God's dealings with Israel that finds its culmination in the Christ.

Whereas Romans has the appearance of being a theological essay, 1 Corinthians deals with a series of problems within the Corinthian community. In Paul's response to these issues, MARIA PASCUZZI finds an entrée to his understanding of God. She argues that, although the Corinthians have been told how God is revealed in Jesus Christ, they have misconstrued what it means to profess, belong, and glorify the God and Father of Jesus Christ. The manner in which Paul answers the problems he encounters at Corinth manifests a theocentric perspective that is radicalized by the cross and so refines the meaning of God's power and wisdom for humanity. God no longer acts in history apart from Christ, and yet the centrality of Christ in Paul's writings does not impinge on God's sovereignty; for it is God who calls into being the new community in Christ. God remains sovereign over humanity, and the sovereignty of God is the point of reference for Paul's ethical teaching. While Paul presents Christ as God's unique agent in creation and redemption, then, he does not exalt him at the expense of God's sovereignty.

In his essay on 2 Corinthians, JOHN GILLMAN notes that, whereas there are more references to Christ than there are to God in 1 Corinthians, in 2 Corinthians there are more references to God than to Christ. Gillman argues that these references are part of Paul's rhetorical strategy to bolster his credibility to a community that has called his ministry into question, for they highlight how God has acted in Paul's life and the life of the Corinthian community. In the opening chapters of 2 Corinthians, God emerges as the central figure who comforts, consoles, and empowers Paul and the community, and raises the dead. These and other activities reveal God as gracious in reconciling the community and the world to God. To defend his ministry to the Corinthians, therefore, Paul argues that, through Christ, *God* is at work in his ministry. Thus, it is Paul's ministry of reconciliation that leads to a fuller understanding of God in 2 Corinthians.

RONALD D. WITHERUP notes that commentaries on Galatians rarely address the topic of God, and yet God is the primary actor who lies behind the events described in Galatians. It is God who elects and calls Abraham, Paul, and the Galatians. It is God who calls and elects people for salvation because of the promises made to Abraham and his posterity. God fulfills these promises by freely and graciously justifying sinners. Paul's teaching on justification by faith, which is the truth of the gospel he preaches, reveals God as the God of Truth who calls the elect into freedom. Two other themes emerge from Witherup's reading of Galatians: the God of Judgment whose justifying grace calls people to live in a new way, and the God of Mercy, the Father of Jesus Christ, who calls people into an intimate relationship that makes them God's dear, adopted children. The portrait of God that Witherup paints is the outcome of a close reading of Galatians that gives attention to the letter's underlying narrative of God who chooses, elects, justifies, and judges in order to extend compassion and mercy.

Whereas the Christ Hymn of Philippians invites commentators to focus on the high christology of this letter, AYODELE AYENI and TIMOTHY MILINOVICH direct their attention to how the Philippians came to know and worship the God of Israel whom Paul proclaimed in Jesus Christ, and how their faith in the God and Father of Jesus Christ reoriented the ethical and worship dimensions of their life. To accomplish this, they present an overview of how this letter portrays the work of God, giving special attention to the worship and glory of God. They note that it is God who, at a specific moment in history, began a good work in the Philippians through the preaching of the gospel that made them children of God whom they now call their Father. As a result of the good work God began in them, the Philippians have been drawn into a community in which they know and worship the God of peace who is sovereign over the entire cosmos. By focusing on the central role God plays in Philippians, Ayeni and Milinovich confirm what other authors of this volume emphasize, namely, that although Paul affirms that God is known through Jesus Christ, God's sovereignty is never endangered by Paul's understanding of Jesus Christ.

Whereas most Pauline interpreters highlight the central role that being "in Christ" plays in Paul's understanding of Christ, MARK J. GOODWIN explores how participation "in God" enriches our understanding of God. Focusing on the opening verse of 1 Thessalonians, which speaks of the Thessalonians being "in God the Father and the Lord Jesus Christ" (1 Thess 1:1), he argues that Paul's use of "in Christ" in a participatory way suggests that "in God" also has a participatory meaning in this verse. Being "in God" highlights the new relationship to God that the Thessalonians have experienced through their participation in Christ, their faith in the word of the gospel, and the presence of the Spirit in their lives, all of which results in an experience of the living God, the Father of Jesus Christ, as their Father as well. The Pauline understanding of God that emerges from this essay is not so much a description of God as an account of how God is experienced through faith in Christ and the power of the Spirit.

Philemon might seem an unlikely place to uncover what Paul teaches about God. The essay of FERDINAND OKORIE, however, shows that, as brief as this letter is, it shares in and reveals Paul's fundamental insight about God: that God is renewing the world and social relations in Christ. Okorie maintains that Paul's plea for Philemon to receive Onesimus is best read in the wider context of what God is doing in the world in Christ. This understanding of God, as shown in Philemon, is all-embracing. It proclaims that God has begun a process of renewal in Christ that touches every household and human relationship because, in Christ, God is intimately involved in the human condition.

In his attempt to find a point of unity in the many ways that Paul speaks of God, NAJEEB T. HADDAD draws attention to the theme of new creation that plays a prominent role in Galatians, 2 Corinthians, and Romans. Paul explicitly refers to God's "new creation" in Gal 6:15 and 2 Cor 5:17, and he presupposes it in Romans 8 when he speaks of the promised renewal of not only humanity but the whole of God's creation. While the new creation comes into being through the death and resurrection of Christ, its theocentric dimension can sometimes be overlooked. For, while God reconciles humanity in Christ, God remains the primary agent in the unfolding drama of the new creation brought about by Christ's death and resurrection. Given its breadth and scope, Paul's understanding of God, who brings about the new creation in Christ, is a unifying theme.

Although MARY T. BRIEN'S essay focuses on Romans, it examines a theme that unifies Paul's understanding of God, namely, that "the gospel of God" that Paul preaches is *God's* good news for all people, for Jews and gentiles alike. To support her claim, Brien focuses on five rhetorical questions that point to the universality of the gospel of God: (1) Are Jews any better off than gentiles; is there an advantage to circumcision? (2) Will the infidelity of some negate God's fidelity to Israel? (3) Is "God" the God only of the Jews? (4) Has God failed to keep the promises made to Israel? (5) Has God rejected the people of Israel? The manner in which Paul responds to these questions reveals that God is One and therefore wants all to be saved, gentile as well as Jew. God's promises have not failed, and God has not been unfaithful. The all-embracing plan of God announced in "the gospel of God" that Paul proclaims is unfolding and will include all. Like other essays of this volume, which also highlight the sovereignty of God, this essay reminds us that God is the author and origin of all that has happened in Christ.

ELLIOTT C. MALONEY addresses the question that must be asked by any interpreter who seeks the Pauline understanding of God: How do we know God? Drawing on texts from several of Paul's letters, Maloney argues what other essays of this volume affirm, that, for those who are in Christ, knowledge of Christ is the epistemological key to knowing God. To be sure God is revealed in creation and the law as Paul notes in Romans, but the power of sin prevented humanity from acting according to this knowledge. Therefore, God chose to reveal divine wisdom and power in the weakness and folly of the cross. Maloney concludes, "Paul completes the process of revelation with the circle of true knowledge of God coming through creation, made explicit in the Law, but responded to and acted out in the daily lives of those who unite themselves to God in imitation of the cross of Christ, empowered by the Spirit." Maloney's epistemological study provides readers with an insightful way to unify Paul's theology of God.

While readers of this volume will draw their own conclusions about Paul's understanding of God, I highlight three. First, God is known in and though the cross and resurrection of Jesus Christ and the power of the Spirit. Second, although God is known through Christ, God remains sovereign, the Lord of history and creation, whose gift of salvation in Christ is universal and ongoing. Third, by being known, called, elected, and loved by God, believers come to know the God whom they cannot know apart from the Son and the Spirit of God.

1

The Story of God in Romans

TIMOTHY MILINOVICH

■ INTRODUCTION

The matter of God's activity or characteristics in the Letter to the
Romans remains largely unaddressed in critical study. This seems
paradoxical since God (θεός) occurs over 120 times in Romans and is
regularly the main subject in the text. In addition, there are roughly 150
more instances where God is the active entity but is referred to with pro-
nouns or other titles (e.g., "Lord") or is implied by use of the divine passive, bringing the total references to θεός to around 270. Even in a letter
of considerable length at 429 verses, it is clear that God is a major player
in the text's line of argument. It is likely, as James D. G. Dunn has noted,
that God's omnipresence in Paul's narrative thought world contributes to
this disproportion.[1]

While there are a variety of ways by which one could critically assess
God's role in the letter, in this chapter I will use a narrative-critical
approach to reconstruct God's activity and character traits and to explore
how the narrative thought world that Paul crafts for his addressees coor-
dinates with the letter's persuasive aims and rhetorical construction.[2]

1. James D. G. Dunn, *Theology of Paul the Apostle* (Grand Rapids: Eerdmans,
1998) 21.

2. For an excellent narrative reading of Romans, see A. Katherine Grieb, who
engages each section as a separate smaller story within the larger arc of God's plan to
save Israel and the gentiles (*The Story of Romans: A Narrative Defense of God's Righteousness* [Louisville: Westminster John Knox, 2003]). On narrative readings of Paul's

11

That is, while Paul addresses key topics in a systematic or topical approach in the letter, I will attempt to place God in the center of the stage upon which Paul unfolds the cosmic drama of those in Christ and to consider the εὐαγγέλιον τοῦ θεοῦ ("good news of God") that Paul proclaims not just as God's message but as the story about God, and God's people, as well. This "story" about God—how God fulfills the plan to redeem and save those who are in Christ—is the narrative thought world that influences how the implied audience receives the letter's argument as it is performed.

The Community in Rome

The situation and identity (ethnic and/or religious) of the addressees remains a debated point.[3] The target audience was composed of Jewish Christians, gentile Christians, and gentile proselytes or God-fearers who have had a deep connection with the Jesus movement and teaching that originated in Jerusalem.[4] There is, therefore, a firm grounding in the richness of the traditions and observance of Judaism.

Paul's reasons for writing to the Romans were likely multivalent: to defend himself against harsh criticism; to prepare for a future trip to Spain via Rome; to present his gospel in his own terms; to offer his own (pastoral) advice for their current challenges, albeit without wishing to presume authority over them; and to lay groundwork to evangelize in Rome as well.[5] It is very possible that Paul's challenges in Galatia required one or both of the following: a direct response to criticisms of his approach to the law in that letter; and/or a community of his own in Rome to affirm his credentials as the "apostle to the gentiles."

The exact nature of the addressees' situation is just as complicated as their identity and was likely impacted by a number of factors. House

---

letters, see also Richard B. Hays, "Is Paul's Gospel Narratable?," *JSNT* 27 (2004) 217–39; and Grant R. Osborne, "Hermeneutics/Interpreting Paul," *DPL*, 495. See also Richard N. Longenecker, *The Epistle to the Romans: A Commentary on the Greek Text* (NIGTC; Grand Rapids: Eerdmans, 2016) 10.

3. On the complicated matter of ethnic identity, see Rafael Rodriguez, *If You Call Yourself a Jew: Reappraising Paul's Letter to the Romans* (Eugene, OR: Cascade, 2014) 7–11.

4. Raymond E. Brown and John P. Meier, *Antioch and Rome: New Testament Cradles of Catholic Christianity* (1983; repr., Mahwah, NJ: Paulist, 2004) 46–52; Joseph A. Fitzmyer, *Romans: A New Translation with Introduction and Commentary* (AB 33; New York: Doubleday, 1992) 32–36; Longenecker, *Epistle to the Romans*, 8–9. Rodriguez offers an intriguing alternative view that Paul's audience is primarily gentile-Christian (*If You Call Yourself a Jew*, 7–11).

5. Fitzmyer, *Romans*, 79–80; Longenecker, *Epistle to the Romans*, 9–14.

churches and the Jesus movement in synagogues could have begun anytime in the 40s C.E. The expulsion of Jews by Claudius from the city due to social disturbances over a "Chrestus" (Suetonius, *Claudius* 25), and their return after Claudius's death in 54, no doubt created tension between some Jewish Christians and gentile proselytes who favored a more traditional approach to the Jewish customs and new gentile converts.[6] Unbalanced portions of these groups in house churches could make gatherings and worship smolder with talking points and counterpoints to their fellow believers and likely intensified the conflict across the city's faithful.

Regardless of whether there was a substantial known problem in Rome, and whether Paul was aware of its details, the social environment at the time Paul wrote indicates a delicate intracommunity situation. Paul now needs to defend his apostleship without the presumption of authority over the audience and to demonstrate that his gospel is both an extension of the Jewish traditions he still holds dear and can be relevant in resolving present internal disputes in Rome. In addition, he must say what each of the three key demographics in the audience wishes to hear without overbalancing and favoring one group over another, so that they will evaluate him positively. It is, situationally speaking, one of his most daunting rhetorical challenges.

The Narrative

Our narrative reading will add to this sociorhetorical background the lens of an overarching thought world that unfolds through the argument of the letter. We can deduce four stages in Paul's general outline of God's story: (1) before creation; (2) from Adam to Moses; (3) from Israel to the advent of the Messiah; and (4) now, as the Spirit animates the churches in Rome as they await Christ's return.

This narrative is inherently dependent on and informed by the Jewish Scriptures. While Paul displays his knowledge of these texts in many of his letters, in Romans we find a peculiar opportunity in which Paul uses Scripture voluminously, likely to connect with his audience. Paul's view of God's activity and the world is singular: God has been intimately involved in human history, from creation to its end, and intervenes in extraordinary ways. Much of this view relies on Paul's rereading of God's activity as described in Jewish Scripture. Now, however, Paul tells anew for the diverse Roman audience the accounts of Adam, the patriarchal families,

---

6. Brendan Byrne, *Romans* (SacPag 6; 1996; repr., Collegeville, MN: Liturgical Press, 2007) 10–13; Robert Jewett, *Romans: A Commentary* (Hermeneia; Minneapolis: Fortress, 2007) 70–72.

Moses, the law, the prophets, and the life of Israel through the lens of God's extraordinary intervention through Christ. This story encompasses cosmic and human spheres of history, as well as the plan of salvation that supersedes the boundaries of time and space. The characters and stories remain static, but they are illuminated now by the light of Christ and the imminence of the resurrection. For example, whereas Adam initiated sin and condemnation that corrupted the world at creation, in Christ God has initiated new life and righteousness for those who believe. The story is still one that coheres with Jewish Scriptures and traditions, but now Paul looks backward, from the end of time to the beginning, to reinterpret these texts and traditions in a new light for the Jews, gentiles, and God-fearers who call on the name of Christ in Rome.[7]

■ PAUL'S GOSPEL OF GOD AS THE STORY OF GOD

Before Time

God's relationship with those in Christ began before creation. Whereas Genesis 1 relates that God made the heavens and the earth in the beginning, Paul begins the story with God foreknowing, predestining, and conforming those in Christ to the image of the Son prior to the creation of the world (Rom 8:28–30). Douglas A. Campbell notes that this small kernel of text sums up the totality of "God's great plan that lies at the heart of the cosmos."[8] This key point, not revealed until midway through the letter, sits as the foundation of the rest of the narrative thought world presented in Paul's argument.

This narrative factor recenters the totality of Paul's recounting of Scripture and circumvents challenges to gentile inclusion in Christ-believing communities that may have been occurring in Rome. The life of Israel, the law, and the role of the gentiles are tied not to genealogical rules of the world or human codes but to God's own will. To counter the readings of Scripture that might preclude gentiles in Roman communities, throughout the letter Paul will point to texts where the law and prophets have spoken of this plan. So while this plan has stood mainly outside of human

7. On how Paul's retelling of Old Testament Scripture is related to his new perspective on the world and salvation history through the lens of Christ, I follow Normand Bonneau, "Stages of Salvation History in Rom 1:16–3:26," *Église et Theologie* 23 (1992) 177–94.

8. Douglas A. Campbell, *Pauline Dogmatics: The Triumph of God's Love* (Grand Rapids: Eerdmans, 2020) 84.

perspective, it is revealed in the power of the gospel now for the Roman addressees, Jew and gentile alike.

From Adam to Moses: God's Relationship with Early Humanity

Paul does not recount the creation of the cosmos and of Adam in detail but instead focuses on the fall immediately after. Sin entered the world through Adam's transgression and reigned with death as a terminal dyad over humanity "from Adam to Moses" (5:12–14). Adam's transgression initiated a progression of humanity's saturation in sin and the corruption of all creation (5:18; 8:19–24).[9]

God permitted this degradation within a larger plan that would see opportunities for renewal, but until then humanity could not recognize God's divine sovereignty as Creator because their perception was warped by sin. Amplifying Adam's example, humanity entered a spiral of sinfulness in which they worshiped idols rather than God, with the result that God "handed them over" to their desires in an escalation of their evil behavior toward one another (1:20–28).[10] While Paul has in mind here all of humanity, the implied audience—Jew and gentile alike—would recognize their imperial environment's ideology of *religio* in this denunciation of improper worship.[11]

Yet humanity's Creator did not forget them. Paul recounts the traditions of Genesis 12–17 with a special emphasis on God crediting Abraham with righteousness because of his faith (even while he was still uncircumcised) and promising an inheritance for his heirs (4:2, 9–13). Because of Abraham's faith that God can bring life out of death, God appointed him as father of many nations and affirmed that his offspring may receive the promise the same way Abraham had—through the righteousness of faith, whether circumcised or not (4:13, 22–23).[12]

9. Frank J. Matera, *Romans* (Paideia; Grand Rapids: Baker Academic, 2010) 139.

10. Consistent with other Hebrew views of idolatry, humanity's misplacement of glory made them avatars of their sinful desires rather than reflecting the glorious image of their forgotten Creator (1:28–32). See Longenecker, *Epistle to the Romans*, 223–24; Douglas J. Moo, *The Epistle to the Romans* (NICNT; Grand Rapids: Eerdmans, 1996) 106–10.

11. On Roman religious concepts and deities, see Mark Reasoner, "Rome and Roman Christianity," *DPL*, 850–55; Valerie M. Warrior, *Roman Religion* (Cambridge Introduction to Roman Civilization; Cambridge: Cambridge University Press, 2006) 3–5; Clifford Ando, *The Matter of the Gods: Religion and the Roman Empire* (Transformation of the Classical Heritage 44; Berkeley: University of California Press, 2008) 128–38.

12. Thomas H. Tobin, *Paul's Rhetoric in Its Contexts: The Argument of Romans* (Peabody, MA: Hendrickson, 2004) 148.

Paul's retelling makes clear that it is God, not human generation, that determines the heir to the promise. God established that Isaac would be heir from among Sarah's children, and Jacob from among Rebekah's. This decision was God's own to show that those who are called in the future need not be selected by their deeds or lineage.[13] God ensures that God's own word remains definitive and resolute, even when some humans might fail or try to interfere (9:6–12).[14] Likewise, as with Pharaoh, God can raise up antagonists to set in relief God's own greatness for the whole world to see (9:17, 22).[15]

From Israel to the Messiah: Moses, the Law, and the Prophets

Although Paul continues to recount the pentateuchal traditions from the patriarchs to the exodus tradition, his narratives of Moses and of the law are not central to God's salvific plan. Instead, Paul's account focuses on what God has done to ensure that the promise to Abraham and those in Christ remains effective, essentially demoting the law and Moses to the status of subplots in a larger plan. The subtle manner in which Paul manages this shift demonstrates his awareness that, for gentile converts, neither dismissing the law as an antagonist (as he did in Galatians) nor keeping the law's stipulations is possible here; instead a narrow middle path is required.

Paul is careful to note that God informed Israel of the law's purpose at the time of its reception (Rom 10:19; Deut 32:21).[16] Moses wrote that those who do the law will live by it (Rom 10:4; Lev 18:5), but the message of faith was also announced in the law and is already "in your mouth and in your heart," so that one can believe and testify that Jesus is Lord and glorify God's sovereignty over the earth (Rom 10:8–9; Deut 30:14).[17]

Israel's status with God is clear and unassailable. It is through Israel's prophets and Scriptures that God first proclaimed the gospel (1:2) and

13. Byrne refers to this as "the 'Elective/Promise' pattern of God's action in the past" that has impact still on Paul's audience (*Romans*, 290).

14. James D. G. Dunn states that Paul makes this case in a way that his Jewish Christian audience would have readily accepted, since they did not see Ishmael or Esau as heirs of the promise, despite their lineage (*Romans 9–16* [WBC 38B; Waco, TX: Word, 1988] 547).

15. Thomas R. Schreiner, *Romans* (BECNT; Grand Rapids: Baker, 1998) 510–15.

16. Byrne, *Romans*, 325.

17. Jean-Noel Aletti, "Interpreting Rom 11:14: What Is at Stake?," in *Celebrating Paul: Festschrift in Honor of Jerome Murphy-O'Connor, O.P., and Joseph A. Fitzmyer, S.J.* (ed. Peter Spitaler; CBQMS 48; Washington, DC: Catholic Biblical Association, 2011) 245–64, here 264.

made Israel to be a living exemplar of God's glory and divinity to all other nations, with the result that the whole world is accountable to God's will in the law (3:19). The oracles and Scriptures, which God gave as an advantage to Israel (3:2), testify against humanity and validate God's just judgment. The salvation and wrath that Scripture offers to the penitent and the recalcitrant, respectively, are the same message Paul now proclaims anew as God's gospel (1:18; 2:6–10; 3:6, 9–10).[18] In this way Paul is able to negotiate his gospel so as not to contradict the values of his addressees, who retain an appreciation of Jewish traditions and interpretations of Scripture.

Yet, Paul reminds the audience, Israel's relationship with the law was complicated, even when the people's group identity was concretized under a monarchy. In that time God continued to express through the prophets the law's message of faith, but with a new emphasis that others would be hardened. David, a progenitor of the messianic line (and a prophet, in Paul's view), pronounced this promise (1:4–7) and righteousness by faith in Abraham's example (Rom 4:6–8; cf. Ps 32:1–2). Isaiah joins David in proclaiming that God hardens the hearts of some in order that those who were called might be enlightened and might glorify God with their faith (Rom 11:7–13; Isa 29:10; Ps 69:22–23; also Deut 29:4).

Those who focus only on the letter of the law will stumble, but those who believe in the justice of the law can achieve its righteousness (9:33).[19] The result of this divine selection is that God will be found by a people who did not seek God, and will appear to them because God has intentionally and often reached out to an unbelieving people (10:20; see also 10:4, 12). Therefore, while God put some in Israel into a deep sleep so that they would not perceive God's glory fully (11:8), God proclaimed that a remnant of Israel and gentiles will be able to return to God in the future. The unloved will become beloved, those shown no mercy will be given mercy, and those who were not-my-people will be adopted as God's own children (9:25; 11:4).[20] The divine teleology dictates that, by causing some in Israel to stumble, God has brought the opportunity of salvation to the gentiles. By this logic, God's reclamation of Israel at the end-time will bring salvation and resurrection for all of creation (11:11–15; also 8:18–25).

18. C. E. B. Cranfield, *A Critical and Exegetical Commentary on the Epistle to the Romans* (2 vols.; ICC; New York: T&T Clark, 1975–1979) 1:146–52; Schreiner, *Romans*, 113–15.

19. John Paul Heil, "Christ, the Termination of the Law (Rom 9:30–10:8)," *CBQ* 63 (2001) 484–98, here 487–89.

20. Longenecker, *Epistle to the Romans*, 821–22, 859–60.

Now: God Sends Christ and the Spirit

In accordance with God's plan that was promised to Abraham and proclaimed in the law and the prophets, at the proper time God sent Christ
to redeem those in him and the Spirit to preserve them. Since the law,
which is holy, just, and noble (7:12), was unable to justify humanity under
sin's dominion (8:3–4), God manifested righteousness by setting the Son,
who had been indicated beforehand in the law and prophets, as an offering for all. The proclamation of this gospel to all makes possible the
forgiveness of sins previously committed and the redemption of those
justified (3:21–25).[21] In justifying the faithful by setting Christ as a sin
offering, God completes what the law could not do and condemns sin in
the flesh (3:25; 8:3).[22]

Christ's incarnation is revolutionary but also intricately tied to other
parts of God's plan. God sent Christ in the image of sinful flesh to coun-
teract Adam's transgression, which remained apparent in humanity's sinfulness, and to condemn sin in the flesh (5:12; 8:3). God sent the law to
increase the offenses that Adam's transgression initiated and to identify
many as sinners (5:20), but Christ's obedience to God's plan to offer him
up increased God's grace even further to address the law's condemnation
(5:15, 19).[23] Christ's incarnation also interfaces with God's promise to
Abraham regarding his heirs. Christ must be incarnate to die and be
resurrected so that God can credit with righteousness those who believe,
like Abraham, that God can raise the dead to new life (4:23–25).

In addition to humanity's initial representative, Christ also bears a
connection to Israel's emblematic king. God had the Son descend through
the Davidic line (according to the flesh) so that the root of Jesse may rule
over nations and the gentiles may hope in David, to whom God promised
an everlasting kingdom (1:3; 15:12).[24] This narrative brings into alignment
how God directly fulfills promises made to Abraham, the patriarchs (15:8),
and David, and fulfills what was spoken through the law, the prophets,

---

21. Fitzmyer, *Romans*, 342. The alternative reading of "faithfulness of Christ" is
also viable: see Teresa Morgan, *Roman Faith and Christian Faith: Pistis and Fides in the
Early Roman Empire and Early Churches* (Oxford: Oxford University Press, 2015) 154–
58; Longenecker, *Epistle to the Romans*, 408–13.

22. Fitzmyer, *Romans*, 358–62, 400.

23. Felipe de Jesús Legarreta-Castillo, *The Figure of Adam in Romans 5 and 1 Corinthians 15: The New Creation and Its Ethical and Social Reconfiguration* (Emerging
Scholars; Minneapolis: Fortress, 2014) 156–65.

24. Longenecker, *Epistle to the Romans*, 65; Byrne, *Romans*, 432; Dunn, *Romans
9–16*, 853.

and the Scriptures to Israel and the world by offering up Christ to allow entrance of the gentiles into the worship community of Israel.

Christ's death is not the end of his story but the beginning of God's impact for the faithful, which continues when God raises Jesus from the dead and declares him God's Son in power through the Spirit (1:3–4). Now the process of baptism replicates God's dual activity in Christ for each believer in order that the faithful might walk in new life (6:5). Through the death and resurrection process actualized in baptism, God liberates the faithful who are under slavery of sin and, as their new master, grants them the gift of everlasting life (6:15, 23) so that they might work and bear fruit on God's behalf (7:4).[25]

The resurrection highlights how God also intervenes for those in Christ through the Spirit. God poured the Spirit and grace into the hearts of the faithful (5:5) to indwell and animate believers in their new life (6:5, 11–14).[26] Paul describes God's grace and the Spirit as liberating believers: by grace God delivered believers from the law in their members that wars against God's law in the mind (7:25); and by the law of the Spirit of life (an apophasis for God), God liberated humanity from sin and death (8:2).[27] God's indwelling Spirit holds multiple benefits for those who belong to Christ (8:9). In addition, it is by this Spirit that God raises them from the dead (8:11).[28] As Joel prophesied, the Spirit does not distinguish Jew from gentile or God-fearer but comes to all who call upon God's name and are therefore God's adopted children (Rom 8:14–15; 10:13; Joel 2:32).

Now, at the time that this letter is being read to the Roman churches, God's wrath is being revealed to all humanity because of their senseless abandonment of God and glorification of idols (1:18–19). The mercies God had shown humanity before in abiding their sins gave time for repentance and acknowledgment of God's sovereignty (2:1–5). Soon God will judge every person according to what they have done, including whether and how they accept God's sovereignty as Creator.

Those who stubbornly resist God's call to return will receive just judgment according to their works, as Scripture has made known (Ps 62:12; Prov 24:12). This judgment will show no partiality: Jew and gentile alike will suffer or succeed based on what they have done. The law itself will not be the only arbiter for this evaluation since the main require-

---

25. C. K. Barrett, *A Commentary on the Epistle to the Romans* (HNTC; New York: Harper & Row, 1957) 123.

26. Moo, *Epistle to the Romans*, 368–72.

27. Matera, *Romans*, 179–90.

28. Ibid., 196. See also Timothy Milinovich, "Once More, with Feeling: Romans 8,31–39 as Rhetorical *Peroratio*," *Bib* 99 (2018) 525–43, here 532–33.

ments of the law are written on the hearts of all people (Rom 2:14–16). Those who serve themselves, who deny the truth, and who do evil will find God's wrath and anger. But those who pursue God's glory and immortality by doing good (i.e., doing God's will) will receive life in the new age (2:6–11). Since sinfulness grows with idolatry, with the rejection of God's glory, and with lack of faithfulness (1:20–21), God's judging humans by their actions and justifying them by their faith are not contradictory.[29] God's love is freely given; but God's wrath must be earned.

■ THE CHARACTER OF GOD IN ROMANS

From this narrative account we can observe four characteristics of God that Paul demonstrates for his addressees: (1) God loves those who were called before time and space and moves cosmic events and human history to effect their salvation and keep the promise to glorify them. (2) God is One and, as sole Creator, is sovereign over all creation and humanity, so that there can be no distinction or favor of one people over another. (3) God is just and the final judge. And (4) God is faithful to the end.

God's Actions Driven by Love

God's actions in 8:28–30, motivated by love, initiated a chain of benefits for the beloved that precede material time and space. Those God foreknew—that is, knew relationally before creation—were conformed to the Son at that point, with the result that they might be called, justified, and glorified.[30] This relationship that God forms protects the faithful from spiritual, cosmic, or terrestrial forces inhibiting their relationship with God (8:36–39).

The prequel to Genesis in Rom 8:28–30 showed that the promise God made to Abraham is tied to God's love for the people before time and space, not circumcision, which Abraham took as a sign of righteousness. In the second stage of the plan, Abraham's faith confirms his righteousness before God, and the path he walks shows a way forward for the faithful who remain uncircumcised in Paul's time (4:9–12; cf. 2:28–29). By the precedent of the faith of the father of many nations, God's promise can be transmitted to those in Christ through faith-righteousness, not

---

29. Fitzmyer, *Romans*, 297–98.
30. Karl Barth identifies the love of God as the central point of 8:28–30 and the totality of the Christian faith (*The Epistle to the Romans* [trans. Edwin C. Hoskins; Oxford: Oxford University Press, 1968] 317–20; German original, 1919).

national or biological lineage (5:14–19).[31] And just as God's offering of Christ negated Adam's transgression, so too does God justify and raise those who believe in the one who raised Jesus—even the ungodly. Moses, David, other prophets, and even the law testified to Paul's gospel that those in Christ are not only those who are biologically Abraham's children, those who are circumcised, or those who follow the law; and those who will stand condemned by God are not only those who do not have the law. Instead, it is faith—knowing God as sovereign Creator and abiding faithfully with one's fellow creatures—that actualizes the plan God set in motion for those who love the Creator—the Creator who first loved, foreknew, and predestined them for glory.

God Is One and Sovereign over All Humanity and Creation

While the religious context in which Paul's audience lives recognizes many gods of varying personalities and degrees of divinity, Paul announces a story in which one God crafts a singular reality that, though corruptible, can be renewed by this God's singular sovereign will.[32] Rather than a cacophony of despotic deities utilizing humans as collateral in their own divine contests, Paul's story follows one God who creates and maintains a relationship with this creation to its completion. The singularity of God's purpose parallels the oneness of God's self. And although the audience's situation may seem chaotic, they can take comfort in that, just as they have one origin, they will have one destination—redemption and peace with God—and one pathway, through Christ, to get there.

The other axiom that flows from this concept is that God creates. As the active originator of all things seen and unseen, God is the only rightful receptor of glory and honor from living creatures (Rom 1:21–23). God's creative process in Paul's story implies, if not requires, three other characteristics: a benevolence to love and care for this creation; a will to ensure this creation's development and completion; and an innovativeness to re-create when new challenges arise. That God not only creates, but continues to re-create by forging new pathways forward for these creatures to attain redemption and glory, offering solace and encouragement for an audience inundated with new challenges.

Now, knowing that the time of judgment is at hand, Jewish and gentile believers alike can fulfill the whole law (i.e., God's will) by loving one another (Rom 13:8–14). In addition, they also fulfill God's plan in Christ—

---

31. Pheme Perkins, "Adam and Christ in the Pauline Epistles," in Spitaler, *Celebrating Paul*, 128–51, here 143.

32. Reasoner, "Rome and Roman Christianity," 850–55.

who became a servant for the Jews and a gateway for gentiles—in order for God to fulfill the promises made to the patriarchs (15:7–9), and that all peoples might glorify God the sovereign Creator (15:10–13).

God Is Just and the One Who Justifies

As creator and sovereign over creation, only God can define what is justice, who can be justified, and on what grounds. God demonstrates this justice not only in fulfilling the promises made, but also in the means by which this justification was made possible through Christ. God is the main actor behind and surrounding the incarnation. God's sending the Son in the likeness of sinful flesh is causally parallel to the initial action of conforming the faithful to the image of the Son, whose death then justifies them and makes possible their glorification.

Christ's death is effective for those who believe because of how God set out to fulfill the plan that began before time and space (8:28–30). At this time, division is revealed between those who are condemned for their sinfulness and lack of faith, and those who will receive glory, honor, and peace for having faithfully pursued the goodness that God revealed to them and to which God called them (2:7–10).[33] The lines are not drawn between Israel and non-Israel, because showing favoritism to a specific nation and judgment to others in an arbitrary manner would be unjust. Rather, God demonstrates total righteousness by judging all nations on how they have accepted and lived according to the spiritual and ethical knowledge that is now universally revealed (Rom 2:1; 3:9–10).

God Is Faithful to the End

Since the endpoint is as near as it is certain, even as they and creation groan during the birth pains of the liminal space, the faithful in Rome should take heart and anticipate the reification of their adoption in the redemption of their bodies (Rom 8:21–25). Since they have been justified by faith and now have peace with God through Christ, they should have no fear of condemnation (5:1–2; 8:1–4). Instead they can boast in the present sufferings, which build character and strengthen their hope that nothing can separate them from God's love (5:3–4; 8:27–30).

From before time to the end of time, God's purposeful promise to care for Abraham's heirs remains intact. God's resurrection of Christ prefig-

33. Sarah Whittle, "Jubilees and Romans 2:6–29: Circumcision, Law Observance, and Ethnicity," in *Reading Romans in Context: Paul and Second Temple Judaism* (ed. Ben C. Blackwell, John K. Goodrich, and Jason Maston; Grand Rapids: Zondervan, 2015) 46–51, here 49.

ures the glory and inheritance those in Christ will receive, and so they can have confidence that God will complete the plan that has played out on the stage of creation and find them returned to the Creator who first loved them, foreknew them, and called them to faith at this moment in God's own time.

■ THE STORY OF GOD WITHIN PAUL'S RHETORIC

The Correlation of God's Role in the Letter's Narrative Thought World and Rhetorical Structure

Paul constructs his arguments for the audience, mindful of the narrative lens through which they are to understand the presentation. Scholars have suggested various outlines for the letter, with several agreements or points of departure.[34] This chapter favors the rhetorical cues in the occurrences of *peroratio*s throughout the text for structuring the letter.[35] Between the introduction (Rom 1:1–17) and closing (16:1–25), the body

---

34. Various rhetorical structures have been offered for the letter, ranging from a topical/argument-based system (Tobin, *Paul's Rhetoric*, 10–13; Byrne, *Romans*, 9–13), to those that center on the specific characteristics of speech (Ben Witherington III, *Paul's Letter to the Romans: A Socio-Rhetorical Commentary* [Grand Rapids: Eerdmans, 2004] 21–22). The former system often does not take into account the techniques that were used to delimit oratorical performance, whereas the latter often rigidly applies the generic criteria without appreciation for variation or internal nuance. The system used here focuses on the specific rhetorical element of *peroratio*. This was used to conclude internal sections as well as the entire speech. It could be identified by specific generic criteria, including terminological repetition, recapitulation of key previous arguments, stylistic shift (rhetorical questions, incomplete sentences, poetic verse), emotive language, and a call to action or decision for the audience (*adfectus*). See Quintilian, *Inst.* 6.2.1–9; Cicero, *Part. or.* 15.52–55; 17.59; *De or.* 2.52.213–16; Witherington, *Paul's Letter to the Romans*, 17; Milinovich, "Once More, with Feeling," 525–30.

35. Based on the criteria described above, *peroratio*s can be discerned at several key turning points: Rom 1:29–32; 2:17–29; 3:21–31; 4:23–5:11; 7:7–24; 8:31–39; 10:5–21; 11:25–36; 13:8–14; 15:7–13 (concludes 14:1–15:6); 15:14–33 (concludes 12:1–15:6, and arguably the entire letter).

Several previous studies have investigated the presence and role of *peroratio*s in Romans and Paul's letters. See A. H. Snyman, "Style and the Rhetorical Situation of Romans 8:31–39," *NTS* 34 (1988) 218–31; Andrzej Gieniusz, *Romans 8:18–30: Suffering Does Not Thwart the Future Glory* (University of South Florida International Studies in Formative Christianity and Judaism 9; Atlanta: Scholars Press, 1999) 49–51; Jewett, *Romans*, 474; Andrew T. Lincoln, "'Stand Therefore': Ephesians 6:10–20 as Peroration," *BibInt* 3 (1985) 99–114.

of the letter can be divided into three large units. The first main unit (1:18–3:31) addresses the idolatry of gentiles and its consequent sinful behaviors (1:18–32), followed by an explanation of how Jews can still find the law problematic despite having God's favor and knowledge of God's will (2:1–29). This section concludes by asserting that all of humanity is sinful (3:1–20) and therefore requires Christ for salvation (3:21–31).

The central section (4:1–8:39) supports Paul's main thesis that those in Christ have a new relationship with God that is grounded in the law and the prophets by walking back through time with examples from Abraham (4:1–5:11), to Adam (5:12–7:25), to a point outside of time before creation (8:1–39). The third part of the letter (9:1–15:33) returns to the first section's topics of Jews and gentiles with a new focus and reorganization. Whereas 1:18–32 and 2:1–29 spoke of the gentiles' and Jews' respective relationships with God in the past and present, 9:1–11:35 and 12:1–13:13 will look to these groups' relationships with God in the new era (in reverse order), following God's intervention through Christ. The closing of the letter's body in 14:1–15:35 regarding all of humanity restates 3:1–31, but here also the emphasis is on how this new life in Christ is realized in the gathering of believers at worship—both Jew and gentile.

The *peroratio* of the central section (8:31–39) holds the beginning of the overall story and, therefore, acts as a turning point for the audience. It is at this point that the Roman audience is being called to recognize their relationship to God in Christ and the capacity to maintain that relationship in the Spirit in a way that confirms that no created entity—cosmic, earthly, or human—can separate them from the God who called them.

Paul walks the audience from the theological and cultural crises of their own time (1:18–3:31) back through the story of the world (8:28–30)—moving from Abraham, to Adam, to the time before creation. The organization of this narrative within the letter's argumentation emphasizes Paul's climactic point in 8:31–39: God has called from before time Jews and gentiles alike to be conformed to the image of the Son. Adam's fall could not derail this because of God's promise to Abraham (reinterpreted by Paul through the key point of 8:28–30) and Christ's salvific death.

While 1:1–3:31 and 4:1–8:39 move the audience through time from their present situation to before creation, 9:1–15:15 restates Israel's relationship with God and development in history from Moses to the time of the Roman Jewish and gentile Christians' table fellowship in the present day. In 9:1–10:13 Paul gives evidence from the law and the prophets how

God's relationship with Israel remains strong but is more complicated than it may appear on the surface. The citation of Joel 2:32 punches home the point that, while God is loyal to Israel, God will save all those who call on the Lord's name and believe. To Paul, the righteousness that comes through faith was made clear in the Deuteronomic texts that emphasize the faith in the heart (Rom 10:11). In this capacity, there is no distinction between Jew and gentile (10:14). This saving faith is achieved through receiving the message about Christ (10:16–18). These gentiles are like wild branches grafted onto an olive tree. They were once separate but now are made part of the whole and receive as much nourishment (i.e., grace) from the roots as the original branches (11:13–24).

It is in the mystery of Christ that Paul can glory in the riches of God's mercy that all of Israel will be saved (11:33–36). The ingrafted gentile branches can live according to the expectation of God's adopted heirs by sacrificing their bodies in a form of worship that is true and proper and therefore does not conform to the worldly *religio* customs of their Roman neighbors (1:18–32). Building up the community through one's gifts, living in love with all, and respecting appropriate civil authorities can fulfill the law for gentiles who are now God's adopted children (13:1–9). Just as the new branches can participate in this covenant through love, so too should the original and new branches live together without judging one another on matters of food and drink (14:19–23). As with emphasizing the oneness of God, Paul's instruction has the benefit of encouraging unity and patience among the communities without explicitly requesting it or choosing sides in the matter.

Paul as God's Authorized Storyteller

The story and the character of God that Paul conveys to the Roman Christians includes his mission. Whereas those in Christ were called by God to hear and believe the message, God called Paul to be an apostle and to proclaim the gospel to the nations (1:1, 14–15).[36] To this end, Paul now makes the story about what God has done in recalling the faithful from under the enslavement of sin and death and to new life in the Spirit and justification through Christ.

Paul makes sure to explain to his audience that this message is not of his own making, nor his own interpretation. God has already spoken it beforehand in the Scriptures—the law and the prophets. This account is not only for Jews who hold the Scriptures and already await the enthronement of David's descendant. God made Paul an apostle to call the faithful

---

36. Matera, *Romans*, 23.

from among the gentiles—many of whom number among his audience in Rome. By preaching the gospel about what God has done for them in Christ, Paul serves a priestly role before God for the faithful gentiles (15:14–22). It is in this priestly capacity that Paul intercedes on their behalf through prayer and now writes to tell them of their salvation and place in God's story—a story that is quickly coming to a close (1:7–8).

Paul is confident that the faithful in Rome are already filled with knowledge and goodness (15:14), and he has no interest in treading over other missionaries' territory (15:20–21), yet he writes now to remind them that God favored him to be an apostle of Christ Jesus to the gentiles. It is his duty to proclaim the story of God to the faithful scattered among the gentiles and to make them into an acceptable offering to God, sanctified by the Holy Spirit (15:15–16).[37] While the audience may have heard of Christ from other missionaries before, they had not received the full story of how they fit into God's plan until they heard it from Paul.

Paul will continue his role in God's story when he visits Rome soon to complete and confirm what he announces now in this letter. In Rome he will be able to share spiritually with those who already believe and gather new fruit from among the gentiles there who have not yet heard the message, before continuing on to Spain (15:27–29). Paul's own biographical sketch aligns with his account of God's story: just as the Roman audience can rest assured that God set this plan in motion to redeem and raise them in glory, so too can they rest in the hope that God has duly commissioned Paul to proclaim this message and continues to work through him to complete the promises to those in Christ.

■ CONCLUSION: THE GOSPEL OF GOD AS THE STORY OF GOD

A narrative reading of Paul's letter to the Romans benefits one's perception of its argument from the end-time looking back. Extending the reader's view to a point before time and space, one can see how God initiates the full chain of events, from pre-creation to final judgment, in a loving relationship to regain the faithful who were trapped under sin's hold. Yet God worked to regain the relationship—through historical events, promises to the patriarchs, the law, the prophets, the Scriptures, and finally with Christ. God's sending and offering of Christ undid sin's manipulation of humanity and completed what the law could not—so, just as Abraham had been an example for his descendants from the nations, God now can

37. Dunn, *Romans 9–16*, 859.

justify those in Christ through faith. This justification reconciled them to God in a relational sense, renewing their status as co-heirs with Christ, just as they had been conformed to Christ's image when they were fore-known by God before creation. While sin had enslaved God's beloved due to Adam's disobedience, now God's redemption of them through Christ's blood makes it possible for them to be adopted and, by the Spirit God poured into their hearts, empowered to self-identify as God's heirs.

There remain necessary questions about the role of God in Romans. How do we consider the analogy of God as father in a relational and theo-logical sense today? How do we align the imperial power dynamics to which Paul connects God's sovereignty? And how can one discuss righteousness in churches when the image of God and God's authority in this letter (esp. 13:1–7) is so often used to dissuade voices who speak out to identify injustice and call for change? These questions deserve their own chapter-length attention.

For now, I have focused on the literary and rhetorical overview of God in Romans. The story that Paul tells the complex communities in Rome is one of a loving God who is sole Creator and sovereign over all things, who will justify and judge creatures in a mysterious but impartial manner, and who will be faithful to the end for those who accept the invitation to return to peace. Before time and space began, God's plan was already purposefully unfolding. And so nothing that exists in the material or spiritual realms can overrule God's love of the faithful. This is the story that Paul has set out with a perceived mandate to tell, and its expression in Romans remains a testimony to Paul's own sense of his calling from God, and his ability to articulate to the ends of the earth the character of the Creator and sovereign of all things

2

"God from Whom All Things Are and for Whom We Exist" (1 Corinthians 8:6): Paul's Portrayal of God in 1 Corinthians

MARIA PASCUZZI, CSJ

Paul's theology, taken in the strict sense to refer to his understanding of God, is indebted to, and shaped by, both his Jewish faith and his encounter with the risen Christ whom God was pleased to reveal to him (Gal 1:15–16). As other essays in this volume show, however, how Paul expresses himself about God and what he chooses to say about God in his letters are also shaped by the issues and exigencies peculiar to each community to which he writes.

In this essay, I focus on Paul's understanding of God as reflected in 1 Corinthians, a letter written to a community composed mainly of gentiles evangelized by Paul on his first visit to Roman Corinth, ca. 50–51 C.E.[1] Problems arose in this community after Paul left Corinth and relocated to Ephesus, whence he wrote 1 Corinthians ca. 53–54 C.E. His responses to the problem of factionalism (1 Cor 1:10–4:21) and the denial of the resurrection (chap. 15) frame his comments on a series of issues affecting the day-to-day life of this nascent community (5:1–14:40). Scholars agree that misunderstanding about the gospel was at the heart of these problems, although they do not agree about what factors contributed to the misunderstanding.[2]

1. The NAB translation is used throughout unless otherwise noted.
2. Prominent hypotheses are summarized in Gordon D. Fee, *The First Epistle to the Corinthians* (NICNT; Grand Rapids: Eerdmans, 1987) 13–15.

28

■ θεός IN 1 CORINTHIANS

Of the 548 occurrences of the term θεός ("god") in the Pauline corpus,[3] 101 occur in 1 Corinthians.[4] Forty-eight of those occurrences are concentrated in chaps. 1–4, with twenty in chap. 1 alone. The other fifty-three occurrences are spread across chaps. 5–15. With few exceptions,[5] what Paul had to say about God has not commanded the same attention as other aspects of this letter, which, according to Gordon Fee, contains "little reflection on God's character as such."[6] He attributes this to the fact that "this is the symbolic universe the Corinthian believers, even though Gentiles, share with Paul through the gospel and the scriptures that had become a fixed part of their religious life."[7] Fee's comments about 1 Corinthians cohere with those of other scholars who claim that Paul's letters offer no new, or remarkable, insights about God.[8]

Granted, the letter does not dwell extensively on the "character" of God, if what Fee intends is an ordered reflection on the inner nature of God. It does, however, contain one of the most exposited passages in the Pauline corpus about God's character (1:18–31), and there are other passages where, in the process of arguing his points and exhorting his audience, a theocentric perspective is prominent. The rationale Fee offers, which depends on a shared symbolic universe, is also overstated. If Paul's new Corinthian converts shared his symbolic universe to the degree Fee suggests, one would expect this sharing to be demonstrated, at the very least, in behavior that adhered to the norms and values associated with this God. But the divisive and immoral behavior exhibited by the

3. James D. G. Dunn, *The Theology of Paul the Apostle* (Grand Rapids: Eerdmans, 1998) 28.

4. Divine passives and occurrences in Old Testament citations are not included in this tally.

5. See, e.g., Neil Richardson, *Paul's Language about God* (JSNTSup 99; Sheffield: Sheffield Academic Press, 1994) esp. 94–138; also Pheme Perkins, "God's Power in Human Weakness: Paul Teaches the Corinthians about God," in *The Forgotten God: Perspectives in Biblical Theology; Essays in Honor of Paul J. Achtemeier on the Occasion of His Seventy-Fifth Birthday* (ed. A. Andrew Das and Frank J. Matera; Louisville: Westminster John Knox, 2002) 145–62.

6. Gordon D. Fee, "Toward a Theology of 1 Corinthians," in *Pauline Theology*, vol. 2, *1 & 2 Corinthians* (ed. David M. Hay; Minneapolis: Fortress, 1993) 37–58, here 41.

7. Ibid., 41 n. 15.

8. See, e.g., Dunn, *Theology of Paul the Apostle*, 28; also E. P. Sanders, *Paul and Palestinian Judaism: A Comparison of Patterns of Religion* (Philadelphia: Fortress, 1977) 509.

Corinthians continued to reflect values and behavior associated with their pre-conversion lives (6:9–11a).

On his founding visit to Corinth, a thoroughly polytheistic city,[9] Paul, in addition to proclaiming the risen Christ's lordship, had obviously insisted, as he had elsewhere, that belonging to Christ involved rejecting idols, professing the one true God, and living in a manner pleasing to God (see, e.g., 1 Thess 1:8–9; 4:1). In fact, belief in the one true God is a shared premise in Paul's discussion of idol food, made clear by the emphatically placed "for us" in 1 Cor 8:6a. Paul himself had testified to this God and what God willed for the Corinthians (2:1; 15:15). Further, the rhetorical questions, which begin with the introductory formula "do you not know . . . ?," functioned as reminders of what Paul had already taught. Thus, the Corinthians were aware that they were indwelt by God's Spirit (3:16; 6:19), and that inappropriate behavior in God's kingdom in the present would, at the eschaton, disqualify them from inheriting the kingdom of this God (6:9–11).[10] Though they had some idea about God, and what God willed, the letter's contents reveal that they had misconstrued what it means to profess, belong to, and glorify this one particular God, and to live as sanctified members of the assembly that God called into being in Christ.[11] They also apparently failed to recognize God's sovereignty and to understand the relationship between God and Christ.[12] All of this misunderstanding contributed to the friction reflected in almost every chapter of this letter.

In response, Paul offers a series of clarifications, instructions, and exhortations, all revolving around an absolute, sovereign God whose salvific will is accomplished in Christ's death and resurrection. Here, as elsewhere in his letters, Paul intertwines the language of God and Christ. He emphasizes Christ's centrality in the plan of salvation, but never without an accompanying emphasis on God, the initiator of the plan to redeem

---

9. Nancy Bookidis, "Religion in Corinth: 146 BCE to 100 CE," in *Urban Religion in Roman Corinth: Interdisciplinary Approaches* (ed. Daniel N. Schowalter and Steven J. Friesen; HTS 53; Cambridge, MA: Harvard University Press, 2005) 141–64.

10. On Paul's "kingdom of God" language, see Frederick D. Carr, who sets Christ's work in the context of God's sovereignty ("Beginning at the End: The Kingdom of God in 1 Corinthians," *CBQ* 81 [2019] 449–69, here 452 n. 15).

11. Karl Barth expressed the Corinthian problem this way: "they believed, not in God, but in their own belief in God" (*The Resurrection of the Dead* [trans. H. J. Stenning; Eugene, OR: Wipf & Stock, 2003] 15; German original, 1924).

12. As Wayne A. Meeks observed, Paul had to explain not only the implications of belief in one God but also what Christ crucified had to do with God's salvific purposes (*The First Urban Christians: The Social World of the Apostle Paul* [New Haven: Yale University Press, 1983] 180).

and save. Despite the fact that God is so prominent in this letter, arguably one of Paul's most theological, sparse attention has been paid to his portrayal of God and the decidedly theocentric perspective that pervades this letter.[13] It is prominent in chaps. 1–4, and again in chap. 15, but it is also threaded throughout chaps. 5–14. After a close reading of these chapters focused on Paul's theocentric perspective, I will consider Paul's portrayal of the relationship between God and Christ, and then offer summary comments about what 1 Cornthians reveals about Paul's understanding of God.

▪ Paul's Theocentric Perspective in 1 Corinthians

Paul's theocentric perspective is immediately evident in the epistolary salutation, where he grounds his apostolic calling in the will of God, with the emphasis on God (1:1). He identifies his Corinthian addressees as the "church of God," further qualified as those "sanctified in Christ Jesus" and "called holy," that is, recognized by God as God's own people and set apart for God's service.[14] Paul's prayer of thanksgiving reinforces this emphasis on God. He begins by acknowledging God's grace bestowed on the Corinthians, evident in their manifold spiritual gifts (1:4), and concludes with an emphasis on God's initiative in calling believers into the fellowship of his Son, Jesus Christ our Lord (1:9).[15] God's call, mediated through the gospel proclamation, invites belief in a God whose saving activity reveals itself as wisdom and power in a crucified Messiah. For Paul, understanding God through the cross was fundamental to reuniting the community and redirecting it to live in a way consonant with God's will.

Partisan allegiance and competitive boasting contributed to the factionalism that characterized Corinthian community life (1 Cor 1:10–17). In response to this situation, Paul deals with two fundamental, interrelated misconceptions concerning (1) the nature of the gospel and (2) the role of ministers. He begins by inviting the Corinthians to reconsider who God is in light of the "word of the cross." Using the categories of wisdom and power, Paul exposes the paradoxical ways of this God who exhibits

13. See Richardson, *Paul's Language about God*, 114–15.
14. See Raymond F. Collins, *First Corinthians* (SacPag 7; Collegeville, MN: Liturgical Press, 1999) 46.
15. Despite the thanksgiving's theocentric framework, some scholars read it exclusively through christological lenses. See, e.g., Calvin Roetzel, *Paul: The Man and the Myth* (Minneapolis: Fortress, 1999) 111.

divine wisdom and power not simply in the risen exalted Christ, but in Christ crucified (1:18–25). God's wisdom and power, revealed in the proclamation of Christ crucified, divide humans, and defy and destroy the wisdom of this age by which they live (1:18–19). God exhibits this same paradoxical logic in calling into the assembly of saints those of unremarkable social status. In this display of divine initiative, God disregards human evaluative criteria (1:26–29). Thanks to that initiative, those whom God has called, and who are united to Christ, have acquired a new identity insofar as God has made Christ their wisdom, righteousness, sanctification, and redemption (1:30). As those whose lives were now infused with both the cross and the resurrection, the Corinthians were expected to live differently in the present, beginning with the cessation of the boasting and contentiousness that were dividing the community.

There are a few important things to signal here. First, in 1:18–31 the term θεός occurs fourteen times. Moreover, in the citation of Isa 29:14 in 1:19, God is clearly the subject of ἀπολῶ ("I will destroy") and ἀθετήσω ("I will nullify"). Beyond this remarkably concentrated use of θεός, the repeated positioning of ἐξελέξατο ὁ θεός ("God chose") at the end of vv. 27a, 27b, and 28a obviously puts the emphasis on God's prerogative. Second, in 1:18–31 Paul portrays a supreme God whose wisdom and ways are unfathomable. God's wisdom is of such an entirely different order that it is perceived only by God's own Spirit, or by humans gifted with God's Spirit, that is, the spiritually mature (2:6, 12, 13). To those without the Spirit, God's wisdom is mere foolishness (2:14). Unable to perceive the mystery unfolding before their eyes, the unspiritual fail to recognize the Lord of glory (2:8). Why does God act this way? Is it simply to exercise sovereignty in order to bring humans down a peg? Yes, in the sense that it deprives humans of their grounds for boasting (1:31). But God's ultimate purpose is to save humans, whose wisdom is a wisdom of this age, incapable of bringing them to recognize God's self-revelation in the cross (1:21). Third, the God portrayed here, who shames the wise and powerful, and calls the lowly, is a God attested throughout the Old Testament (see Jer 9:23–24; 1 Sam 2:1–10). But everything known thus far about God is radicalized in the cross. In the cross, God does not simply act contrary to human wisdom but destroys and nullifies it. God makes human wisdom foolish (1 Cor 1:20), rendering it so devoid of any sense or persuasive force that even God's "foolishness" is wiser than human wisdom and God's "weakness" is stronger than human strength.[16] Ultimately,

16. Richardson considers ἀθετήσω (v. 19) and ἐμώρανεν ("made foolish," v. 20) "divine put down language" drawn from the Old Testament (*Paul's Language about*

the God who is discovered in the gospel proclamation is radically free and sovereign, unconstrained by the limits or dictates of human reasoning.

When Paul returns to the problem of partisanship and discusses his and Apollos's respective roles in the life of the Corinthian community, he continues to underscore God's sovereignty (3:5–23). He and Apollos are fellow workers, active in the unfolding of God's salvific plan in the life of believers. He plants; Apollos waters; but God alone gives the growth (3:7). The community's foundation is Christ (3:11). However, the community, variously described as θεοῦ γεώργιον, θεοῦ οἰκοδομή ("God's field, God's building," 3:9), as well as the ναὸς θεοῦ ("temple of God," 3:16–17), belongs to God and owes its existence exclusively to the will and work of God. The agricultural image of field and the architectural image of building recall the associated images of agriculture and construction scattered throughout the Old Testament (e.g., Josh 24:13; Jer 18:9), which describe God's activity and underscore God's sovereignty.[17] Beyond expressing the community's possession by God, these images also remind them that they are God's own work: the field that God works, the building that God builds. Note how the architectural metaphor also underscores God's agency. Paul laid the foundation but was enabled to do so "according to the grace of God" (1 Cor 3:10), whose grace is the source of every charism in the community (see 1:5–7; 12:6). The construction rising from the foundation is a temple, not a static structure but a pulsating community in which the Spirit of God dwells (3:16–17). Like the Jerusalem temple, the community, now imagined as a privileged place of God's dwelling, has the attendant obligation to maintain its sacrosanct state.

At the end of this discussion in which Paul provides a correct understanding of the relationship between the Corinthians and their ministers, he concludes by reaffirming the sovereignty of God, even over Christ: ". . . you belong to Christ, and Christ belongs to God" (3:23; my translation). This statement will be considered again below.

Though chap. 4 contains the fewest occurrences of θεός in the unit comprising 1:10–4:21, God's centrality continues in this chapter where Paul defines apostles as "stewards of the mysteries of God," that is, as those entrusted with preaching God's gospel of salvation in Christ crucified (see

---

God, 12–25, 132–33). He also observes that, when Paul speaks of God's "foolishness" and "weakness" (v. 25), he introduces language about God with no parallels in Jewish or Greco-Roman literature.

17. Noted by Max-Alain Chevallier, "La construction de la communauté sur la fondement du Christ (1 Co 3,5–17)," in *Paolo a una chiesa divisa, 1 Co 1–4* (ed. Lorenzo De Lorenzi; Monographic Series of "Benedictine": Biblical-ecumenical Section 5; Rome: Abbazia di S. Paolo fuori le mura, 1980) 109–36.

2:7–9). As God's steward, Paul is accountable only to God and will be judged on whether he has been trustworthy (4:2–3). Therefore, the Corinthians' judgment of Paul in the present is of no consequence. What matters is the eschatological judgment, when praise will come to each from God (4:4–5). Paul admits that his trial-laden ministry appears to all, whether humans or angels, as an abject failure; however, he sets it within a theological frame. God has exhibited apostles as last of all and continues to work through human weakness to accomplish his salvific plan (4:9; see 1:18–31).

■ THEOCENTRIC PERSPECTIVE AND MOTIVES IN PAUL'S ETHICAL TEACHING AND EXHORTATIONS

In comparison to his dense use of θεός in chaps. 1–4, Paul employs the term only fifty-three times across the next ten chapters, as noted above. Despite the sparser usage, Paul's theological perspective remains prominent in these chapters.

He demands the expulsion of the πονηρός (evil person, 1 Cor 5:1–13) because the Corinthians form one holy community, a leaven-free lump of dough (5:6–7a). Through Christ's death (5:7b), the community exists as a sanctified community willed by God whose Spirit indwells it. Sin, which pollutes the community, renders it an inhospitable dwelling for God's Spirit, whose animating presence must be preserved (5:5). When Paul takes up the problem of lawsuits among believers, he reminds them that they are responsible for judging the world (6:2). Why? Because as οἱ ἅγιοι ("the saints"), already reigning with Christ, they must demonstrate kingdom behavior in the present, or they put at risk the inheritance of God's kingdom, which Paul holds out as an eschatological goal.[18]

The exhortation to flee πορνεία ("unlawful sexual intercourse; my translation) (6:12–20) is framed by theocentric motives: believers are destined to be raised by God, who raised the Lord (6:14), and they are bought (by God) with a price (6:20a). In the Pauline corpus, this is one of the most concise and dramatic expressions of God's absolute claim on believers, which Paul will repeat in 7:23. Believers are not self-determining but are under the sovereignty of a new owner. Therefore, Paul exhorts the Corinthians to glorify God, each in one's own body, which is an individual temple indwelt by God's Spirit (6:19–20). In chap. 7, God's call to faith is

---

18. On present "kingdom behavior" required for kingdom inheritance, see Carr, "Beginning at the End," 450–64.

the decisive criterion for determining one's social status (7:15, 17, 20). Paul insists that one's status at the time of God's call remains the appropriate one in which to live out that call. The only thing that matters is to "keep God's commands" (7:19) and "remain with God" (7:24). After a lengthy discussion concerning food offered to idols, the final and decisive motivation Paul offers for the proper exercise of Christian freedom is theocentric: "So whether you eat or drink, or whatever you do, do everything for the glory of God" (10:31).

In 11:3 Paul explains the relationship between a woman and a man on analogy with Christ's relationship to God, whom Paul describes as "the head of Christ."[19] As recognized, this verse and the discussion that follows concerning appropriate liturgical dress for men and women are fraught with exegetical difficulties. The concern beneath the particulars, however, is that Christian behavior, even in the context of worship, should reflect God's design for man and woman and should align with the hierarchy and order established by God (11:7, 12).

In denouncing abuses at the Lord's Supper, Paul cites God's future judgment, which entails the possibility of chastisement and condemnation as motives for desisting from community-destroying behavior at the Eucharist (11:27–31). When establishing guidelines for the use of spiritual gifts, Paul reminds the community of the sovereignty of God, who "activates all of them in everyone" (12:6 NRSV). Further, within the framework of God's sovereignty, Paul invites the Corinthians to acknowledge God's positioning of each member in the one body (12:18). Both God's disregard for human evaluative criteria, evident in assigning greater glory to the inferior parts, and the mention of σχίσμα (NRSV "dissension," 12:25) link this discussion to the beginning of the letter (1:10–31). In addition to arranging the members, God's sovereign choice accounts for the diversity of gifts given for the service of the community. Regardless of the gift one receives and the service associated with it, God is the origin and animating force of each gift and so is at work in the life of each believer.

God is not explicitly mentioned in chap. 13. Nevertheless, this encomium to love is profoundly theological. The love lauded is not an abstraction, nor is it sensual and self-interested.[20] Rather, it is the active love

---

19. However κεφαλή ("head") is rendered (see Anthony C. Thiselton, *The First Epistle to the Corinthians: A Commentary on the Greek Text* [NIGTC; Grand Rapids: Eerdmans, 2014] 816–21), what is insinuated in v. 3, as elsewhere in this letter in 3:23 and 15:28, is that God is preeminent and Christ is, in some way, dependent on, or subordinate to God.

20. On Christian ἀγάπη ("love"), see Anders Nygren, *Agape and Eros* (trans. Philip S. Watson; Philadelphia: Westminster, 1953).

characteristic of God that is manifest in Christ crucified.[21] That self-sacrificing, other-regarding love is what counts and what Paul expects the Corinthians to incarnate and demonstrate toward others. At the eschaton, when God's plan is completely unveiled, the other spiritual gifts of the present aeon will be rendered unnecessary, brought to an end (by God).[22] Believers will encounter God face-to-face and will know God fully as they have been known fully (by God).[23] Only love, grounded in the very nature of God and which defines eschatological existence, will never be modified or superseded (13:13).[24]

For Paul, all the various spiritual gifts are of equal importance because all are divinely allotted and animated (12:6, 11).[25] In chap. 14, however, where he focuses on two particular gifts and on what each contributes to the community, Paul clearly states a preference for prophecy over glossolalia (14:5, 19). The last of the three reasons he gives for his preference is theocentric, namely, that prophecy can move unbelievers to convert, to prostrate themselves, and to worship God (1 Cor 14:25).[26] In concluding his instructions on the order and purpose for which those with various gifts may speak in the assembly, Paul reminds the Corinthians that such order accords with the will of God, who is "not the God of disorder but of peace" (14:33).

Though the Corinthians' denial of Christ's resurrection elicited Paul's discussion in chap. 15, the sovereignty of God is ultimately at stake here. In a concise rebuttal of their position, Paul signals its two key problems: first, in denying Christ's resurrection, they are not denying any work of Christ but the sovereign will and salvific work of God, who is the subject of Paul's testimony; second, denial renders faith useless, with disastrous consequences for both the living and the dead (15:12–19). After this

---

21. In 13:4, the verbs μακροθυμέω ("to be long-suffering") and χρηστεύομαι ("to show kindness"), rendered adjectivally in English ("patient and kind"), are qualities associated with God (see Rom 2:4); in believers, they are evidence of Spirit-guided lives (Gal 5:22). Χριστός does not occur in this chapter; however, the love exalted is also profoundly christological.

22. Divine action is implied in the future passive forms of καταργέω ("to be brought to an end"), used twice in 13:8 and once in v. 10.

23. "By God" is also implied in the aorist passive ἐπεγνώσθην ("I have been known," 13:12).

24. Thiselton, *First Epistle to the Corinthians*, 1073.

25. I agree with Fee (*First Corinthians*, 619) that glossolalia's placement last in the list in v. 28, and second from last in the list contained in vv. 8–10, is not meant to diminish its value relative to the other gifts.

26. Paul's other reasons: (1) the prophetic word is directed to others for their upbuilding, etc., v. 3; and (2) it is immediately intelligible to all, v. 5.

refutation, Paul lays out the consequences of Christ's resurrection and then describes the unfolding of eschatological events. When Christ comes again, he will hand over the reign to God. Until then, God's sovereignty is exercised in history through Christ, who will destroy every earthly authority, including death (15:24–26). But, at the end, after subjecting all things to the Father,[27] the Son will be subjected to God the Father who placed all things in subjection to Christ, so that God may be all in all (15:28). In the divine political order envisioned here, God's consummate sovereignty is affirmed. Paul's insistence that God establishes the sequence of eschatological events, which climaxes in the subjection of all things to God—including Christ, whose lordship ends when God's purposes are ful-filled—stands out as perhaps the most radically theocentric passage in the Pauline corpus.

The same theocentric focus continues throughout chap. 15. When Paul turns to the question of the nature of the resurrection body in v. 35, he addresses his interlocutor as a fool, able to understand the rudiments of farming yet unable to recognize God's agency and power over death. To each seed, Paul insists, God gives an appropriate new body as God pleases (15:38; see also 12:11). God brings forth new life from what is dead, whether seed or the human body, because God is sovereign over death. In the chapter's final unit, Paul again assures the Corinthians of God's sover-eignty over death and of their own impending transformation/resurrec-tion, which will take place according to God's eschatological timetable. The parousia will entail the transformation of both the living and dead who will put on immortality, signaling the annihilation of death. With that, God's plan is completely fulfilled, and God's reign fully established (vv. 50–57). Though Christ is the agent, God is the victor over death. Thus, Paul directs his thanks to God for gifting believers with a share in this victory, which they will experience fully in the future (v. 57).

■ THE RELATIONSHIP BETWEEN GOD AND CHRIST

Paul makes three separate statements in this letter—in 3:23, 11:3, and 15:28—which, prima facie, stress God's sovereignty even over Christ. Some New Testament scholars are concerned with whether the subordi-nation expressed in these passages is ontological or functional.[28] Others

27. See references to the fatherhood of God in articles in this volume by Witherup (71–72) and Okorie (123–24).

28. Most consider the subordination functional, e.g., Barrett, *First Corinthians,*

question why such statements occur only here in the entire letter and offer various explanations to account for them. For example, Richard B. Hays claims that 3:23 was necessary to counter Corinthian boasting in an exalted wisdom via the Stoic understanding of the wise person as possessing all things. He maintains that the Corinthians failed to include God in their assessment of reality and to recognize God's sovereignty. Thus, Paul had to remind them that they belong to no human but, like Paul and Apollos, belong to Christ, through whom they belong ultimately to God, the source of everything they have.[29] Hays does not consider 11:3 or 15:28 to have been necessitated by the same problem addressed in 3:23. Of 15:28 he says only that Paul was operating with what would later be called a subordinationist christology.[30] Hans Conzelmann identifies the problem behind the Corinthian factions as a pneumatic exalted christology. With reference to 3:23, he notes only that "Christological subordinationism emerges in reference back to God," but he mentions no link between 3:23 and the problem of exalted christology.[31] Neil Richardson agrees that exalted christology was a problem at Corinth and suggests that, in addition to his concentrated use of θεός in chaps. 1–3, Paul used the affirmation in 3:23 to correct a Christ party for whom Christ was a hero and God insignificant.[32] Richardson, only parenthetically, associates Paul's comment in 11:3 and 15:28 with the need to correct the Christ party.[33] Anthony C. Thiselton agrees with others that one reason Paul asserted the ultimacy of God lay in his opponents' zeal to regard Christ as one manifestation of divine, eternal wisdom.[34]

Underlying these hypotheses, each with a degree of plausibility, is the recognition that what Paul affirmed was a simple truth: belonging to the one true God, from whom are all things, is inseparable from belonging to

---

97–98; Fee, *First Epistle to the Corinthians*, 155, 159–60; also Gordon D. Fee, *Pauline Christology: An Exegetical-Theological Study* (Peabody, MA: Hendrickson, 2007) 142.

29. Richard B. Hays, *First Corinthians* (IBC; Louisville: Westminster John Knox, 1997) 60–61.

30. Ibid., 266.

31. Hans Conzelmann, *1 Corinthians: A Commentary on the First Epistle to the Corinthians*, Hermeneia (Philadelphia: Fortress, 1975) 34.

32. Richardson, *Paul's Language about God*, 115. In his case against the existence of a "Christ party," James Prothro rejects the possibility that 3:23 was meant to correct the Christ party, arguing that Paul would be effectively affirming the partisanship he has already denounced as a problem ("Who Is 'of Christ'? A Grammatical and Theological Reconsideration of 1 Cor 1.12," *NTS* 60 [2014] 250–65, here 254). Paul's statement in 3:23, however, does not conclude by promoting partisan belonging to Christ, as Prothro argues, but by affirming that all, including Christ, belong to God.

33. Richardson, *Paul's Language about God*, 115.

34. Thiselton, *First Epistle to the Corinthians*, 329 n. 150.

the crucified and exalted Christ, and belonging to Christ is inseparable from belonging to God, whose sovereignty is unparalleled. After two millennia of theological reflection, it requires some effort to understand that an early community of believers, for reasons that cannot be known with certainty, failed to understand this and needed to have it repeatedly inculcated.

Finally, the creedal formula in 8:6 also raises questions about the relationship between God and Christ. Apparently, some Corinthians, knowing that no idol exists, argued for the right to eat food offered to idols. Paul agrees with his debaters that no idol exists and that there is no God but one (8:4). Even if, in the culture of religious polytheism, so-called gods were thought to inhabit the heavens and the earth, Paul insists that "for us"—that is, for Christ-believers, there is only "one God, the Father, from whom are all things, and for whom we exist" (v. 6a). Here Paul not only rephrases the monotheistic profession of faith articulated in the *šĕmaᶜ* but expands it in v. 6b to include the profession that "there is one Lord Jesus Christ through whom all things are and through whom we exist." The prepositions Paul uses in v. 6 distinguish the role of God the Father from Jesus Christ the Lord.[35] But in distinguishing these roles and assigning the title Lord to Jesus, which in Israel's profession of faith was reserved exclusively for God, was Paul effectively identifying Jesus with God, declaring his divinity and going beyond the pale of Israel's monotheistic faith?

Fee claims that Paul sees no tension between his monotheistic faith and the clear distinction he draws between the roles of the Father and the Lord Jesus Christ.[36] Richard A. Horsley turns to Jewish wisdom speculation and the link between wisdom/Sophia and the possession of knowledge of God. He maintains that Paul was attempting to redirect the Corinthians' focus on heavenly Sophia to God's real Sophia, Christ, as their ethical guide and authority.[37] Others resolve the tension by noting that first-century Judaism's profession of monotheistic faith was flexible, able to accommodate belief in various divine intermediary figures.[38]

---

35. In v. 6ab ἐκ/εἰς (NRSV "from"/"for") stress God as both the source and goal of existence, while διά (2x) ("through") stresses the Son's role as agent or mediator.
36. Fee, *First Corinthians*, 375.
37. Richard A. Horsley, *1 Corinthians* (ANTC; Nashville: Abingdon, 1998) 116–20.
38. See esp. Larry W. Hurtado, *One God, One Lord: Early Christian Devotion and Ancient Jewish Monotheism* (Philadelphia: Fortress, 1988); also Dunn, *Theology of Paul the Apostle*, 31–38. On the debate concerning the definition of first-century Jewish monotheism and its implications for christology, see Brandon R. Smith, "What Christ

Given that, the argument goes, the proclamation of the divinity of Jesus would have been perceived without affront to Israel's monotheistic faith.[39] Richard Bauckham argues that Paul does not add the one Lord to the one God, which would result in ditheism, but includes Jesus in the unique identity of the one God.[40] According to Bauckham, once this is understood, there is no need for theories of divine agents to keep Paul within the boundaries of Jewish monotheism, which was reshaped by the first believers to include Christ, thus creating what Bauckham and others refer to as christological monotheism.[41] James D. G. Dunn, who finds in 1 Cor 8:6 evidence of an early identification of Christ with divine wisdom, maintains that there is no identification of God and Christ in this verse, which indicates only that Christ has been given a share in God's lordship.[42] Contra Dunn, Francis Watson insists that, when Paul assigns the title "Lord" to Jesus he is identifying Jesus with God.[43]

1 Corinthians 8:6 presents a number of interpretive possibilities.[44] However, beyond agreement that Paul's language suggests a close relationship between God and Christ, no one can say with certainty what Paul intended to communicate or what his audience would have understood by this statement. Did he mean to communicate only that Jesus shared in the lordship of the creator God, or that Christ was incorporated into the oneness of the one God, and was God? Was he identifying Christ with preexistent Wisdom? Or was he claiming that Christ was a preexistent divine agent who shared God's attributes and was worthy of worship, which Hurtado considers indicative of divine status, though a status

---

Does, God Does: Surveying Recent Scholarship on Christological Monotheism," *CurBR* 17 (2019) 184–208, esp. 196–204.

39. According to Hurtado, the first Jewish Christians used "the divine agency category to grant Christ a position of enormous importance while still protecting the uniqueness of God" (*One God, One Lord*, 98).

40. Richard Bauckham, *Jesus and the God of Israel: God Crucified and Other Studies on the New Testament's Christology of Divine Identity* (Grand Rapids: Eerdmans, 2008) 182–232.

41. Ibid., 184.

42. Dunn, *Theology of Paul the Apostle*, 252–54, 272–75; idem, *Christology in the Making: A New Testament Inquiry into the Origins of the Doctrine of the Incarnation* (2nd ed.; Grand Rapids: Eerdmans, 1989) esp. 180–83.

43. Francis Watson, "The Triune Divine Identity: Reflections on Pauline God-Language, in Disagreement with J. D. G. Dunn," *JSNT* 80 (2000) 99–124. Watson's comment was made in reference to the use of "Lord" in Phil 2:10–11, but it applies here as well. In Watson's view (117), Dunn's problem is that his concept of monotheism cannot abide being transgressed by christology.

44. For a review of positions regarding early christology, see Smith, "What Christ Does," esp. 184–96.

not equivalent to God/Yhwh?[45] On this last point, it is worth noting that 1 Corinthians contains sparse evidence that Jesus was worshiped.[46] There are no christological hymns or exhortations to praise and glorify Christ. Moreover, besides the fact that prayer and thanksgiving are directed to God alone (see 1:4; 6:20; 10:31; 15:57), where Paul does refer to the Lord's Supper (1 Cor 11:17–26), he states only that the first believers remembered Jesus and proclaimed his death.[47] Further, in chap. 14, where Paul focuses explicitly on Christian worship, Christ is never mentioned and all worship is directed to God (14:2, 18, 25, 28). These observations concerning 1 Cor 8:6, coupled with the texts just reviewed, especially 1 Cor 15:28 with its dramatic depiction of the eschaton when everything, including Christ, is subject to God's dominion, should caution against reading 1 Cor 8:6b as a statement of divine identity that accords Christ, the Lord, a status equivalent to that of Yhwh.

■ CONCLUSION

From this brief study, a few salient features about Paul's portrayal of God in 1 Corinthians begin to emerge. First, the God depicted in 1 Corinthians is a God who no longer acts in history apart from Christ; yet Paul leaves no doubt about God's absolute sovereignty, which is evident in God's actions.[48] God calls into being the community in Christ. God is the author of salvation in Christ crucified, and God makes foolish the world's wisdom. God reveals through the Spirit and gives the Spirit, enabling humans to fathom God's wisdom and ways. God is the source of believers' life in Jesus. God grows the superstructure, the community of believers, built on

45. Hurtado does note that Jesus was not worshiped as a second god with his own cult, but always with reference to God (*One God, One Lord*, 138, 151).

46. Even where 1 Corinthians is filled with the kind of literary evidence Hurtado finds elsewhere in Paul to support his thesis that early Christian faith was binitarian (see *One God, One Lord*, esp. 99–114), the question remains: Are texts evidence of practice? Hurtado eventually replaced binitarian with dyadic; see Larry Hurtado, "'Ancient Jewish Monotheism' in the Hellenistic and Roman Periods," *Journal of Ancient Judaism* 4 (2013) 379–400.

47. The phrase "Our Lord, come" (16:22) is addressed to the Lord (Jesus); but Dunn questions whether this is a prayer or an appeal (*Did the First Christians Worship Jesus? The New Testament Evidence* [Louisville: Westminster John Knox, 2010] 34).

48. In chaps. 1–4 alone, God is the subject of sixteen active verbs (1:8, 19 [2x], 20–21 [3x], 27–28 [3x]; 2:7, 9, 10; 3:6, 7, 17, 20) and is elsewhere the named or unnamed agent of an action (1:1, 2 [2x], 4, 9, 24; 4:5c, 9). By contrast, Christ/the Lord is the subject of only two verbs in these chapters (1:17 and 4:19).

the foundation of Christ. God raised the Lord Jesus. God provides the charisms and ministries needed for the continued upbuilding of the church, and it is God, the faithful one, who will strengthen and provide believers with what is needed to overcome temptation. God destines believers for resurrection and, through Christ's coming at the end, will complete believers' salvation and bring them into the kingdom, when God will be all in all. From the beginning to the end of this letter, God initiates, saves, and sustains the people God has called and destined for eternal life.

Second, as noted above, despite Paul's sparser use of the term θεός in chaps. 5–14, he does rely on theological criteria to motivate the behavior of Christ-believers. Paul invokes God's law (5:13), God's intention to raise believers' bodies, and God's absolute claim on them (6:12–20), as well as God's call (7:17), God's glory (10:31), and God's own peaceful nature, which demands peace (14:33; cf. 7:15b). Paul presupposes God's hierarchical ordering in creation as the starting point for his teaching in 1 Corinthians 11 (vv. 3, 7–9). Further, in 1 Corinthians 12, the concord that is to characterize the life shared by those who form one body in Christ depends on God's action in apportioning gifts (12:4–11) and arranging members (12:12–20). Though Paul's ethical teaching in chaps. 5–14 is set within a christological context, the texts just cited underscore the theocentric foundation of Christian existence. Thus, the Christ-believer is dependent on God's sovereign power and purposes and is responsible to live in accord with the will of God (7:19), glorifying God in every way (6:20; 10:31).

Third, with regard to the interpretation of 1 Cor 8:6, two methodological concerns are worth raising. First, when scholars comment on the so-called subordinationist passages (3:23; 11:3; 15:28), the focus is usually on the function of these formulations in the unfolding of Paul's argument. The same is not the case with the statement in 8:6. Concern for its significance in the context of Paul's practical argument takes a backseat to concern over its theological significance. N. T. Wright, for example, is adamant that 8:6 is no dogmatic aside or maxim cited to advance a pragmatic argument, but, foremost, a statement of monotheistic divine identity. This assertion ties into his argument that early Christians understood Jesus to be divine because he fulfilled their expectations concerning Yhwh's return to Zion.[49] In context, however, 8:6 does function as a counterpoint to what is stated in v. 5, and its primary purpose is to serve the argument

---

49. N. T. Wright, *Paul and the Faithfulness of God* (2 vols.; Christian Origins and the Question of God 4; Minneapolis: Fortress, 2013) 2:663–64, and further, 633.

Paul advances concerning the consumption of food offered to idols, as various scholars have indicated.[50] Second, before interpreting 8:6 in concert with other passages in the Pauline corpus to construct a Pauline christology, Paul's statement in 1 Cor 8:6 first needs to be interpreted in the context of this letter, especially those passages where God's preeminence in relation to Christ is stressed. To assume that, by calling Jesus Christ "Lord," Paul intended to identify him as Yhwh/God requires ignoring the subordinationist passages, especially 1 Cor 15:24–28, where Paul envisions the end of Christ's lordship and stresses Christ's submission to God, who reigns supreme. This will come about once Christ has accomplished his purpose and handed over the kingdom to God. Further, by interpreting 8:6 ontologically rather than functionally, an unnecessary opposition is created between Paul's portrayal of the relationship between God and Christ in this verse and his portrayal of that relationship in the subordinationist passages. But, in fact, Paul portrays Christ as functionally subordinate, even in 1 Cor 8:6.[51] Christ is affirmed as God's agent in creation and redemption, but God remains the unique source and destiny of all that exists. If there was a tendency in the Corinthian community to exalt Christ at the expense of reverence, devotion, and obedience to God, Paul has made it eminently clear in this letter that Christ does not challenge or eclipse the sovereignty of God "from whom all things are and for whom we exist" (8:6).

---

50. See, e.g., Hays, *First Corinthians*, 136–40; Pheme Perkins, *First Corinthians* (Paideia; Grand Rapids: Baker Academic, 2012) 115. If 8:6 was directed wholly to the situation in Corinth to underscore the inseparability of the creator God from the Lord of believers, as Dunn claims (see *Christology in the Making*, 180–81), this would reinforce what was suggested above, namely, that the Corinthians failed to recognize the connection and its implications.

51. See n. 35 above.

3

God in 2 Corinthians

JOHN GILLMAN

Paul elevates God's prominence to new heights in 2 Corinthians, where "God" occurs more frequently than "Christ," unlike in 1 Corinthians, where the opposite is true.[1] Forced to defend his apostleship (2:14–7:4) to an alienated community that prefers aggressive outside "superapostles" (11:5), Paul draws upon deeply held theological convictions to bolster his credibility and to achieve reconciliation. In a sustained and dramatic reframe, Paul masterfully places God and not himself at the center of his rhetorical strategy. Persistently this embattled apostle calls upon God as the trustworthy anchor and witness to his ministry. Thus, Paul endeavors to preserve his authority among those who doubted his sincerity (1:15–22) and diminished his status (11:5). The apostle's rhetorical "weapons of warfare" have "divine power" (10:4).

Central to the apostle's understanding is his conviction about the oneness, unity, and uniqueness of God, a fundamental belief shaped by his formation in Judaism (see 1 Cor 8:4, 6).[2] Thoroughly embedded in his Jewish tradition, Paul recasts basic theological beliefs from his ancestral

---

1. Although most commentators conclude that 2 Corinthians is a composite of two or more letters, I accept the integrity of the letter, for, among other reasons, there is no evidence in the manuscript history that indicates the contrary. For a recent defense of the integrity of the letter, see Stanley E. Porter, *The Apostle Paul: His Life, Thought, and Letters* (Grand Rapids: Eerdmans, 2016) 269–78. See also Jan Lambrecht, *Second Corinthians* (SacPag 8; Collegeville, MN: Liturgical Press, 1999) 7–9.

2. It would be fair to categorize this fundamental belief as a Pauline conviction or self-evident truth. See David M. Hay, who distinguishes between convictions, doubts, and warrants ("The Shaping of Theology in 2 Corinthians:; Convictions, Doubts, and Warrants," in *Pauline Theology*, vol. 2, *1 & 2 Corinthians* [ed. David M. Hay; Minneapolis: Fortress, 1993] 135–55). James D. G. Dunn states that God is "the

religious heritage for a predominantly gentile community in light of how the one God of Israel has acted definitively in Jesus Messiah.

This essay will address Paul's theological perspective in three sections: (1) God's prominent debut in chap. 1 of the letter; (2) God's agency, attributes, and authority; and (3) God's relationship to Christ, the Spirit, and Paul and the Corinthians. The third section will highlight God's initiative in reconciliation, a theological theme rather unique to the letter.

■ GOD'S PROMINENT DEBUT

God emerges as the lead actor on center stage in the opening chapter (salutation, blessing, 2 Cor 1:1–11; Paul's sincerity, 1:12–24). For his gentile recipients Paul portrays a God who is magnificent, engaged, and invested in humankind. Paul's identity as apostle, implying election, is grounded in the will of God (1:1); he is jointly commissioned by Christ Jesus and by God. Further, the ἐκκλησία in Corinth originates from and belongs to God (1:1). Paul effectively brings himself and the Corinthians into a close relationship based on their intimate connection with the divine.[3] God functions as the authenticating authority.

Paul concludes the prescript by affirming that grace (χάρις) is from God; hence he can speak regularly of the grace of God that reverberates throughout the letter. Paul testifies that he conducts his ministry "by the grace of God" (1:12), urges the Corinthians not to receive "the grace of God," understood here as the "gospel," in vain (6:1), states that "the grace of God" has been received by the Macedonians (8:1),[4] and underscores the surpassing nature of the "grace of God" (9:14). In the last two instances, χάρις refers concretely to the collection that Paul undertakes to bring about reconciliation between his gentile communities and the

---

primary subtext of all [Paul's] writing" (*The Theology of Paul the Apostle* [Grand Rapids: Eerdmans, 1998] 28).

See Suzanne Nicholson, who asserts that "all of Paul's arguments about justification, grace, the will of God, and ethics derive fundamentally from his convictions regarding the oneness of God" (*Dynamic Oneness: The Significance and Flexibility of Paul's One-God Language* [Eugene, OR: Pickwick, 2010] 241).

3. See Randall K. J. Tan, "Color outside the Lines: Rethinking How to Interpret Paul's Letters," in *Paul and His Theology* (ed. Stanley E. Porter; Pauline Studies 3; Leiden: Brill, 2006) 153–87, esp. 170–71; Beverly Roberts Gaventa, "Apostle and Church in 2 Corinthians," in Hay, *Pauline Theology*, 2:182–99, here 194.

4. See the repeated uses of χάρις in chaps. 8—9, often referring to the collection (8:1, 6–7, 19), but with other meanings as well, including thanksgiving, blessing, and gratitude (grace) (8:16; 9:8, 14–15).

Jerusalem church (chaps. 8–9). God's grace is the dynamic source of the Corinthians' generosity in the collection, for grace begets grace. Paul emphasizes that "the cheerful zeal of the Macedonians" to participate in the collection is a divine "indescribable gift."[5]

Paul portrays God as the compassionate one who offers consolation in the midst of affliction, a theme that echoes throughout the blessing. The logic is straightforward: Paul emphasizes that God comforts "us" (Paul and Timothy) in all "our" affliction so that "we" can be empowered to comfort others who are afflicted. How? Precisely through the same consolation that "we" have received from God (1:4). Theologically Paul ingeniously appeals to the mutuality in suffering experienced and consolation offered as the basis for a reconciled relationship. God's consolation is no less abundant than that of the sufferings of Christ (1:5). Paul's own affliction is for the consolation of those who suffer in the same way he does (1:6–7). The theme of consolation is reintroduced regarding the arrival of Titus (7:6–9). God consoles the downcast Paul, afflicted with external conflicts and internal fears, when Titus arrives bringing good news that the wayward Corinthians through their *metanoia* have been reconciled to Paul.

Continuing with the benediction, Paul employs the same verb (ῥύομαι, "to rescue") three times to acclaim the rescuing activity of God (1:10). First, Paul affirms that God has rescued the apostles from "so deadly peril," then expresses his expectation that God will continue to rescue "us," and finally states his conviction that God will rescue us still again, the definitive rescue being at the resurrection from the dead (4:14). The dual themes of consolation and rescue shape the constant pattern of God's activity. Paul's concluding wish is that, through the prayers of the Corinthians, thanks may be given (to God)[6] for the gracious gift that has been granted to "us" (1:11).

Perhaps defending himself against those who accuse him of acting according to "human standards" (10:2), Paul protests that his "simplicity and sincerity" are from God and that he has acted "by the grace of God" (1:12). Then, in a spat about the yes and no of his travel plans, Paul invokes God's covenantal faithfulness as the trustworthy source for his word:

5. Antony Binz, "'He Who Supplies Seed to the Sower and Bread for Food': The Pauline Characterization of God in 2 Corinthians 8–9," in *Theologizing in the Corinthian Conflict: Studies in the Exegesis and Theology of 2 Corinthians* (ed. Dominika Kurek-Chomycz, Ma. Marilou S. Ibita, Reimund Bieringer, and Thomas A. Vollmer; Biblical Tools and Studies 16; Leuven: Peeters, 2013) 305–17, here 307.

6. Cf. Lambrecht, who translates, "(God) may be thanked . . ." (*Second Corinthians*, 21).

"God is faithful" (1:18) and the witness over Paul's life (1:23); Paul avers that his integrity—his intention, his love, and his honesty—is known to God (cf. 5:11; 11:11, 31). Before God (ἐνώπιον τοῦ θεοῦ, 4:2), Paul commends himself, does what is right (8:21), and speaks in Christ (κατέναντι θεοῦ, "before God," 12:19). Paul is fully transparent to God as he hopes to be fully transparent to the Corinthians (5:11). When Paul was "out of his mind" (12:2–4), it was for God (5:13). God has a history of fidelity which Paul brings into focus by recalling the totality of "the promises of God" (1:20; see also 7:1). In a rhetorical crescendo, Paul employs four participles (connected paratactically, καί . . . καί . . . καί), to underscore dramatically God's sustained activity in "us" (1:21–22): God is the one who establishes/strengthens us into Christ, has anointed us, has sealed us, and has given us the first installment, that is, the Spirit (see also 5:5).[7] The last three aorist participles may recall what believers, possibly also Christ, have experienced from God at baptism.[8] The play on words between "Christ," who is God's anointed one, and "anointed" can hardly be missed. The anointing itself comes through the reception of God's spirit, which in turn explains how God strengthens believers.

The presence of God played out so prominently across Paul's theological stage in the opening chapter pervades the rest of the letter, which illuminates God's agency, characteristics, and authority and sets the foundation for God's reconciling action through Christ.

■ THE AGENCY, CHARACTERISTICS, AND AUTHORITY OF GOD

Paul presents God's agency in multiple instances (46x), regularly with θεός as the expressed nominative (13x), half of these (23x) occurring in the aorist.[9] Ten of the total occurrences are found in scriptural citations (discussed below). In addition, as many as nine divine passives appear in different forms.

---

7. The durative aspect of the present participle (ὁ δὲ βεβαιῶν, "the one strengthening") suggests that God's work is ongoing. See Mark A. Seifrid, *The Second Letter to the Corinthians* (Pillar New Testament Commentary; Grand Rapids: Eerdmans, 2014) 65 n. 244.

8. Note the trinitarian flavor of 1:18–22: God (4x), Christ (2x), and Spirit (1x). Cf. 13:13.

9. This includes those instances when God is either the expressed nominative (see below) or unexpressed subject of verbs. Not included in this tabulation are the divine passives or the two instances when "Lord" in 2 Corinthians refers to God (6:17–18; although see also possibly 3:16–17; 8:21; 10:17) and not to Christ.

The apostle is intentional about highlighting the activity of God (giving, encouraging, rescuing/raising up, and reconciling) globally across time: past, present, and future. God gives (δίδωμι, 4x) the Holy Spirit (1:21; 5:5), the ministry of reconciliation (5:18), earnestness in the heart of Titus (8:16), and righteousness to the poor (9:9; see also the possible divine passive in 12:7). These examples specify the quality of God's grace announced in 1:2. Integral to God's identity is the action of reconciling not only Paul and the Corinthians but also the world (καταλλάσσω, "to reconcile," 5:18–19; see the divine passive in 4:1); God puts into believers the "word of reconciliation" (5:19; see below).

In 2:14, Paul co-opts Roman triumphal imagery, portraying God—not a victorious Roman emperor—as the one who is "leads us in triumph in Christ" (2:14). This much-debated metaphor portrays the manner in which God celebrates the divine victory over us. Further, God is the one who makes ministers of the new covenant (3:6), has caused divine light to shine in our hearts (4:6), prepares us for the future life by giving us the Spirit (5:5), increases the harvest of righteousness (9:10), and assigns the ministry field for "us" to work in (10:13).

The abundant manifestation of God-in-action contributes to a multiple array of divine attributes, often identified with the genitive ([τοῦ] θεοῦ).[10] Paul accentuates God's grace and power, both of which he names as beyond all comparison (see ἡ ὑπερβολὴ τῆς δυνάμεως, "the surpassing power," 4:7; διὰ τὴν ὑπερβάλλουσαν χάριν, "because of the surpassing grace," 9:14). In three instances χάρις, meaning "thanksgiving," is to be given to God in response to divine action: (1) for leading the apostles in triumphal procession (2:14); (2) for the eagerness God has put into the heart of Titus (8:16); and (3) for God's "indescribable gift," namely, salvation (9:15). The Corinthians' "great generosity" produces "thanksgiving to God" (9:11), heightened in the next verse with the emphatic plural: "through many thanksgivings to God" (9:12). For Paul, God is "the one who sets in motion and facilitates a human response," that serves as the rationale for thanksgiving being expressed to God.[11]

Unlike Paul, who is weighed down ὑπὲρ δύναμιν ("beyond [our] strength," 1:8), "the power of God" (δύναμις τοῦ θεοῦ) is all-surpassing in

10. Through a cascade of genitives throughout the letter, Paul names the grace and power of God most frequently (4x each), followed by word, will, glory, and temple of God (2x each). And in thematic groups, Paul mentions once each the Spirit, the Son, and the image of God; the sincerity, righteousness, and love of God; the gospel (compare "word," 2x) and promises; the knowledge of God (compare the verbal expression "God knows," which appears 4x); the servants; and the fear and jealously of God.

11. Binz, "He Who Supplies Seed,'" 308–9.

comparison to the earthen vessel of the apostles (4:7). For Paul, in stark contrast to the culturally conditioned expectation, divine power is revealed in human weakness (4:7–11; 6:2–10; 12:8–10). His ministry comes in the power of God (6:7), named the κύριος παντοκράτωρ ("Lord Almighty," 6:18). Through Paul's own weakness and suffering, divine power is revealed in the person of Christ (12:9–10). Just as Christ, crucified in weakness, lives by the power of God, so too will Paul (who boasts of his own weakness) and the apostles live by the power of God (13:4).[12] With divine power comes glory. Having contrasted the glory associated with the ministry of Moses, Paul can speak of the surpassing glory (3:7–11) that is none other than "the glory of the Lord [Christ]" (3:18) and "the glory of God" (4:6). Fittingly, the Corinthians glorify God by their obedience to the gospel (9:13; see also 8:19).

In several other instances, Paul uses "God" as an attributive genitive. Confronting critics who malign his ministry, Paul defends his integrity along with that of fellow apostles as "ministers of God" (6:4) and defends his preaching of the "word of God" (2:17; 4:2), also called "the gospel of God" (11:7). The Corinthians are Paul's letters written by "the Spirit of the living God" (3:3). Twice Paul associates "building," understood metaphorically, with God. At the future resurrection believers will have a building from God (5:1), not made with hands, while in the present Paul and other believers are "the temple of the living God" (6:16, discussed below).

Paul invokes "the promises of God" (1:20; see 7:1), names "the righteousness of God" (5:21; see 9:9–10), and underscores "the knowledge of God" (10:5).[13] He sees a role for "the fear of God" (7:1) and "the jealously of God" ("divine jealousy," 11:2). Having affirmed that "God loves" a cheerful giver (9:7) and that God is "the God of love and peace" (13:11), Paul concludes by highlighting "the love of God" (13:13).[14] In three instances Paul uses adjectives to fill out his portrait of God, who is notably blessed (1:3), faithful (1:18) and living (3:3; 6:16), and who speaks with singular authority.

---

12. Three of the four occurrences of "power of God" are anarthrous (6:7; 13:4 [2x]; cf. 4:7).

13. See "knowledge of him" in 2:14, where the whole expression functions as an epexegetical genitive to "fragrance." The possessive "of him" probably refers to God rather than Christ (note the 2:14 and 4:6 inclusion). Thus, Lambrecht, Second Corinthians, 39.

14. Love is also a hallmark of Paul (see 8:7 "our love in you," attested in P46 and B, versus "your love for us" in א C D F) and of the Corinthians (8:8, 24).

Paul implicitly, yet emphatically, by invoking divine authority as manifested in Scripture, reminds his gentile converts that the God they profess is the God of Israel. God's own voice (4:6; 6:2, 16–18) brings linguistic force and compelling authority to Paul's argument.[15] Scripture serves as a "stand-in" for God. Almost one quarter (22%) of the instances of God's agency occur in echoes of (4:6) or citations from (6:2, 16) Scripture.

Placing a premium on the word of God, Paul affirms that, unlike those who huckster the word of God, "we" speak in Christ out of sincerity as persons sent from God standing before God (2:17).[16] The theological character of Paul's ministry resounds. "We" (the co-authors) have renounced shameful things, refused "to practice cunning or falsify God's word," but as an open manifestation of truth commend "ourselves" to all "in the sight of God" (4:2). The "logos" (named "the gospel of God" in 11:7) he preaches with firm conviction is divine in its origin and a manifestation of truth.

The first time Paul quotes God directly is in 4:6: "Let light shine out of darkness." With echoes of Gen 1:3 and Isa 9:2, Paul implies that the God of creation who made light shine in the original sphere of darkness (Genesis) and the God of redemption (Isaiah) is the One who illuminated his own heart at his call and the hearts of the Corinthians (v. 6b). God's explicit word (v. 6a) anchors the expansive reference to light, knowledge, glory, and ἐν προσώπῳ ['Ιησοῦ] Χριστοῦ ("in the face of [Jesus] Christ") in v. 6b and anticipates the new creation in Christ in 5:17.

In 6:2a Paul invokes God's past definitive action of helping Israel in its restoration (Isa 49:8a LXX) and through a dramatic shift applies God's past action to the present ("behold, now," v. 2b). Paul adds καιρὸς εὐπρόσδεκτος ("acceptable time"), emphasizing that God is acting favorably on the Corinthians' behalf.[17] The "day of salvation" refers to the saving work of Christ, specifically his role in God's reconciling activity (5:18–21).

---

15. The three instances of God's direct speech are expressed in verbs in the present tense (4:6), the aorist (6:2), and the future tense (6:16–18). See Katja Kujanpää, who explores the variety of functions quotations perform, their rhetorical effects, and Paul's technique in framing quotations in his argument ("From Eloquence to Evading Responsibility: The Rhetorical Functions of Quotations in Paul's Argumentation," *JBL* 136 [2017] 185–202).

16. The phrase ὡς ἐκ θεοῦ is elliptical and can be read either "as persons sent from God" (NRSV) or "as those who speak words coming from God" (Lambrecht, *Second Corinthians*, 40). The NAB translates simply "from God."

17. See Lambrecht, *Second Corinthians*, 108–9.

The most sustained use of Scripture occurs in 6:16–18, where Paul combines Old Testament motifs three times (Lev 26:11, 12 [Sinai covenant] and Ezek 37:27 [new covenant] in 6:16; Isa 52:11–12 and Ezek 20:34 in 6:17; and 2 Sam 7:14 and Isa 46:6 in 6:18) to demonstrate that God's future promises have been fulfilled in believers who are the temple of the living God (v. 16a).[18] Not Paul's authority, which agitators sought to undermine, but God's anchors his ministry of reconciliation. Paul extends the covenantal promise made to Israel (2 Sam 7:14; see the covenantal statement: "They shall be my people, and I will be their God," Jer 32:38) to the community of the gentiles, who constitute the whole family of God, collectively understood as the temple of the living God (6:16a). God will be "their God," and believers shall be "my people" (v. 16b). In adoption language, God will be "your father" and they will be "my sons and daughters" (v. 18). Reconciliation is effected.

In 9:9, Paul cites Ps 111:9 (LXX): "He scatters abroad, he gives to the poor . . . ," which he applies to God, the supreme benefactor (see 9:8 and 11). Eliciting support for the collection, Paul musters up three arguments: first, God loves a cheerful giver (9:7); second, God has the power to provide every blessing in abundance, and hence the Corinthians are to share abundantly (9:8); and, third, as attested by Scripture, God gives to the poor, and therefore the Corinthians are to do likewise (9:9).

Invoking the authority and power of God, Paul appeals for the collection and its contribution to reconciliation with Jerusalem. Paul stresses that God—cast in the agrarian role of seed-scatterer—is the ultimate source of generosity, and this is to be manifested in the abundant sharing of believers with those in need, thus participating in God's beneficence. Through divine action, God's "righteousness endures forever" (9:9b), which in turn increases "the harvest of [the Corinthians'] righteousness" (9:10b), deriving ultimately from the justice of God. Thus, they are enriched (9:11a, divine passive).

Through their generosity, Corinthians produce thanksgiving(s) to God (9:11). They glorify God by "their confession to the Gospel of Christ" (9:13), who is God's "indescribable gift" to them (9:15).[19] To summarize, in 9:8–15 God's agency in human affairs is exercised in multiple ways: having the power to provide every blessing, giving to the poor, increasing righteousness, and enriching the community in every way, particularly through Christ, God's preeminent gift.

18. See James M. Scott, "The Use of Scripture in 2 Corinthians 6:16c–18 and Paul's Restoration Theology," *JSNT* 17 (1994) 73–99.
19. For other interpretations of the subject of the participle "glorify," see Binz, "'He Who Supplies Seed,'" 314.

- **GOD'S RELATIONSHIP TO CHRIST, (THE) SPIRIT, AND PAUL AND THE CORINTHIANS**

Remaining one and unique, God's identity is to be understood fundamentally in relationship to Christ and to the Spirit. The divine claim extends to Paul and the Corinthians, whose identity is radically defined by this claim.

God in Relationship to Christ

Integral to the identity and activity of God is God's relationship with Christ, through whom reconciliation is achieved. God and Christ share the same divine qualities, such that for Paul the very identity of God includes Christ. Paul's monotheism is fundamentally christological. He creatively reinterprets the binomial expression "Lord God" from the Septuagint, applying "Lord" most often to Christ, and understanding "God" theologically (see 1 Cor 8:6). Thus, Paul conformed "to the witness of Scripture when he applied language to Christ that was functionally equivalent to the language he uses of God."[20]

Christ shares divine prerogatives.[21] The blessing of "grace and peace" comes from both God the Father and the Lord Jesus Christ (2 Cor 1:2), who identifies his gift to Paul as "my grace" (12:9). Paul's ministerial actions are conducted ἐν προσώπῳ Χριστοῦ ("in the presence of Christ," 2:10); the apostles commend themselves ἐνώπιον τοῦ θεοῦ ("before God," 4:2; see 9:12). Power is an attribute of God (4:7; 6:7; 13:4 [2x]) and of Christ (12:9), who is powerful among the Corinthians (13:4). The "good news" is identified most often as that of Christ (2:12; 9:13; 10:14), yet also is God's (11:7).

God and Christ are characterized by glory (for God, 4:6; for Christ, 4:4; 8:23; see "glory of the Lord, 3:18; 8:19), both of which are closely associated with light (compare 4:4 and 4:6). Indeed, the knowledge of God's glory is on the face of Jesus Christ (4:6). Paul affirms that he and the apostles are "servants of God" (6:4) and implies that they are also "servants of Christ" (11:23). Both "the love of Christ" (5:14) and "the love of God" (13:13) are dynamic realities; the former "holds us in its grip,"[22] and the latter, Paul prays, is "to be with you all."

---

20. Nicholson, *Dynamic Oneness*, 245.

21. In contrast to "Christ," Paul uses "Jesus" (without "Christ" or "Lord") six (possibly seven) times in 2 Corinthians 4 when referring to his suffering and death (vv. 5b, 10a, 10b, 11a, 11b, 14b).

22. Translation from Lambrecht, *Second Corinthians*, 94.

The hallmark of Paul's theology is what God has done in Christ, having raised him from the dead (4:14).[23] The connection is familial: God is the "Father of our Lord Jesus Christ" (1:3; 11:31), Jesus Christ is the Son of God (1:19), and Christ is the image of God (4:4).[24] For Paul, neither God nor Jesus can be understood apart from the other. The yes of Christ (1:19) is proof that God is faithful—a hallmark of God in the Hebrew Scriptures—and that Paul's word is reliable (1:18).

Paul affirms that Christ is the "image of God" (4:4; see 3:18). In both his humanity and divinity, Christ is the perfect image bearer of God. Believers behold the glory of the Lord not directly but as in a mirror, and this image, perceived in the proclamation of the gospel, is none other than the "image of God." In 1 Corinthians the image of Christ, the heavenly one, is contrasted with Adam, the earthly one (1 Cor 15:49; see Gen 1:26–27). Christ is the true image of God, in stark contrast to "the god of this world" (4:4).[25] Thus, the identity of God is known fundamentally through relationship with Christ. Paul's gospel to the fractured ἐκκλησία in Corinth is that followers of Christ experience through him reconciliation with God, bringing them into full relationship with the divine (5:18). As evidence, Paul impresses upon them the new reality God has created in their hearts by anointing and sealing them with the gift of the Spirit (1:21–22).

God in Relationship to (the) Spirit

The Spirit the Corinthians have received is none other than the Spirit of God. In addition to 1:21–22, Paul brings together God and Spirit twice (3:3; 13:13; see also the much-debated 3:17).[26] In a polemical argument

23. See, e.g., Gordon D. Fee, *Pauline Christology: An Exegetical-Theological Study* (Peabody, MA: Hendrickson, 2007; repr., Grand Rapids: Baker Academic, 2013) 161.

24. The portrayal of God as Father is deeply rooted in the Jewish Scriptures. God is presented preeminently as the Father of Israel (Deut 32:6; Isa 63:16; 64:8; Jer 3:4, 19; 31:9; Mal 1:6; 2:10); Israel is called God's (firstborn) son (Exod 4:22; Hos 11:1) and is referred to as God's children (Deut 14:1; Isa 1:2–4; 63:16; Jer 3:14, 22; 4:22; 31:20). See Murray J. Smith, "The Thessalonian Correspondence," in *All Things to All Cultures: Paul among Jews, Greeks, and Romans* (ed. Mark Harding and Alanna Nobbs; Grand Rapids: Eerdmans, 2013) 269–301, here 286.

25. This may well refer to the deified emperor Augustus, whose image was everywhere in public spaces. See Frederick J. Long, "'The God of This Age' (2 Cor 4:14) and Paul's Empire-Resisting Gospel at Corinth," in *The First Urban Churches*, vol. 2, *Roman Corinth* (ed. James R. Harrison and L. L. Welborn; WGRW 8; Atlanta: SBL Press, 2016) 219–69.

26. For a recent discussion of this problematic text, see Wesley Hill, *Paul and the Trinity: Persons, Relations, and the Pauline Letters* (Grand Rapids: Eerdmans, 2015) 143–53. While many commentators prefer a christological interpretation, Hill suggests

(2:14–3:6), Paul contends with those who imply that he lacks the required letters of recommendation (3:2). Using a series of interconnected antitheses drawn from images in the Jewish Scriptures, Paul argues that the Corinthians themselves are his letters of recommendation from Christ, written not with ink on tablets of stone but on tablets of human hearts with the "Spirit of the living God" (3:3).

Paul creates the novel expression "Spirit of the living God," *hapax* in the Bible, by combining Spirit and God, already familiar to the Corinthians,[27] and adding the descriptor "living," connoting that God is "the originating power behind the Spirit."[28] Since both God and Spirit are life-giving (1 Cor 6:14; 15:45), it is a small step to the expression "Spirit of the living God" (3:3; see 3:6, "the Spirit gives life"). The gospel was embraced in Corinth through the activity of the Spirit, who is God's first installment (1:22; 5:5). That God is a living God echoes the God of Israel, who initiated the covenant.[29] As the origin of life, God raises the dead (1:9)—confirmed in having raised Jesus (4:14a)—rescues from danger (1:10), and will bring believers into the divine presence (4:14b).

God acts through the Spirit, by whom the "letter" was written (3:3). The Corinthians themselves are the (invisible) letter written on the hearts of Paul and his co-workers as well as the (visible) script (fruit) of his apostolic labor, known and read by all (3:2).[30]

In the concluding benediction, Paul brings together Jesus Christ, God, and the Holy Spirit (13:13). The triadic sequence represents "a very early already beautifully balanced 'trinitarian' formula."[31] "The communion of the Holy Spirit"—which may be an objective genitive (see 8:4; 1 Cor 10:16; Phil 3:10)—refers to the participation of the ἐκκλησία in the life of the Spirit. God's love makes possible fellowship, understood as from/in the Spirit.[32] The sequence Christ–God–Spirit[33] affirms that the

---

that the tide is turning toward a theological interpretation, which he opts for along with others.

27. For God, see the multiple occurrences in 1 Corinthians 1 and throughout the letter; for Spirit, see, e.g., 2:4, 10; 12:1–13; for Spirit of God, see, e.g., 2:11; 12:3.

28. Mark J. Goodwin, *Paul, Apostle of the Living God: Kerygma and Conversion in 2 Corinthians* (Harrisburg, PA: Trinity Press International, 2001) 187.

29. Ibid., 161–89.

30. With "known and read," Paul reverses the logical order of normal letter reading: first reading, then knowing.

31. Lambrecht, *Second Corinthians*, 238.

32. See ibid., 228; Raymond F. Collins, *Second Corinthians* (Paideia; Grand Rapids: Baker Academic, 2013) 268.

33. Note also a similar sequence "Christ–God–God–Spirit" in 3:4–6. Paul's confidence is through Christ, toward God, who has made him competent for the Spirit, who gives life.

Spirit is divine in intimate communion with God and is the source of unity (see 1 Cor 6:17) for this splintered community in need of reconciliation.

God in Relationship to Paul and the Corinthians

What God has done through Christ in the Spirit is paradigmatic of the way God extends divine grace to all humanity, and, in our case, to Paul and the Corinthians. Originating from the Lord (i.e., Christ), Paul's apostolic authority empowers him to build up and not tear down (10:8; 13:10). Thus, Paul and his co-workers preach Jesus Christ and not themselves (4:5). In their ministry, they have conducted themselves in "simplicity and godly sincerity,"[34] empowered "by the grace of God" (1:12). Hence Paul's gospel is to be evaluated by the divine standard and not by that of "earthly wisdom" (1:12) or any "different gospel" (11:4). God is the one who has apportioned to him and his collaborators, "according to the measure of canon" (10:13), an expression interpreted either literally (NRSV: "mission field") or metaphorically ("competence").[35] If the former, which is more likely, then God is the one who gave the apostles the authority to build up the ἐκκλησία.

The source of Paul and his co-workers' "competence/sufficiency" (ἱκανότης, 3:5) is God, who has made them "competent/sufficient" (ἱκά–νωσεν) to be "ministers of the new covenant, not of the letter but of the spirit" (3:6). They are servants for Jesus's sake (4:6), specifically "servants of God" (6:4), in the midst of much affliction. Through the lens of this identity—concretely illustrated with a vivid *Peristasenkatalog* (6:4b–5) and moral and spiritual qualities (6:6–8a), including "the power of God" (6:7)—Paul commends himself (6:4).

With an emphatic "we" Paul asserts that he and the Corinthians are "the temple of the living God" (6:16b; cf. 1 Cor 3:16; Eph 2:21).[36] He identifies the community metaphorically with the sacred dwelling place of God in Jerusalem, still existing in all its glory. Unlike the boundaries delineated in the historical temple, this metaphor communicates "a vision which eliminates divisions within, such as the quarrels that threatened to destroy the Corinthian community."[37] The living God (ζῶντος is emphatic),

34. A genitive of quality, also called the Hebrew genitive.
35. See Lambrecht, who prefers a metaphorical meaning (*Second Corinthians*, 165–66).
36. In the GNT[5] the editors raised the likelihood of this variant reading to {B}, "the text is most certain," from that of {C}, "the Committee had difficulty in deciding," in the previous edition (1975).
37. John R. Levison, "The Spirit and the Temple in Paul's Letters to the Corinthians," in Porter, *Paul and His Theology*, 189–216, here 213.

who dwells in the Jerusalem temple, now dwells among the Corinthian believers and, by extension, in small communities of faith that have sprouted up around the eastern Mediterranean.[38]

The agency of the living God reaches its climax in 5:18–21, when the apostle puts on full display the reconciling activity of the divine, using repeatedly καταλλάσσω.[39] God acts in an unprecedented manner in the drama of salvation through the death of Christ on behalf of the apostles, the believers, and, more broadly, humankind.[40] By "not counting their trespasses against them" (5:19) and by making Christ to be sin (5:21), God radically reshapes the destiny of the world and specifically reconciles Paul and the Corinthians to one another. Through a complex array of prepositional phrases naming God, Christ, and "us," Paul accentuates God's intimate involvement in "changing" (the root meaning of "reconciliation") alienation into a relationship of harmony and rejoicing (7:16).[41]

Figuring prominently in 5:18–21, God actively engages in five different modalities: (1) reconciling "us" (5:18)/the world (5:19), (2) having given the ministry of reconciliation (5:18)/having entrusted the message of reconciliation (5:19), (3) not counting their trespasses (5:19), (4) appealing through "us" (5:20), and (5) having made Christ to be sin (5:21). Unlike other religious contexts where offending humans take the initiative offering prayers, sacrifice, repentance, and conversion to reconcile themselves with the divine (e.g., 2 Macc 8:29), for Paul God takes the initiative.

"All things" (τὰ πάντα) in 5:18 come from God. These refer to the preceding verses, particularly 5:14–15 regarding the salvific Christ-event.[42] Then, evidently the first to use reconciliation language in a Christian context, Paul affirms that God is the one who reconciled "us" to the divine.[43] God accomplished this διὰ Χριστοῦ, an instrumental phrase that

---

38. See N. Thomas Wright, *Paul and the Faithfulness of God* (2 vols.; Christian Origins and the Question of God 4; Minneapolis: Fortress, 2013) 1:437.

39. From κατά + ἀλλάσσω, literally a monetary term meaning "to change/exchange," this verb occurs five times in 5:18–20. In the New Testament, reconciliation vocabulary occurs only in Paul (see also Rom 5:10–11; 11:15; 1 Cor 7:11; cf. Eph 2:16; Col 1:20). On the use of reconciliation in warfare contexts, see Lisa M. Bowens, "Divine Desire: Paul's Apocalyptic God of Rescue," *Theology Today* 75 (2018) 9–21.

40. In these four verses θεός occurs five times and Χριστός four times. God is the agent; Christ is the instrument by whom God's actions are accomplished.

41. Four different prepositions are used with either God (1x), Christ (5x), or "us" (3x) as the object: ἐκ, "from" (God), διά "through" (Christ, "us"), ἐν "in" (Christ [2x], "us"), and ὑπέρ "over" (Christ [2x], "us").

42. See Lambrecht, *Second Corinthians*, 97.

43. See Stanley E. Porter, "Paul's Concept of Reconciliation, Twice More," in *Paul and His Theology*, 131–52, here 150.

is shorthand for Christ's death and resurrection (see 5:14–15).[44] Having initiated the process of reconciliation, God then entrusted "the ministry of reconciliation" to "us."

The following verse, an emphatic restatement of 5:18 with important additions, underscores through a periphrastic construction God's ongoing reconciling activity, ἐν Χριστῷ.[45] In 5:19 the recipient is the "world," understood not in a cosmological sense but in a broad anthropological sense. Acting as a divine bookkeeper, God has removed an obstacle to reconciliation by "not counting their trespasses against them." Then God placed the message of reconciliation "in us" (ἐν ἡμῖν), recalling "in your hearts" in 3:2. The "ministry/word" of reconciliation (5:18–19) gives specific content to the "diplomatic" mission of Paul and his co-workers in their function as "ambassadors for Christ" (5:20). In direct response to God's appeal, Paul offers this imperative: "Be reconciled to God." God has accomplished the divine portion; now the addressees are to do theirs, namely, be reconciled to God.

In 5:21 Paul highlights God's action in having made Christ "to be sin"—radically and shockingly—identifying Christ with the dark side of humanity. This is done not that "we" might know, believe, or receive.[46] Rather, it is done more fundamentally that "we" might "become the righteousness of God."[47] In a remarkable Pauline interchange text, Christ, according to the divine plan, has identified with the human condition so that humanity may become like Christ and thereby be transformed into God's righteousness (see also 8:9).[48] God's unconventional action brings reconciliation to a fractured world. No longer alienated from each other, God has given everything to bring about relational healing between Paul and the ἐκκλησία in Corinth.

---

44. See Stanley E. Porter, "Reconciliation and 2 Cor 5,18–21," in *The Corinthian Correspondence* (ed. Reimund Bieringer; BETL 125; Leuven: Leuven University Press, 1996) 693–704, here 701.

45. The phrase ὡς ὅτι at the beginning of 5:19, indicates something that is traditional and already well known.

46. Contrast the multiple cognitive statements in the preceding context with Paul/we as subject: 5:1, 6, 11, 14, 16, pointed out by Luke Timothy Johnson, "'God Was In Christ': 2 Corinthians 5:19 and Mythic Language," in *Myth and Scripture: Contemporary Perspectives on Religion, Language, and Imagination* (ed. Dexter E. Callender Jr.; RBS 78; Atlanta: SBL Press, 2014) 201–11, here 205.

47. See Richard B. Hays, *The Moral Vision of the New Testament: Community, Cross, New Creation; A Contemporary Introduction to New Testament Ethics* (New York: HarperCollins, 1996) 24.

48. See Morna D. Hooker, *From Adam to Christ: Essays on Paul* (Cambridge: Cambridge University Press, 1990) 26.

■ CONCLUSION

In 2 Corinthians, Paul writes a compelling script that shapes the character of God in a way that serves his rhetorical purpose of achieving reconciliation. He calls upon God as his star witness, who testifies to his integrity, sincerity, and function as an apostle. To those who discredit Paul or his gospel, Paul demonstrates that God through Christ is working in his ministry of reconciliation. Thus, to discredit Paul is to deny the very identity of God who has entrusted the apostle with this ministry. In all circumstances, especially through the sustained defense of his apostleship, Paul trusted God, the faithful one.

The images and motifs throughout the letter serve the dominant theme of reconciliation. For example, the two images—(1) of God leading Paul (and the apostles)—the aroma of Christ—in a triumphal procession (2:17) and (2) of God conferring upon Paul (and the apostles) the highest-ranking office, namely, ambassadors for Christ (5:20)—contribute mightily to establishing Paul's divine credentials as a minister of reconciliation. In the metaphorical role of head of state, the God of power and glory, and not the Roman emperor, is the Lord who acts with supreme authority in his apostle.

The theme of divine comfort, reverberating throughout the benediction (1:3–7) and again with the good news brought by Titus (7:6–9) echoes the dominant theme of reconciliation. The invocation of the Father's mercy (1:3)—integral to God's identity—at the beginning of the letter is a verbal prelude to the theme of reconciliation richly proclaimed in 5:18–21. God's gift of reconciliation made possible through Christ serves as the high point and anchors the entire communiqué.

Paul's theology in 2 Corinthians is profound and well developed. The character of God, expressed through multiple characteristics and decisive actions, serves as a firm foundation for Paul's multivalent appeal in the letter for reconciliation. The dynamic relational power of the living God has radically transformed Paul and enables an alienated community to experience reconciliation. The ongoing challenge remains for them and for Christians today to embrace this divinely given grace.

4

God in the Letter to the Galatians

RONALD D. WITHERUP, P.S.S.

First impressions of reading any of Paul's letters might suggest that his image of God is basically consistent with his Jewish milieu.[1] While this is true, there is more that can be said. Numerous scholars have noted the "neglect" of this theme in the New Testament in general, but also in Paul's letters.[2] A search of available commentaries on Galatians did not yield much information on the topic as a separate, identifiable theme.[3] There are, however, discussions of God's role, for instance, scattered throughout some commentaries, though this widely dispersed information makes it difficult to formulate a coherent picture easily.[4] In addition, Richard Hays, whose seminal work has guided Pauline scholarship for

---

1. This is essentially the judgment of Donald Guthrie and Ralph P. Martin, "God," *DPL*, 354–69, among others.

2. See, e.g., Larry Hurtado, who summarizes the limited number of studies on Paul's understanding of God (*God in New Testament Theology* [Library of Biblical Theology; Nashville: Abingdon, 2010] 10–17).

3. One short analysis, under the title "Dio Padre," is found in Albert Vanhoye, *Lettera Ai Galati: Nuova versione, introduzione e commento* (2nd ed.; Libri Biblici NT 8; Milan: Paoline, 2008) 155–56. Five key commentaries I used are the following: J. Louis Martyn, *Galatians: A New Translation with Introduction and Commentary* (AB 33A; New York: Doubleday, 1997); Martinus C. de Boer, *Galatians: A Commentary* (NTL; Louisville: Westminster John Knox, 2011); Frank J. Matera, *Galatians* (SacPag 9; Collegeville, MN: Liturgical Press, 1992); Douglas J. Moo, *Galatians* (BECNT; Grand Rapids: Baker Academic, 2013); and N. T. Wright, *Galatians* (Commentaries for Christian Formation; Grand Rapids: Eerdmans, 2021). See also Ronald D. Witherup, *Galatians: Life in the New Creation; A Spiritual-Pastoral Reading* (Mahwah, NJ: Paulist, 2020).

4. For example, the commentaries of Martyn (*Galatians*, 95–97, 105–6, 116–17, 165–66, 412–14, etc.), de Boer (*Galatians*, 21–25, 28–30, 81, 89–91, 240–47, 260–67, etc.), and Moo (*Galatians*, 49–53, 67–69, 235–37, 249–51).

decades, wrote an essay on the image of God in Galatians and Romans that I became aware of only after completing a first draft of this paper.[5] His conclusions can be summarized succinctly. He finds the image of God as Father as the principal one, and he describes God's activity with the following nine assertions: God made promises to Abraham, gave the law, sent the Son into the world, raised Jesus from the dead, justifies the gentiles through the faithfulness of Jesus Christ, calls believers into participation in the new covenant community, supplies the Spirit, will eventually judge everyone, and is the ultimate recipient of glory. As will be seen, this summary coheres well with my own study, though I have organized the material in a different fashion and have boiled it down to five main categories. Hays's inclusion of "glory" in his summary may be unnecessary. He correctly notes that it is mentioned only in passing in Galatians but is much more fully developed in Romans.[6] For that reason I have not given it prominence in my own description.

For my analysis, I will proceed in four stages. First, I examine the "God" language in the letter. Second, I look at the treatment of God's "identity" in Galatians. Third, I explore five key themes that illuminate God's activity and characteristics. Finally, I briefly propose how Paul's understanding of God impacts the broader rhetoric of the letter.

■ GOD LANGUAGE IN GALATIANS

The mention of God in Galatians can be divided into explicit and implicit references.

Explicit References

Explicitly, the word "God" (θεός) in reference to the one true God—in one form or another—occurs twenty-seven times in twenty-six verses in Galatians. Only two of these occurrences are found in passages with text-critical problems; although the evidence regarding the *explicit* mention of God in these instances is mixed, experts judge that God is the

---

5. See Richard B. Hays, "The God of Mercy Who Rescues Us from the Present Evil Age: Romans and Galatians," in *The Forgotten God: Perspectives in Biblical Theology; Essays in Honor of Paul J. Achtemeier on His Seventy-Fifth Birthday* (ed. A. Andrew Das and Frank J. Matera; Louisville: Westminster John Knox, 2002) 123–43, esp. 125–31.

6. Ibid., 131; cf. 138–39.

subject.[7] In another instance, the word "God" is used in contrast to "beings that by nature are not gods [θεοῖς] at all" (4:8). Paul's strong Jewish, monotheistic perspective holds throughout the letter. In Galatians, Paul uses the title "Lord" (κύριος) only in reference to Jesus Christ (1:3; 5:10; 6:14, 18).[8]

Two other aspects of the letter's language bear notice. One is the close association of God with the image of the Father (πατήρ), the only place where Paul connects the title to his apostolic call.[9] This is a concept that Marianne Meye Thompson has explored at length for the whole New Testament.[10] She rightly calls attention to the closeness of christological and theological thought in Paul, and she also notes the importance of the Aramaic expression ʾAbba in reinforcing the relationship between Jesus and God as his Father (see below under "The God of Tenderness"). At the very beginning of Galatians, this association is mentioned no fewer than three times in quick succession. The first is Paul's greeting, in reference to God being the Father who raised Jesus Christ from the dead (1:1), the only explicit mention of resurrection;[11] the second refers to God, "our Father" (1:3), the "our" implying the Galatians, Paul, and his companions; and the third mentions the "will of our God and Father" (1:4). As we will see, this close connection between God and the image of the Father is not simply a formulaic greeting but is important in the rhetoric of the letter. Moreover, the explicit mention of the resurrection, found only here in Paul in relation to the Father, prepares for the "new creation" (6:15) because it is only by Christ's cross and resurrection that God establishes this new reality.

7. See 1:15 (Ὅτε δὲ εὐδόκησεν [ὁ θεὸς] ὁ ἀφορίσας με, "but when [God], who set me apart, was pleased . . .") and 3:21 (ὁ οὖν νόμος κατὰ τῶν ἐπαγγελιῶν [τοῦ θεοῦ];, "Is the law then opposed to the promises [of God]?" [NRSV]).

8. The ambiguous reference "in the Lord" (5:10) refers to Jesus Christ, not to God the Father. For a balanced study of "Lord" language in Paul, see David B. Capes, *The Divine Christ: Paul, the Lord Jesus, and the Scriptures of Israel* (Acadia Studies in Bible and Theology; Grand Rapids: Baker Academic, 2018), which nonetheless curiously does not discuss this verse.

9. Moo, however, goes on to diminish the importance of the image of God as Father for the rest of the letter (*Galatians*, 69), whereas I think it is key to the whole of Paul's argument.

10. See Marianne Meye Thompson, *The Promise of the Father: Jesus and God in the New Testament* (Louisville: Westminster John Knox, 2000) esp. 116–32 on the letters of Paul.

11. Five other texts likely refer to the resurrection (or new life) more subtly: 2:19–21; 3:19–21; 5:24–25; 6:8; 6:14–15. See Andrew K. Boakye, *Death and Life: Resurrection, Restoration, and Rectification in Paul's Letter to the Galatians* (Eugene, OR: Pickwick, 2017).

The other noteworthy aspect is the closeness in Paul's language between Jesus Christ and God, specifically as Father. The greeting already asserts this relationship (1:1), but it is affirmed elsewhere as well. By the vocabulary of "revelation," Paul affirms God as the one who made "his Son" known to him (1:16, ἀποκαλύψαι τὸν υἱὸν αὐτοῦ, "to reveal his son"). Paul's is thus an authoritative call. Elsewhere Paul explicitly speaks of God sending forth (ἐξαπέστειλεν) God's Son into the world (4:4) for the sake of redemption from sin. This shows that God shares the Son freely, giving him to the world as a gift. Furthermore, in language that already reveals Paul's movement toward the unique trinitarian viewpoint of Christianity, Paul says in the same passage that God sent forth (ἐξαπέστειλεν) the "Spirit of his Son" into our hearts, and this gift is what enables us to recognize that we are truly God's children and that God is our Father (4:6). God's gift of the Spirit allows the Galatians to live by faith, not by the law (3:5; also 5:16, 22, 25).[12]

Although it is beyond the scope of this article, mention can be made of the modern problem that "Father" language evokes in our day. Not only have modern interpreters become hypersensitive to sexist or patriarchally biased language in the Bible, but some opine that, since some human fathers are less than model incarnations of an ideal, the image arrives tarnished and can impede believers trying to relate to God in any meaningful way as a divine Father. Such discussion moves into the complex territory of theological and hermeneutical discourse. For our purposes, what is essential is to note that, in Paul's Jewish context, calling God Father or addressing God as Father is simply a given in his culture, although Jesus's use of the Aramaic address ʾAbba may add a layer of intimacy.[13] The value of such language is that it is *personal* and *relational*. God is not merely a vague entity, an aloof spirit, or a distant tyrant who toys with humanity but a close, inviting, and life-giving individual. Moreover, in the context of the Galatians' having been attracted to other "gods" and natural forces, emphasizing this personal dimension of God's identity is a way of challenging their prior adhesion to what amounts to idols (4:3, 8–11).

Implicit References

God is also implicitly present in Galatians in multiple passages, especially through the use of verbs in the passive voice of which God is the implied

---

12. The participle ἐπιχορηγῶν ("one who supplies") does not have an explicit subject, but the NRSV rightly indicates it is God (also NET, NIV).

13. See Thompson, *Promise of the Father*, 40–55.

subject (e.g., "entrusted," 2:7; "given," 2:9; "justified," 2:16–17 [4x]; also 3:11, 24; "reckoned," 3:6; "blessed," 3:8; "added" and "promised," 3:19; "known," 4:9; "formed," 4:19; "called," 5:13). Also apparent are the attributions to the sacred Scriptures (γέγραπται, "it is written," 3:10, 13; 4:22, 27). These verbs are directly connected to other themes I will address below, but the combined explicit and implicit passages on God reinforce the impression that the theme permeates the letter, from start to finish.

■ IDENTITY

Most scholars agree that Paul does not spend time describing God. Basically, all of Paul's letters—Galatians included—*presume* the Old Testament background about God's nature rather than exploring it. James Dunn, for instance, labels Paul's ideas on God as "all too axiomatic."[14] Dunn asserts that Paul's view of God is entirely what his Jewish counterparts would also have accepted, albeit with certain christological nuances that obviously arose from Paul's coming to know the Lord Jesus. Francis Watson critiqued this viewpoint strongly, however, by pointing out that, whenever Paul speaks of God, he means "the God and Father of our Lord Jesus Christ" and thus not simply the God of Israel.[15] Watson insists that Paul makes this assertion without detriment to his fundamental monotheism. Inevitably, Paul's language raises questions about the relationship between his theology and his christology. They are intimately connected, yet in such a way, as Watson insists, that monotheism is not jeopardized. Indeed, we also need to add into the mix Paul's pneumatological perspective, which gives the Holy Spirit a prominent role and which also plays an important part in his argumentation in Galatians. Watson is correct, I believe, to emphasize that this "triune divine identity" goes beyond the level of standard Jewish conceptions of God without threatening a monotheistic outlook.

Another assumption often in play concerning the content of Paul's arguments is that, for the most part, his hearers/readers would have shared the same basic approach, although the Galatians, as gentile converts, would

14. James D. G. Dunn, *The Theology of Paul the Apostle* (Grand Rapids: Eerdmans, 1998) 28; see also Guthrie and Martin, "God," 354–55. Richard N. Longenecker emphasizes Paul's typical Jewish emphasis on God's "functions" rather than on ontology, but also notes the nuance of Paul's christological connections between God and Jesus.

15. See Francis Watson, "The Triune Divine Identity: Reflections on Pauline God-Language, in Disagreement with J. D. G. Dunn," *JSNT* 80 (2000) 90–124.

perhaps have had less familiarity with Jewish ideas than their Jewish-Christian counterparts. This would be so because in Paul's preaching—his gospel—he would have used many terms with scriptural background that would have been at his disposal but which were also likely used by his opponents in Galatia. In any event, Paul affirms a few basic aspects of God's identity in the letter.

The first is that "God is one" (3:20; Deut 6:4). Although the statement occurs in the context of a complicated sentence whose precise meaning is disputed, Paul's assertion appears connected to the contrast of God's oneness with multiple false "gods" (4:8), which in the case of the Galatians included elemental powers to which they became enslaved (4:8, 10; cf. 4:3, where Paul applies a similar enslavement of all humanity pre-Christ, including himself [ἡμεῖς], to "elemental powers of the world").

Another aspect of Paul's teaching includes several positions that are consistent with his Jewish context. Thus, God rightly receives "glory" (ἐδόξαζον, 1:24) from human beings; God shows no "partiality" in dealing with human beings (2:6)—an important idea for the gentile Galatians to grasp; God has a kingdom or reigns over the universe (5:21);[16] and God is not to be "mocked" or treated with contempt (μυκτηρίζεται, 6:7). All of these expressions conform to a standard Jewish understanding of God's identity, although Paul applies some of them specifically to the Galatian context in which he is writing. From a strictly Christian standpoint, Paul affirms that the Galatian "churches" (1:2) are now, by implication, part of "the church of God" that he had persecuted (1:13) before his divine commissioning to be the apostle to the gentiles (1:11–16).

A more problematic phrase is the unique expression "the Israel of God" in the context of the final wish for peace and mercy (6:16). This famous *crux interpretum* can be taken in several ways, with two main possibilities.[17] The common sense of the expression out of context would seemingly be the Jews, God's chosen people—Israel. But it could also mean "Israel" in a metaphorical sense of both Jewish and gentile believers who now constitute one "family of faith" (6:10). Although Paul nowhere asserts that the church is the new Israel, this latter interpretation could fit with his overall argumentation of insisting that the Galatians remain

---

16. Galatians 5:21 is one of the rare instances in the undisputed letters of Paul where the familiar Gospel expression βασιλεία θεοῦ ("kingdom of God") occurs; cf. Rom 14:17; 1 Cor 4:20; 6:9, 10; 15:50; and "the kingdom" in 1 Cor 15:24.

17. See the lucid discussions in de Boer, *Galatians*, 405–8; Martyn, *Galatians*, 574–77; Matera, *Galatians*, 232, and especially the detailed article of Susan Grove Eastman, "Israel and the Mercy of God: A Re-reading of Galatians 6.6 and Romans 9–11," *NTS* 56 (2010) 367–95.

faithful to the gospel message in which *all* find a new identity (3:25). Nonetheless, historical Israel is probably to be preferred in line with Paul's understanding, expressed later in Romans, of God's gratuitous mercy (Rom 11:30–32). Moreover, the unusual expression "God's Israel" would draw attention to God's faithfulness, implying that God does not abandon the chosen people in the midst of the outreach to the gentiles.[18]

- ### ACTIVITY AND CHARACTERISTICS

In my reading of Galatians, I identify a collection of activities and characteristics that encompass five major subthemes that predominate the letter and show how Paul conceives of God as the prime mover behind his teaching: the God of election and promise, of justification, of truth and freedom, of judgment, and of tenderness.

The God of Election and Promise

This may well be the controlling image for God in Galatians, and it is noticeable on several levels. First, and most evident, the beginning of the letter emphasizes Paul's insistence that he writes as one with the authority of God alone, and not simply from a human viewpoint. The greeting itself denies human source or agency in his selection as an apostle (both ἀπό, "from," and διά, "through") and at the same time affirms his selection "through [διά] Jesus Christ and God the Father who raised him from the dead" (1:1). The mention of Jesus Christ does not discount the fact that it is God the Father who acts behind the scenes, for Paul explicitly asserts that God "revealed" God's Son to him (1:16). All that Paul recounts is done in accord with the will (θέλημα, 1:4) of the Father. To reinforce his point, Paul reiterates his strong affirmation that God has chosen him to preach the gospel and that human agency was not involved. Twice he affirms that what happened to him was according to divine revelation (1:12, 16; 2:2).[19] There can be no mistaking that God is the origin of his call and his message. Using language that echoes the vocation of prophets before him, Paul describes his apostolic commissioning as a prophetic call (1:15; cf. Isa 49:1; Jer 1:4–5).[20] In typically Pauline fashion, he attributes

18. De Boer, *Galatians*, 408; Wright, *Galatians*, 369.
19. See the expression δι᾽ ἀποκαλύψεως ("through a revelation," 1:12); Jesus Christ is the content of the revelation, but the implied source is God, who is also the subject of the infinitive in 1:16.
20. I include the language of Paul's being sent as an apostle (ἐξαποστέλλω, 4:4, 6; also 1:1; 2:8) as related to this theme.

his call to "grace" (χάρις), which is God's mysterious power at work in the universe, and especially in the hearts of believers.[21] Paul affirms that he and his colleagues have personally been given God's grace for their ministry (2:9, δοθεῖσαν, passive voice). Moreover, Paul claims that his motivation is entirely to please God and not simply human beings (1:10).

The God of election is not merely active in Paul's life. He also insists that it was God who called (καλέσαντος; cf. also 5:8, 13) the Galatians—by the "grace of [Christ]" (1:6)—a call they are in danger of abandoning because they are being seduced away from the gospel Paul preached (1:8; 2:2).[22] This gospel is nothing less than what God has done in Christ for the salvation of the world, and ultimately for its "freedom" in the Spirit (5:1). It is the "gospel of Christ" (1:7) that certain unnamed interlopers and "false brothers" are attempting to pervert (2:4). This is what has angered Paul so greatly and is the principal reason he writes the letter. Paul is also quite perceptive at one point concerning God's initiative, affirming that the Galatians had come to "know" God, but quickly correcting himself, "or rather to be known by God [ὑπὸ θεοῦ]" (4:9; also 1 Cor 8:2–3; 13:12). God initiates the relationship, and being chosen by God includes being known by him.

A major aspect of Paul's affirmation of the God of election is found in the person of Abraham, who dominates the body of the letter.[23] Abraham is Paul's primary scriptural defense of his position because God called Abraham, who "'believed God,' and it was credited [passive voice] to him as righteousness" (3:6). God's election of, and covenant with, Abraham lies behind the image, but Paul, for understandable reasons, does not evoke the covenant explicitly (its sign was circumcision!). He is less interested in the fact that God chose Abraham to be the father of a multitude than in the fact that Abraham responded freely and immediately to this divine election.

Closely tied to election and to the figure of Abraham is the idea of "promise" (ἐπαγγελία, 3:14, 17, 18, 19, 22, 29; 4:23, 28). Paul asserts that, just as God was faithful to the promise God gave Abraham and to his son Isaac, the "heir of the promise," so too is God faithful to the Galatians, whom God calls to faith, and who are "children of the promise" (4:28–

---

21. See 1:3, 6; 2:9, 21; 5:4; 6:18.

22. Whether God or Christ is meant as the source of the call is not entirely clear in 1:6, but in either case, Paul was merely the instrument by his proclamation of the gospel. Note, however, that some manuscripts are missing Χριστοῦ.

23. See Hays's treatment of the figure of Abraham ("God of Mercy," 126–27).

29). In both instances, it is God who "credits" Abraham as righteous (3:6) and God who stands by this promise.[24]

Another dimension of this theme is the subtle allusion to baptism and the "new creation" that resounds in the letter. The most explicit mention is obviously Paul's assertion that baptism into Christ means being "clothed" in him (3:27) in such a way that the standard human distinctions of Jew/gentile, slave/free, male *and* female do not hold, because "all are one in Christ" (3:28). This is an "election" in the sense that by baptism "we belong to Christ" (3:29, literally, Χριστοῦ).[25] It bestows a new identity on the Galatians. By baptism and the Holy Spirit, they become adopted children, true heirs (4:6–7). Indeed, Paul later insists that only the "new creation" counts (6:15; cf. 2 Cor 5:17). His teaching disabuses the Galatians of any naïve idea that accepting circumcision will bestow a proper identity upon them in order to be true followers of Christ and members of the covenant community. They do not need this "mark" of identity in Christ; this was contrary to Paul's gospel. They, like Paul, are marked rather by the cross of Christ (2:19; cf. 5:11; 6:12, 14, 17). Christian identity comes from being in Christ through the Holy Spirit, according to God's grace.

The God of Justification

One of Paul's enduring understandings of God's activity is his notion of justification (or rectification; the root δικαι-; 2:16 [3x], 17; 3:8, 11, 24; cf. 5:4; Rom 2:13; 3:24; 5:1, 1 Cor 6:11; etc.).[26] Justification is one of the most important fruits of God's plan in the cross and resurrection of Jesus, intimately tied to salvation, redemption, atonement, reconciliation, and sanctification. Prescinding from the Catholic/Protestant discussion of whether one is *declared* or *made* righteous (justified or rectified), what is clear is that God is the actor and human beings the recipients (3:8; cf. also passive voice in 2:16 [3x], 17; 3:11, 24). God, through the self-offering of the faithful Son Jesus on the cross, has given humanity a new way to overcome the power of sin and death. The new creation (6:15) has already begun.

24. Paul normally uses the singular "promise," employing the plural (promises) only in 3:16 and 21, perhaps having in mind there both Abraham's descendants (Gen 17:2–6) through Isaac *and* the gift of the promised land (Gen 17:7).

25. Notice how Paul includes himself in this expression ("we").

26. "Rectification" has less historical "baggage" than "justification." For a clear defense of the need to move beyond a forensic understanding of this concept, see Thomas D. Stegman, "Paul's Use of *DIKAIO-* Terminology: Moving Beyond N. T. Wright's Forensic Interpretation," *TS* 72 (2011) 496–524.

Paul is so adamant on this point because he has realized that "works of the law" are no longer needed for salvation (2:16). Christ's faithfulness by the "grace of God" is sufficient. Believers' actions do not earn salvation but concretely witness to God's salvific activity on behalf of humanity through God's Son. He warns the Galatians away from the temptation of accepting circumcision and obedience to the law, precisely because it would drain Christ's salvific action of all its meaning (2:21; 5:2). God's justification of sinners is essentially a compassionate sign that God does not want to leave us to our sinful inclinations; God restores right relationships.

The God of Truth and Freedom

A third aspect of Paul's teaching is the underlying insistence that the gospel message he and his colleagues have preached is entirely true. He is urgently writing this letter to call the Galatians back to the "truth of the gospel" (2:5, 14). Because it comes from God, the message can be nothing other than the truth. Paul even calls upon God as a witness that he himself is telling the truth (1:20). One may assume that perhaps some in the Galatian community were, under pressure from the agitators, asserting that it was Paul who was distorting the gospel, not them. Paul firmly rejects such a notion. The gospel he preached was authentic "good news" because it came from God (1:11). Furthermore, the authorities in Jerusalem, who were apostles "before" Paul (πρὸ ἐμοῦ, 1:17), had approved his message (2:2). Even though the Jerusalem agreement had confirmed the twofold ministry of preaching the gospel—one to the Jews and one to the gentiles (2:9)—there is clearly no difference in the truth of the gospel, because it comes from God. Paul knows that it can be distorted, but he insists that there is no "alternative" gospel (1:6, 9). This is what makes the situation in Galatia so dire. In abandoning the authentic gospel message, the Galatians are in danger of wandering far from the truth, and thus from God. One suspects that the importance of honesty in dealing with the gospel is why Paul is so upset with Kephas and with his own colleague Barnabas (2:11–14). They "were not acting consistently with the truth of the gospel" (2:14). Their waffling on table fellowship with gentiles seriously undermined Paul's message.

Galatians reinforces the notion of the God of truth in two other ways. One is by Paul's use of Scripture (Old Testament), which is extensive. If the letter does not contain a clear statement about the ongoing validity of the Scriptures (as in Rom 15:4), nonetheless underlying Paul's entire argumentation is that the Scriptures come from God and embody the truth. It is probable that Paul uses some of the same scriptural quotations or images as the agitators. They are likely involved in a debate over how the Scriptures are to be best understood. In fact, sometimes Paul virtually personifies "the Scripture" (ἡ γραφή) as able to "foresee" (προϊδοῦσα, 3:8) that "God would justify the gentiles by faith," and to foretell "the gospel to Abraham" (3:8). Paul even claims that Scripture "imprisoned [συνέκλει-σεν] all things under the power of sin" (3:22, here understood as a cosmic power that enslaves). If the image is odd, Paul sees in it a positive outcome: "so that [ἵνα; result rather than purpose; cf. Rom 5:20] through the faithfulness of Jesus Christ what was promised might be given to those who believe" (cf. also Rom 11:32).[27] Like the law's temporary function as a pedagogue (3:24), Scripture can function as a kind of disciplinarian for the paradoxical purpose of making the "promise" a reality.

Paul's use of Scripture in Galatians is important.[28] It forms a vital underpinning for his principal argumentation, though he supplements his arguments with his own autobiographical testimony. Galatians cites Scripture (usually the Septuagint) eleven times (3:6, 8, 10, 11, 12, 13, 16; 4:22, 27, 30; 5:14), mostly associated with Paul's explanation of the importance of Abraham and the promise.[29] As elsewhere, Paul has a predilection to precede his citations with the passive voice expression, "it is written" (γέγραπται, 3:10, 13; 4:22, 27; cf. Rom 1:17; 2:24; 3:4; etc.), which signals God's authorship. Yet Paul is selective in the way he cites Scripture in order to bolster his argumentation. In rabbinic fashion, he can take the Scriptures in ways inconsistent with the original sense. The sequence in 3:6–13, for instance, illustrates this point. His use of Scripture is somewhat dizzying, because he cites passages that essentially say the exact opposite (Lev 18:5; Hab 2:4) but are now employed to verify his main point: faith, not the law, is what leads to righteousness before God.

27. The whole question of the phrase πίστις Χριστοῦ (2:16) and its variants is extremely complex and highly debated, though in recent decades the interpretation as a subjective genitive has dominated, that is, "faith of Christ." This is an instance where the expression διὰ πίστεως Ἰησοῦ Χριστου should properly be considered in this fashion (also 2:20; 3:22–26). I believe, however, that Paul's concept of faith is larger than this expression. Paul's thought also emphasizes in other contexts faith or believing *in* Jesus Christ, especially in regard to the verb πιστεύω, as in this same verse (also 3:22). Note that πίστις in 5:22 is not faith but trustworthiness, a fruit of the Spirit. "Faith working through love" (5:6) can apply to both Christ and all believers (cf. 2:19–20 where faithfulness and love occur together).

28. For an overview of Paul's complex use of Scripture, see Ronald D. Witherup, *Scripture and Tradition in the Letters of Paul* (BSCBAA 4; New York: Paulist, 2021) 1–79.

29. It is debated whether 2:16 constitutes a proper citation of Scripture (Ps 143:2). For the present chapter, I attend to more explicit citations, since possible scriptural allusions, legitimate though they may be, are notoriously difficult to define.

He also adds an echo of the crucifixion ("hung from a tree," 3:13; Deut 21:23) to reinforce his teaching that Christ's saving action on the cross is the vehicle through which "the promise of the Spirit through faith" (3:14) has been given.

Paul is equally creative scripturally in the famous allegory (ἀλληγορού–μενα, 4:24) of the two covenants (4:21–31). The entire argumentation pivots around two key passages Paul employs: a creative use of Isa 54:1 (v. 27) to tie into God's promise to give Abraham progeny, and a direct citation from the Abraham story to send away the slave woman (v. 30; Gen 21:10). By the ingenious use of these two citations, Paul interweaves the story of Abraham and his two wives, by whom he had two sons, with the story of the Galatians. They would surely recognize the authoritative voice of Scripture in application to their own circumstance: drive away those promoting slavery and not freedom!

In addition to the importance of truth, Paul emphasizes that God has "called" the Galatians to freedom (5:13, ἐκλήθητε), which is tied to the preceding message (4:21–31). The passive voice in 5:13 indicates divine origin, although Paul is even more explicit that Christ is the one who, as God's agent, has "set us free" (5:1). But this freedom brings with it responsibility. It is not for self-service but so that the Galatians can "serve one another" (δουλεύετε ἀλλήλοις, 5:13). There is profound irony in Paul's teaching on freedom, for true freedom in Christ means paradoxically becoming a "slave of Christ" (Χριστοῦ δοῦλος, 1:10; cf. 1 Cor 7:22). Being freed from the constraints of following every aspect of the law paradoxically allows believers to live more freely for others. Paul then fleshes out what freedom means concretely by walking in the Spirit (5:16–25), which requires adhering to certain ethical standards.

The God of Judgment

Paul also does not hesitate to employ a warning to the Galatians by reminding them that God also judges. Paul charges them to mend their ways and return to the truth of the gospel or face serious consequences. Twice near the beginning of the letter, Paul invokes the threat of ἀνάθεμα (literally, anathema) (1:8, 9), which here is used in the sense of bringing a curse from God. It is clearly directed against the false preachers who are seducing the Galatians away from the gospel message, but it would have raised a warning flag to Paul's hearers/readers that straying from the gospel can bring divine consequences. It is worth noting more explicitly Paul's warning of "judgment" against the agitators (5:10, κρίμα). More subtly elsewhere, Paul's language evokes a possible curse by God when he cites a warning from Scripture: "Cursed be everyone who does not observe and do all the things written in the book of the law" (3:10; Deut 27:26). He is warning them that to take on the law is to take on the *whole* law, and not fulfilling it will bring negative judgment upon them (also 5:3).

Probably the clearest depiction in the letter of the God of judgment is in the extensive paraenetic teachings of 5:13–6:10, through Paul's famous contrast of flesh (σάρξ) and Spirit (πνεῦμα). The detailed list of the "works of the flesh" leads to the warning that those who do such things "will not inherit the kingdom of God" (5:19–21). By contrast, those who follow the impulse of the Spirit will bear proper fruit (καρπός, sg.), running the gamut from love to kindness to generosity to self-control (5:22). Paul ties these admonitions to the behavior of the Galatians among themselves, urging them to be gentle with backsliders (6:1) and also to "bear one another's burdens" (6:2; cf. Col 3:13).

The next passage continues the theme of judgment. By citing the contrast between sowing and reaping (6:7–9), Paul insists that the Galatians will reap only what they sow, which embodies an explicit warning of judgment if they do not concretely put their freedom in Christ into action toward their neighbor (cf. 5:13–14; Matt 25:31–46). While there may be a hidden allusion to Paul's desire to have the Galatians help him in his task of the famous collection for the poor in Jerusalem (1 Cor 16:1; Gal 2:10), the context also points to a divine accounting in order to "reap eternal life" (6:8). Never tiring from doing good, especially to the "family of faith," will ensure a proper "harvest" (καιρῷ, 6:9–10).

The God of Tenderness

Perhaps the most surprising characteristic of God in Galatians, which is clearly a stern or even angry letter, is that God is compassionate.[30] This feature appears in several ways. First, as was noted above, there is the overarching image of God as "Father." God as Father was an important dimension of Paul's gospel message, for a remnant of the liturgical life of the community remains in the Aramaic word 'Abba, the tender way in which believers can address God through the "Spirit of his Son" (4:6). The context of the passage is important, for Paul is emphasizing that the Galatians have become true children of God by adoption (υἱοθεσία, 4:4–5), in

---

30. If the language of compassion (οἰκτιρμός) is rare in Paul (e.g., 2 Cor 1:3; Phil 2:1; Rom 9:15 [Exod 33:19]; Col 3:12), he does speak of God's mercy (ἔλεος), even at the end of this stern letter (6:16). See Ronald D. Witherup, *Mercy and the Bible: Why It Matters* (New York: Paulist, 2018) 78–86. Paul also invokes God's mercy in relation to Israel in Romans 9–11; see Dunn, *Theology of Paul the Apostle*, 513; and Eastman, "Israel and the Mercy of God," 376–79.

words that are mirrored in Paul's later teaching in Romans in a similar setting (cf. Rom 8:15). God bestows a profound identity on the Galatians through the Son Jesus Christ. They are not slaves but children, true heirs of a true Father (3:26; 4:6), which is why Paul is appealing to them not to abandon this gracious identity to become slaves by adopting prescripts of the law or by reverting to former pagan practices (4:8–10).

Paul reinforces the Father image in another way. It is not only that God acts as Father to the Galatians, as he does to all God's children, but Paul himself has been acting as a surrogate parent for his own wayward children. He has been both father and mother to them, trying to facilitate their birth into the new life of faith, while also giving them a guiding hand as their founding father (cf. 1 Thess 2:7b–12). Thus, throughout the letter, frustrated and fearful though Paul is that the Galatians are not heeding his teaching (4:11), he nonetheless affirms their initially loyal response to him (4:12–14). He offers them what we might call "tough love," but he never abandons using familial language. Although called to account, they remain his brothers and sisters (1:2, 11; 3:15; 4:12, 28, 31; 5:11, 13; 6:1, 18). In the tender image of a woman in labor, he even cries out: "My children [τέχνα μου], for whom I am again in labor pains until Christ be formed in you!" (4:19).[31]

Cohesion of Themes

These five interrelated themes serve Paul's purpose well in Galatians. Emphasizing "election" helps him trace God's gracious action toward humanity, from Abraham to his own apostolic call, to that of the Galatians, and through Jesus Christ to all humanity—Jew and gentile alike— who constitute a "new creation." This divine election takes place because God is faithful to the "promise"—God's Word is faithful and will ultimately bear fruit. By means of "justification," which God has enacted through the precious gift of God's own Son, the faithful one whose death on a cross wrought salvation and all its attendant results, all humanity has been set right again. Right relationship with God is reestablished, as with fellow human beings. Through "truth and freedom" Paul can exhort the Galatians to come back to this right and true path, the path of God. He can also urge them not to succumb to slavery but to live as free children, which is their heritage. Through "judgment" Paul can speak from

---

31. Some manuscripts use the diminutive form τεχνία ("little children"), making the image even more tender. See 1 Thess 2:7b–8, 11–12, where Paul juxtaposes the dual roles of (spiritual) father and mother in relation to that community; also cf. 1 Cor 3:1–2; 4:14–15; 2 Cor 6:13; Phlm 10.

his apocalyptic perspective that possessing the "kingdom" is not auto-
matic. If salvation is a free gift because of God's action in Christ and the
power of the cross—he "rescues [ἐξέληται] us from the present evil age"
(1:4)[32]—nonetheless there is responsibility on the part of everyone called
into the family of faith. "Faith working through love" demands an ethical
lifestyle, a life lived "through the Spirit." Finally, through "tenderness"
Paul can emphasize God's very nature as a loving, compassionate, forgiv-
ing Father. Paul himself never abandons his affection for his wayward
children in Galatia but tries to model for them an attitude of compassion.

■ GOD IN THE RHETORIC OF GALATIANS

At this point, it is good to step back from this detailed explanation to
glance at the "big picture" in Galatians. Viewed from its overall rhetorical
argumentation, I suggest that God figures large in the total "narrative"
that underlies the letter.[33]

The precipitating cause of the letter is that certain agitators from outside the Galatian communities (2:4, παρεισῆλθον, "sneaked in"), but from
within the "family of faith" (i.e., believers in Christ), have provoked a
serious crisis. Their preaching the necessity of circumcision—thus enter-
ing the Jewish covenant in order to follow Christ—goes contrary to Paul's
"gospel." He writes with full emotion to correct the situation.

Beginning with a standard greeting, shaped nonetheless to fit the
unique situation in Galatia, he addresses the "churches" in the region as
brothers and sisters in the faith, privileged to be members of God's family by the grace of the Lord Jesus Christ (1:1–5). Then he launches his
counterattack in two ways.

First, he uses his autobiographical narrative—a story the Galatians
may or may not have known well—to show that his call and his message

32. The "present evil age" forms part of Paul's basic apocalyptic worldview that
what God has done in Christ saves us from our corrupt era and prepares us for the
(already inaugurated) age to come—new creation (cf. 1 Cor 1:20; 2:6–8; 2 Cor 4:4; Eph
1:21; Phil 3:20). While I accept a strong apocalyptic overtone in Galatians, I do not
think it is the primary focus of the letter (*pace* Martyn). Interestingly, Paul does not
explicitly contrast the present evil age with the future "age to come"; it is implied but
not explicit in Paul's terminology (see Martyn, *Galatians*, 98). Cf. Jamie Davies, "Why
Paul Doesn't Mention the 'Age to Come,'" *SJT* 74 (2021) 199–208; and Constantine R.
Campbell, *Paul and the Hope of Glory: An Exegetical and Theological Study* (Grand Rapids: Zondervan, 2020).

33. By "rhetorical" I do not mean the rhetorical devices of the letter, which are
multiple, but its argumentative thrust.

came from God and that the content of this divine "revelation" is nothing less than Jesus Christ, the crucified and risen Lord. He recounts numerous details of his attempts to defend the "truth of the gospel" and to live out his apostolic call faithfully. His message is very forceful: he no longer lives his own life, but Christ lives in him—and all this is by "the grace of God" (2:20–21). Moreover, he emphasizes in these verses that his own life in Christ—for it is Christ who now inhabits him—is a life through which he has died to the law so that he might "live for God." Everything Paul stands for and has preached ultimately is "for God" and is accomplished by God's grace. He even affirms that the Galatians had welcomed him as an "angel of God," that is, a divine messenger; in doing so they had welcomed him "as Christ Jesus" himself (4:14; cf. Matt 10:40). Subtly, he is affirming his role as God's chosen instrument for proclaiming the truth that he had preached and that now they are in danger of abandoning.

Second, to strengthen his argument, he sets forth some scriptural testimony, hoping that the Galatians will recognize the force of Scripture as God's Word.[34] Using the figure of Abraham, Paul lays out his understanding of how God worked with this progenitor of faith. God called Abraham, whose response was immediate and unquestioned "faith," for which God credits him as righteous, a key affirmation in Paul's argumentation (3:6; cf. Gen 15:6; Rom 4:3). Paul sees in this action a prefigurement of God's planned destiny to justify, rectify, or make/declare righteous also the gentiles (3:8), of which his Galatians are a prime example. Through complex scriptural argumentation, and by glossing over the covenant of circumcision with Abraham, Paul places the emphasis on the promise(s) of God regarding progeny. God promises Abraham a son—an heir, not a slave—through whom he would become the progenitor of a great family because the true heir is none other than Jesus Christ, who proves himself the faithful Son of God and in whose name the Galatians were baptized into a new creation. This is how they have become "Abraham's descendants, heirs according to the promise" (3:29; also 4:9, "through God" [διὰ θεοῦ]). By virtue of this new life, they become God's adopted children, joined to his only Son. They also prove themselves true heirs of the promise, having received the gift of the Spirit, who enables them to cry out to God as Father (ʾAbba).

Paul bolsters his scriptural argumentation with yet another example from Abraham, in the allegory of the two covenants (4:21–31). Once more, with an imaginative interpretation, Paul reminds the Galatians of

---

34. We should recall that in antiquity, unlike today, arguments from authority held great weight.

the need to choose the right path God has proffered them (cf. Deut 30:19; Psalm 1). They are already justified and are free children, true heirs. They are to remain free and reject slavery to the law (4:31; 5:1).

Key to his argumentation is obviously the question of the law and its relationship to faith. If the law once served to help distinguish right from wrong, it is no longer needed. What Paul urges the Galatians to recall is that their fulfilling the "law of Christ" (6:2)—that is, the law of love (5:14)—is what bears true "fruit" (5:22). As Paul insists, "For in Christ Jesus, neither circumcision nor uncircumcision counts for anything but only faith working through love" (5:6, 13; 6:15).

Paul's scope in Galatians of what God has accomplished in Christ is breathtaking. From the opening lines about "God the Father and the Lord Jesus Christ" to the final "Amen," God is the primary actor behind the scenes. It is God who has been acting on humanity's behalf, from Abraham, continuing through the faithfulness of God's Son Jesus Christ on the cross, and currently acting in the life of the Galatians, who unfortunately have been turning a deaf ear to Paul's pleas to remain faithful themselves. Paul's own message is rooted in "revelation"—God's gracious unveiling of God's own will—and in his own life in Christ, by which he has been "crucified with Christ" even to the point of receiving the wounds of apostleship (6:17; cf. 2 Cor 11:23–28). If Christ's own faithfulness looms large in this picture, Paul is also calling the Galatians to their faith *in* Christ, which they should live out by the law of love, by "walking" in the power of the Holy Spirit.

In sum, Galatians is not merely a bland repetition of standard Old Testament perspectives. Rather, the letter offers a rich panoply of themes surrounding the image of God. Christological, soteriological, and pneumatological insights greatly enhance the portrayal of God in an innovative manner that responds to Paul's experience with the Galatians and his mature theological reflection in the face of opposition to his gospel message.

5

"The One Who Began a Good Work among You": God in Philippians

AYODELE AYENI, C.S.SP.

TIMOTHY MILINOVICH

Of the two images of the divine found in Philippians—God and "Jesus as God"—the latter has received far more scholarly attention and engagement.[1] In order to mitigate this lacuna, in this chapter we will focus on how God plays a prominent role in the theological argument of this letter.[2] It is God the Father, for example, whose divinity is the standard by which Christ's is compared, who exalted Christ, set the stage for universal acknowledgment of Christ's lordship for God's own glory, and has called the Philippians to a new life in Christ.

The first section will outline Paul's description of God in the letter's linear progression. In the second section we will deduce three major characteristics from the overall argument: God is the Philippians' divine "Father," sovereign over creation, and the proper recipient of worship.

---

1. Larry W. Hurtado, *Lord Jesus Christ: Devotion to Jesus in Earliest Christianity* (Grand Rapids: Eerdmans, 2003); idem, *How on Earth Did Jesus Become a God? Historical Questions about Earliest Devotion to Jesus* (Grand Rapids: Eerdmans, 2005); idem, *God in New Testament Theology* (Library of Biblical Theology; Nashville: Abingdon, 2010); idem, *Honoring the Son: Jesus in Earliest Christian Devotional Practice* (Snapshots; Bellingham, WA: Lexham, 2018); Richard Bauckham, *Jesus and the God of Israel: God Crucified and Other Studies on the New Testament's Christology of Divine Identity* (Grand Rapids: Eerdmans, 2008).

2. While arguments that Philippians consists of more than one letter persist (see, e.g., John Reumann, *Philippians: A New Translation with Introduction and Commentary* [AYB 33B; New Haven: Yale University Press, 2008] 8–13), we will treat the letter in its canonical form.

The third section will address how God's numerous gifts impact the audience in Philippi, which include citizenship, peace, and righteousness. In addition, the "good work" God began in the Philippians gives them κοινωνία to bring them closer together as a community and direct them to understand and offer appropriate worship in which all glory is received by God.

■ OVERVIEW: GOD IN PAUL'S MESSAGE TO THE PHILIPPIANS

1:1–11

When he writes to the Philippians, Paul addresses them as God's holy people and presents himself as the duly commissioned messenger who brings to them the peace and grace of God and Jesus Christ. In his joyful prayers, Paul thanks God for the Philippians' partnership in the gospel from the first time he preached it to them (1:3).[3] Paul can write and pray with confidence for the Philippians because they share (κοινωνία) in God's grace with him, whether he is free or in chains. And God can testify to Paul's affection for, and desire to return to, the Philippians (1:7–8). With this prayer, Paul states confidently that the God he introduced to them, and to whom he constantly prays for their well-being, will continue this "good work" until Christ's return (1:6).

This "good work" is defined further as the grace God has given them to have a share in the gospel with Paul and to support his ministry, as well as the love and knowledge that continue to grow in them so that they may be pure and blameless on the day of Christ, filled with the fruit of righteousness (1:9–11). As Bonnie B. Thurston notes, this concept of "brought to maturity" is spatial, moral, and spiritual in scope.[4] Based on v. 6, where God begins a good work in them, the passive πεπληρωμένοι ("be fulfilled") has God in view as the active agent (as with ἦτε, v. 10).[5]

3. Marvin R. Vincent, *A Critical and Exegetical Commentary on the Epistles to the Philippians and to Philemon* (ICC; Edinburgh: T&T Clark, 1985) 7–10; James W. Thompson and Bruce W. Longenecker, *Philippians and Philemon* (Paideia; Grand Rapids: Baker Academic, 2016) 28 (the commentary on Philippians is by Thompson, and that on Philemon is by Longenecker).

4. Bonnie B. Thurston and Judith M. Ryan, *Philippians and Philemon* (SacPag 10; Collegeville, MN: Liturgical Press, 2009) 54 (Thurston is the author of the commentary on Philippians; Ryan on Philemon).

5. Vincent (*Philippians and Philemon*, 14) and Thompson (*Philippians*, 33) imply God's activity in vv. 10–11. Gerald F. Hawthorne (*Philippians* [WBC 43; Waco, TX: Word, 1983] 29) has Christ as the most immediate source of righteousness but also

Just as God assists the Philippians in the growth of their love and knowledge to help them be pure and blameless, so too does God produce the harvest of righteousness within them through Jesus Christ.

1:12–3:1

Paul is in a desperate state as he writes to the Philippians from prison, though he does not speak in detail about his situation. In fact, he describes it opaquely as "what has happened to me" (1:12).[6] But he makes two theological arguments that develop his overall theme of consolation for the audience. First, Paul avers a divine teleology to explain his time in prison. God is still in control: Paul is in prison only because God seeks to gain a harvest among the imperial guard. While Paul's state of affairs leads him to feel death's shadow encroaching on his ministry, he is confident that God will preserve him. God's success already with the Philippians convinces Paul that God will keep him alive in order to help maintain the spiritual growth of the "good work" God initiated and is working toward fruition among them (1:25–26).

Second, Paul groups his and the Philippians' sufferings with Christ's death on the cross under the same umbrella of God's merciful oversight. Since God is sovereign over all things, so too can God bring about their joint deliverance/salvation (σωτηρίαν). God's provision of the Spirit and the Philippians' prayers will deliver Paul from this situation (1:19), and, although the Philippians suffer, God has given (ἐχαρίσθη) them the opportunity to believe and will save them from their toils and this world (1:28–29).[7] Paul's and the Philippians' reciprocal petitionary prayers demonstrate the κοινωνία that God has established among them.[8] In this way, Paul extends the divine teleology regarding his own suffering in prison to the Philippians' situation.

This divine teleology is prominent also in the Christ hymn (2:6–10). While the text is viewed primarily as Christocentric in scope, God is a

---

views God as the initiator of the process. Paul A. Holloway seems to have the right of it when he ties together God's initial good work (1:6), God's continuing work (2:13), with God's righteousness (3:20) to view the righteousness of 1:11 as God's own righteousness (*Philippians: A Commentary* [Hermeneia; Minneapolis: Fortress, 2017] 80 n. 80). He is joined by Reumann (*Philippians*, 158), who points to God's "filling" of believers elsewhere in Gal 3:2, 5; 5:22; Rom 5:1–5; 8:9; 1 Cor 6:11, among others.

6. Or "the things regarding me . . .", so John Paul Heil, *Philippians: Let Us Rejoice in Being Conformed to Christ* [Early Christianity and Its Literature 3; Atlanta: Society of Biblical Literature, 2010] 14).

7. Thompson, *Philippians*, 54.

8. Thurston, *Philippians*, 62.

primary actor in the narrative implied in the hymn. Christ was in the form of God but did not exploit this equality with God. Instead, Christ emptied himself by taking the form of a slave and human likeness. He humbled himself, becoming obedient and dying on a cross. In direct response, God highly exalted Christ and gave him authority over all things.[9] This exaltation is of mutual benefit to God the Father and to Christ. Everyone will acknowledge Christ as Lord and, as a result, will also glorify God, who exalted Christ to this position. As in 1:11, the arc of salvation history is long, but God bends it toward God's own glory.

The Philippians' partnership (κοινωνία) with Paul in the gospel joins them also to Christ's death/exaltation and, therefore, to God's overall plan for salvation. This co-suffering—Paul's in prison, the Philippians' in their own state, and Christ's on the cross—is correlated with familial images and sacrificial terminology, as are Paul's descriptions of how to be pleasing to God. Paul uses two images to explain how the Philippians can be pleasing to God. From the domestic sphere, the Philippians should honor God by being obedient children. From the realm of sacrificial worship, they should be a blameless and innocent sacrifice, whose faith is an offering over which Paul may be poured as a libation—all of which images operate to glorify God (2:14).

Recalling their plight (1:28–30) and the good work God began among them (1:6), Paul calls on the Philippians to continue to work toward their salvation because God is doing good work in them to help them to obey the gospel (2:12–13).[10] Paul Holloway's translation rightly amplifies this point in 2:12: "God . . . is the one producing in you . . . both the ability to will [what is right] and actually do [it]."[11] Paul encourages the Philippians that enduring with faithfulness through their trials with fear and trembling will demonstrate how God's "good work" in them is indeed making them pure and blameless children of God, filled with righteousness, who will shine like stars on the day of Christ (2:15–16).

The familial language continues in 2:19–3:1 with a new emphasis on service and examples of God's grace empowering successful endurance through difficulty. One example Paul offers is Epaphroditus (2:25–30). God's mercy in helping Epaphroditus recover from illness was likewise a relief from Paul's anxiety and worked to the Philippians' benefit in that Paul could send Epaphroditus back to them to increase their joy and

---

9. Thurston reads the echoes of Ps 110:1–2 as imagining an enthronement for Christ within the exaltation scene (*Philippians*, 87).

10. As Thompson notes, ὥστε in 2:12 connects what follows to the ethical exhortations in 1:27–30 (*Philippians*, 77).

11. Holloway, *Philippians*, 131.

decrease their concern. God's act of healing Epaphroditus (who was thought to be near death) so that he could serve others parallels Paul's description of how God exalted Christ to give the opportunity for faith and righteousness among God's own people (2:27–28; cf. 1:11). God's grace is so abounding, and power over the cosmos so complete, that, even when the Philippians wished they could do something to help Paul but were not able due to material constraints, God fills the gap for them (2:29). This theme, in which God saves those who suffer and empowers them to comfort others in God's own plan, remains prominent through the rest of the letter and underscores behavior that Paul views as demonstrating those who are God's pure and blameless children.

3:2–21

In contrast to God's children, Paul offers his own opponents—those who may already be speaking to the Philippians (1:12–18) and those who may soon be intruding on his mission path (3:2–3, 17–19)—as examples of the wrong way to live and serve God.[12] Epaphroditus and Paul, who offer priestly service and worship God by the Spirit, are the true circumcision and have the true demonstration of faithfulness and right relationship with God (3:3). The difference between those who worship and serve the right way, and those who operate deceptively, is their perception of the origin of righteousness. God's children recognize that true righteousness comes from God, who works through those who submit to the gospel (1:6; 2:12–13; 3:9). Moreover, by participating in Christ's sufferings faithfully through their own trials, they can hope to attain God's righteousness and Christ's resurrection (3:9–11).[13]

Paul's invective against the opponents coheres with his message of hope for the Philippians and his defense of his own ministry that began in 1:27–30 and continued through 2:6–11. Just as Christ, God's Son, humbled himself to death on a cross and God exalted him with authority over all things, so too can the Philippians—God's own children—hope that, by submitting to their present challenges with faithful humility and withstanding these opponents, they too will be raised up and exalted to shine like the stars in the sky (3:10–11). This goal is difficult to attain, even for

---

12. Paul is likely referring to two different groups of opponents in 1:12–14 and 3:2–3, 17–19. See Vincent, *Philippians and Philemon*, 17–18, 92; Elsa Tamez, Cynthia Briggs Kittredge, Claire Miller Colombo, and Alicia J. Batten (*Philippians, Colossians, Philemon* [Wisdom 51; Collegeville, MN: Liturgical Press, 2017] 96; the commentary on Philippians is by Tamez; Colossians, by Kittredge and Colombo; and Philemon, by Batten). The community may be facing a third group of their own leaders or neighbors (Thurston, *Philippians*, 117).

13. Ralph P. Martin, *Philippians* (NCB; London: Oliphants, 1976) 133.

apostles like Paul. But believers should attend to God's call through Christ to bring them closer to God, in relational, salvific, and locative senses. This closeness with God crafts a sense of "home" that aligns with the family imagery found throughout the letter.

4:1–23

The primary actor who empowers Paul to persevere in his ministry is God, who also works in the Philippians to bring about their salvation (4:13; cf. 2:13). The gifts the Philippians sent Paul with Epaphroditus are an acceptable sacrifice (4:18), reflecting the proper behavior of those who are God's children and the true circumcision, who worship properly through God's Spirit (3:3), so as to be pleasing to God (like Paul and Epaphroditus themselves, 2:27–28).[14] Likewise, God will meet all the Philippians' needs through God's own glorious riches for them found in Christ. God is the one who gives citizenship to the Philippians and all the faithful and who empowers Christ with authority to bring all things under Christ's control, and therefore God's (1:27; 3:20).[15] So, while the opponents find shameful destruction from their material concerns, those who look to the cross will find family, citizenship, and salvation in the transformation of their bodies to be like the glorious, resurrected body of Christ. A great gift, indeed!

Paul closes the letter by again emphasizing God's identity as divine father and sovereign of all things, who will fulfill the plan that is currently unfolding for the Philippians, God's children (4:20). Since the Lord Jesus is near, the Philippians should temper their anxieties and rejoice, knowing that God's work to fulfill their salvation is close at hand. Instead of worry or despair, they should continue to set forward their prayers of petition and thanksgiving to God. God's presence, which transcends all things, will lead them toward behavior that is right, pure, and noble, as is fitting for God's children (4:8–9). By practicing the gospel they received from Paul, their adoptive divine father—the God of peace and ruler of the cosmos—will continue to preserve them from anxiety.

■ GOD'S CHARACTERISTICS

Paul frames God's relationship with the Philippians as a remarkable ongoing process. God's ultimate sovereignty over creation ensures that the One "who began a good work among you" and initiated their κοινωνία

14. Hawthorne, *Philippians*, 210.
15. Thompson, *Philippians*, 119–20.

will continue in this relationship to foster their reception of the gospel and bring it to completion until the day of Jesus Christ (1:5–6).[16]

God's relationship with the Philippians is defined in the letter by four characteristics that each deserve recognition, though the activities associated with them at times overlap: (1) God is the Philippians' divine father who, at their reception of Paul's proclamation about Christ, adopted this gentile community to be God's children and began a good work in them. (2) God's fatherhood extends beyond the Philippians' household to the cosmic economy. God is sovereign over creation, and the divine gifts to the Philippians can effectively empower them to endure daily hardships and human opponents, while also growing in them the fruits of peace and righteousness. (3) The God Paul reveals to the Philippians is the God of peace, who will offer consolation and strength in the face of opposition. (4) Finally, God is the proper recipient of worship. The grace, peace, and righteousness that emerge with the good work God began in the Philippians can continue to guide them to know and worship God properly as they await the completion of their citizenship on the day of Christ's return.

God as Father

Paul refers to God in the letter's introduction (1:2) and closing (4:20) as the father he, Christ, and all believers share. In the center of his letter, he likewise describes the Philippians as "God's children" (2:15). These three uses of familial terms coordinate to underscore that the gifts of peace God has been giving (and will continue to give) to the Philippians are part of the "good work" being done in them (2:13) throughout the letter's message.

As Elsa Tamez points out, it is important to read this attribution in the context of Paul's and the audience's patriarchal power structures. The powerless situations in which Paul and the Philippians find themselves required such imagery: ". . . within the imperial context, this internalized power is not sufficient; power from above is also needed. In this sense we can see the Divine as Father-God; the emperor cannot claim the role of *paterfamilias* to humanity."[17]

The use of paternal imagery in the opening and closing of the letter brackets this overall impression. God is the Philippians' father in the same way that Christ is their lord (1:2). The image of father defines the God to whom Paul gives thanks for the Philippians' reception and successful

---

16. Hawthorne, *Philippians*, 98–100.
17. Tamez, *Philippians*, 41.

growth in the gospel until Christ returns, when glory and praise can be given appropriately to God (1:3–11). Paul again recalls their initial receipt of the gospel when he thanks the Philippians for their gift, which he deems to be an acceptable sacrifice that is pleasing to God. Just as a parent might reward a loyal child, God the Father will fully supply the Philippians materially just as has been done spiritually for them through Christ (4:18–20).[18]

Although it is not explicit, there is a possible parallel between Paul's example of Timothy and the Philippians' obligations to live out the gospel in 2:19–24. Paul sets Timothy on a pedestal as one who serves alongside him in care of the gospel "as a child with a father" (2:22 NAB). In view of the proximity to Paul's directive for the community to hold on to the word of life in preparation for the day of Christ, his description of them as God's children in 2:12–18, and in light of the emphasis of God's fatherhood and generous gifts to the church in the letter's brackets, one may see in 2:19–24 an implied directive in 2:12–18 for the Philippians to live out the obligations of their divine father in the same way that Timothy loyally works alongside Paul in the gospel.

God as Sovereign over Creation

In addition to the imagery of God as father, Paul underscores God's divine control over all aspects of reality, including assisting Paul in prison, saving Epaphroditus from illness, easing the Philippians' anxiety, and raising Christ from the dead and conferring on him authority over all things. These gifts demonstrate God's power not only over the community but over the cosmos and its eschatological drama as well.

Paul makes clear that the good work that God began in them at the evangelization of the Philippians continues until Christ's return (1:6). This implies that God remains the protagonist of history and directs the course of world events. It is God who works in the Philippians as their moral power and who is responsible for their salvation (2:12b). The reward of citizenship from heaven that God offers to Christians, like the new name God gives to Jesus Christ, indicates God's authority over creation: only the true ruler of the cosmos can grant heavenly citizenship.

God's sovereignty is expressed in many other ways throughout the letter. It is God's divinity that is the standard to which Christ's is compared (2:10). And it is God who can raise Christ from the dead and make him an authority over all of creation (3:20). Just as God can confer on Christ authority over the cosmos, God can also bestow the gift of citizenship on

18. Donald Guthrie and Ralph P. Martin, "God," DPL, 358.

the Philippians in anticipation of their full reception and understanding to live in a manner worthy of the gospel.

On the earthly plane, God can coordinate all things to benefit these faithful citizens in distress and empower them to help one another as well (4:19). After rescuing Epaphroditus from a near deadly illness, for example, God sent the recent convalescent to give Paul comfort in prison and the Philippians relief from their own distress (1:27–30). Even Paul's imprisonment is working out under God's oversight for the benefit of many and the further distribution of the gospel (1:12–14). Likewise, the "good work" that God began in the Philippians moves them to assist Paul while he is in prison to be a better minister of proper worship to offer glory to God (4:17–18) and will hopefully provide him with a reason to boast at the completion of God's work in them on the day of Christ. It is little wonder, then, that Paul can encourage the Philippians to rejoice in what God has begun, and is continuing to do, for them.

God of Peace

Paul also describes God as the "God of peace" whom he asks to remain with the Philippians and guide them to know and live properly. According to Holloway, Paul crafts Philippians as a letter of consolation to encourage the audience, both in their anxiety for him and their own challenges in living out the gospel.[19] While Paul does not explicitly call God "the God of peace" until 4:9, much of the letter conveys this sense. God's peace comes to the church in the form of encouraging news regarding Paul's successful preaching in prison, of Epaphroditus's improved health, and consolation that their steadfast faith will bring them salvation while those who harass them find destruction (1:27–30).

Even Paul's examples of imitating Christ's humility (2:1) are framed in the spirit of encouragement (παράκλησις), solace (παραμύθιον), compassion (σπλάγχνα), and mercy (οἰκτιρμοί). The selection of these terms is likely intended as a rush of emotive language to amplify the sense of consolation—both for himself and for the Philippians.[20] In this light, Paul's request that the Philippians "do nothing out of selfishness" and "regard others as more important than" themselves defines the character of their κοινωνία and releases them from the anxieties of this "crooked and perverse generation" among whom they live and allows them instead to focus on the obligations to live blamelessly and hold on to the word of life (2:15–16 NAB).

19. Holloway, *Philippians*, 31–36.
20. Ibid., 112.

The result of this peace is joy. Paul joyfully prays when he remembers the Philippians (1:3–4; 4:10) and calls on them to rejoice without anxiety (4:4). Instead, when they offer new petitions they should pray with thanks for the favor they have already received. When they do this, God's unfathomable peace will guard their hearts and minds through Christ (4:4–9).

God as the Recipient of Proper Worship

Paul's solution to anxiety is prayer, so it is not surprising to see worship tied so closely to the God of peace.[21] As John Paul Heil has argued, the context of the letter's reception is, spatially and temporally, in the church at the time of worship.[22] These themes and imagery of worship repeat regularly throughout the letter and each time identify God as the sole recipient of proper worship and glory. It is to God that Paul gives thanks for the gospel's success among the Philippians (1:3–4) and to God that Paul petitions that their spiritual growth in the gospel might continue to completion on the day of Christ when the glory and praise of God might be perfected (1:9–11). In turn, the Philippians are called to offer petitions to God with thanksgiving rather than anxiety, keeping their minds on what is honorable and just (4:6–8).

With several terms associated with sacrifice, Paul reminds the Philippians that life in Christ requires that they give God acceptable offerings.[23] For example, the Philippians show their obedience to the gospel by staying blameless and without blemish, while Paul himself may be "poured out as a libation upon the sacrificial service of your faith" (2:17 NAB). Paul, Timothy, and Epaphroditus are described as servants whose activity supports proper worship "through God's Spirit" and not the ways of the flesh (3:3).[24] By imitating their priestly ministers, the Philippians can hope that Christ will change their bodies to conform with his own glorious body by the same power God used to subject all things to him (3:20–21).

Two points arise from this consistent theme of sacrifice. The first is that proper worship requires not only the right mindset and right manner but also the right recipient. Worship, no matter how beautiful, is effective and proper only if it is directed toward one deserving that devotion. As their divine father and sovereign of the universe who gives them

---

21. Ibid., 183.

22. John Paul Heil, *The Letters of Paul as Rituals of Worship* (Eugene, OR: Cascade, 2011) 138.

23. Hawthorne, *Philippians*, 105.

24. Thurston, *Philippians*, 96.

peace, God is the sole proper recipient of this correctly practiced worship.

Second, while much of this language may be found in the Jewish traditions in the Old Testament/Hebrew Bible, it is more likely that Paul is using here what Thurston calls "dual purpose vocabulary," which translates his traditional religious concepts into his gentile audience's own religious context in Roman Philippi.[25] Paul's revelation to the Philippians of this God, who is not only their divine patron but also the true sovereign of the cosmos, allows them to offer more appropriate worship now than they did in their previous lives before receiving the gospel and highlights the centrality of God as both the initiator and final recipient of a life immersed in the gospel.

■ GOD'S IMPACT ON THE COMMUNITY

The good work that God has done for the Philippians includes several elements. God gives them peace and citizenship in heaven in the age to come and peace and righteousness to assist them during their present troubles. God also forms them as a church with κοινωνία to worship God rightly and to share mutual benefits with their ministers and one another. Lastly, the good work begun in them will preserve them for future glory and resurrection. Each of these gifts is granted "in Christ" and may be seen in line with God's identity as a generous father, as sovereign over creation, the God of peace, and as the proper recipient of worship.

Citizenship

God's "good work" for the Philippians makes them citizens of the gospel (1:27) and of heaven (3:20)—and imposes a moral responsibility on them to produce "the harvest of righteousness" (1:11). In other words, God's sovereignty implicates a new form of morality, which Paul refers to as the "imitation of Christ" (2:5). Holloway avers that Paul's use of the verb πολιτεύεσθε ("to conduct one's life") is both unusual and intentional for his Philippian audience: ". . . like Roman citizenship the gospel carries not only privileges but also duties that it would be shameful to neglect."[26] James Thompson agrees, pointing to the need to live "worthily [ἀξίως] of their citizenship," and adds that this would convey an alternative way of life to that found in the Roman commonwealth, often with negative

25. Thurston, *Philippians*, 88: "Paul had a genius for choosing language that had connotations in both Jewish and Hellenistic ideational worlds."
26. Holloway, *Philippians*, 105.

responses from their Roman neighbors who observed the πολίτευμα ("commonwealth") of a Roman colony and expected the same of all those in the city.[27]

Peace and Joy

It is this changed identity that creates tension with the Philippians' neighbors and local leaders. Citizenship in heaven has its obligations, along with negative responses from outsiders, but it also frees them from the constraints of the present world and its numerous sources of anxiety. Paul's letter communicates this peace from God (1:2), even while he is in prison and the Philippians are under duress. God grants the Philippians peace as a part of their κοινωνία (2:1–2), which is demonstrated more specifically in the restored health of Epaphroditus (2:30) and looks toward their being proved right and their persecutors wrong in the future (3:19–20; cf. 1:28).

Just as their moral life grows toward perfection by God's good work, so too does their peace from God grow to become joy. Due to the consolation they have received in the gospel and from the letter, Paul can urge them repeatedly to rejoice, and to continue doing so knowing that the love they share with those in their κοινωνία will be repaid by God, who will give them material success and even more peace amid their anxieties. Their communal joy responds to God's goodness by glorifying the One who began a good work of the gospel among them. Fear is stronger than hope, but it cannot overcome joy. For this reason, the Philippians can be confident and continue to joyfully live in Christ, knowing that God will continue working within them until their total peace is finally realized.

Righteousness

Freedom from worldly anxiety dovetails with freedom from worldly corruption. From their reception of the gospel and accepting the gracious gift of faith in Christ, a knowledge of the cross and potential harvest of righteousness takes root within them. The righteousness that the Philippians receive through Christ is God's own righteousness, not theirs. This righteousness is revelatory: through the Philippians' blameless and obedient living out of the gospel (2:13–15), God is revealed to the world and thus glorified. This righteousness is modeled in, and mediated by, the cross. God's act in exalting Christ serves as a parallel to giving righteousness to the faithful. Both actions are responses to obedient self-denial, even to the point of death; and both point toward the culmination of God's plan in glorifying the faithful on the day of Christ. As God exalted Christ

27. Thompson, *Philippians*, 51–52.

from his lowly death, so too can God raise up to glory those harmed by the harshness of this world.

Κοινωνία and Proper Worship as a Church

The κοινωνία, or partnership, in this sacrificial service that the Philippians share with Paul and his co-workers is a direct result of the good work God began in their midst (cf. 1:3–4).[28] This point underscores the cyclical reality of God's grace and glorification: it is the animation by God's Spirit by which the Philippians can properly worship the sole proper recipient of such devotion, the sovereign of the cosmos.[29]

The central image that defines this proper worship and the life of those in the church is Christ's death, which the letter's theology conveys as a model of true worship and a communion sacrifice. Rather than a worship that focuses on "righteousness under the law" (3:6), mediated by the ritual of circumcision (3:3), the efficacy of Christ's death on the cross mediates the "righteousness from God based on faith" (3:9). Christ's death may also be viewed as a communion sacrifice because of the "communion" (κοινωνία) it creates among the Philippians horizontally (their citizenship and life in Christ) and between God and them vertically.

Paul highlights such intersectionality of communal worship that glorifies God when he thanks the Philippians for their gift. Although Paul does not repay the Philippians, either in cash or in kind, God takes the initiative to repay them. It is here that the nature of the gifts they gave is manifest. The language of sacrifice (ὀσμὴν εὐωδίας, θυσίαν δεκτήν, εὐάρεστον τῷ θεῷ, "a fragrant aroma, an acceptable sacrifice, pleasing to God," 4:18 NAB) is unmistakable here, albeit metaphorical. Paul construes the "gifts" of the Philippians to him as sacrifice offered to God, which God rewards. The remarks of Gary A. Anderson situate Paul's statement within Second Temple Judaism:

> One of the reasons that charity gained such extraordinary significance is that it was understood as more than a horizontal action involving a donor and recipient; it also had a vertical dimension. To give alms was to perform an act of worship of God (avodah). The Greek translation of Hosea 6:6 captured this perfectly: "I desire mercy [toward your neighbor] not [just] sacrificial service." Just as service at the sacrificial hearth provided food for God (as though he suffered from hunger), so donation of goods to the poor is considered a loan to God (as though he has fallen on hard times).[30]

28. Martin, *Philippians*, 65.
29. Hawthorne, *Philippians*, 127.
30. Gary A. Anderson, *Charity: The Place of the Poor in the Biblical Tradition* (New Haven: Yale University Press, 2013) 104.

From the perspective of Second Temple Judaism, Paul makes clear that it is God who receives the sacrifices offered ("a fragrant aroma, an acceptable sacrifice, pleasing to God," 4:18), because God blesses acts of kindness ("I seek the profit that accumulates to your account," 4:17),[31] and answers prayers ("my God will fully satisfy every need of yours according to his riches in glory in Christ Jesus," 4:19) in response to the Philippians' charitable actions. To conclude, Paul suggests that his actions, and those of the Philippians, have a singular destination in offering all glory to their God and Father (4:20).

Resurrection and Future Glory

Finally, there is a summation of God's authority revealed at Christ's return. Christ, exalted for his obedience and death (2:9–11), will return to grant permanent citizenship to the Philippians who remained faithful in "good work" (1:6) by conforming their bodies to Christ's (3:20). The Philippians are encouraged to anticipate their own resurrection and glorification (3:10–11) from God, just as God rewarded Jesus Christ for his fidelity (2:10–11). God glorified Christ for his obedience (2:9) and will reveal, in Christ, the rewards of the faithful at Christ's return (3:21)—that too will be to the glory of God, which seems to be endless—"To our God and Father, be glory forever and ever. Amen" (4:20 NAB).

■ CONCLUSION

As this essay demonstrates, God the father plays a substantial role in the letter's overall message relating to the Philippians' spiritual growth and salvation. While these gifts are mediated to the community through Christ, God is the primary actor in exalting Christ, calling Paul to preach, and initiating a good work in the Philippians. In addition, God will continue to support this growth to bring about righteousness, making them pure and blameless, until the day of Christ.

As part of his effective message of consolation to the Philippians, Paul describes God's key characteristics. God is the Philippians' loving and generous father who has granted them faith and will reward them for blameless and pure living that marks them as God's children. They can rest assured that the good work God began in them will continue to grow and

---

31. Anderson has documented how the language of "charity" or "almsgiving and sacrifice" morphed into financial terms in the intertestamental period, or the so-called Second Temple period. The vocabulary of "the profit that accumulates to your account" (Phil 4:17) goes along those lines. See Anderson's sequel: *Sin: A History* (New Haven: Yale University Press, 2009); and idem, *Charity*, 129–39.

that God will rescue them from their current distress, and Paul from his, because God is the sovereign of the cosmos who oversees all events from Christ's exaltation to Paul's imprisonment. God can even bring good out of difficult situations, like increasing the gospel while Paul is in prison, or healing Epaphroditus to relieve the anxieties of Paul and the Philippians. They can likewise rest assured that the God of peace will free them from the anxieties of their worldly obligations and lead them to live joyfully in Christ. A life receptive to the good work God has begun in them makes their offering to God proper and glorifies the true recipient of worship, who will respond to their petitions and glorify them for their faithful worship.

The good work God initiated in the Philippians perfects them in the knowledge of Christ, nurturing their faith to grow and guiding their behavior to become more righteous. God grants them citizenship in heaven and God's own righteousness. Additionally, they receive peace in this life and hope for future glory in the resurrection. The totality of God's attributes and activities in the lives of the Philippians can bring them to be as confident in the success of their salvation as Paul is. If, while facing despair in the darkness of prison, Paul can see the good work God began in them making them to shine like stars, then the Philippians can also see hope ahead.

It is notable that much of Paul's terminology (citizenship, peace, knowledge of God, sacrifice, proper worship, etc.) has corollaries with the Philippians' own religio-political milieu in a Roman colony. While some may see a neutral use of recognizable terms, it is also possible to see Paul crafting a manner of life and worship that operates as an alternative to that ascribed by their Roman overseers and those in Philippi who are loyal to Roman emblems. It is certainly likely that the Philippians' neighbors who harassed them perceived this alternative as a possible threat and responded in kind. It is no wonder, then, that Paul seeks to console and encourage the Philippians with promises of God's gracious activity in their lives, and even makes his own situation in prison work toward relieving the Philippians' anxieties over their own challenges. In all of this, Paul finds reason to rejoice: if God can work through him to encourage others to live within Christ and work toward the salvation God has prepared for them, then truly Paul's ministry is animated by the sovereign of the cosmos, a loving and gracious father figure, who will reward the faithful with blessing and glory.

6

1 Thessalonians 1:1: Participation in the Living God

MARK J. GOODWIN

In recent decades, 1 Thessalonians has garnered its fair share of scholarly attention as a pastoral letter written by Paul to a fledgling community of gentile converts. As one scholar says, "Paul wrote 1 Thessalonians with a pastoral purpose in mind" and, by doing so, "created something new."[1] Related to this newfound appreciation of the letter's pastoral dimensions is the role of Paul's God-talk within the letter, and how it serves the letter's wider aims. A good example of this is 1 Thess 1:9–10, in which Paul recalls for the Thessalonians their foundational experience of conversion, something that entailed turning "to God from idols to serve a God who is living and true." This conversion to the one God led to a new life of "service," the moral implications of which Paul will unfold subsequently in 4:1–11.

There are, however, other instances of Paul's God-talk in the letter that function in a pastoral way and have remained largely overlooked. Of particular interest for my discussion is the letter's very first reference to God found in 1:1. In this verse, Paul addresses his first-century readers as "the church of the Thessalonians in God the Father and the Lord Jesus Christ."[2] The phrase "in God the Father" is rare in Paul's letters, being found only in the prescripts of 1 and 2 Thessalonians. It presents a puzzle to contemporary interpreters since the Greek preposition ἐν is polyvalent and notoriously fluid in its semantic force.

---

1. Abraham J. Malherbe, *Paul and the Thessalonians: The Philosophical Tradition of Pastoral Care* (Philadelphia: Fortress, 1987) 68.
2. The translation employed here and in subsequent citations is taken from the NABRE.

91

What exactly does it mean for the church of the Thessalonians to be "in God the Father and the Lord Jesus Christ"? In response, many commentators today interpret the phrase instrumentally, understanding "the church of the Thessalonians" to exist "by" or "through" God (and Christ). In doing so, however, they limit the phrase's meaning and overlook other possible nuances. One such nuance was offered by Adolf Deissmann about a century ago; he maintained that the preposition ἐν can designate a locative sense in connection with a "locus" in which believers dwell.[3] This locative sense is typically associated with a mystical experience of union with Christ, in which believers live "in Christ" and somehow "inhabit" the living reality of Christ (Rom 6:11; 8:1; 1 Cor 15:18; 2 Cor 5:17; Gal 3:28; Phil 3:8–9). Today, this locative sense is known as a "participation" in Christ.

My central question is this: Is it plausible that Paul employed the locative-participatory sense of God in 1 Thess 1:1? In response to this question most interpreters are either silent or skeptical. In Pauline studies today there is wide acceptance of participation in Christ as a central part of Paul's theology, but there is little or no acceptance of a corresponding participation in God, given Paul's relative silence on the latter. This scholarly skepticism regarding a Pauline participation in God has influenced the widespread scholarly dismissals of reading 1 Thess 1:1 in a participatory way, that is, as a participation in God.

My argument here bucks this trend of contemporary scholarship by exploring the plausibility of a participatory reading of 1 Thess 1:1, seeking to draw out what it could mean for the believers of the Thessalonian church to participate "in God the Father and the Lord Jesus Christ." While such a reading has been suggested occasionally in the scholarly literature, it has not been pursued in a full-fledged and systematic way, as I intend to do. I will argue that a participatory interpretation of "in God the Father" not only is grammatically plausible but makes sense within the letter's wider context.

■ THE PLAUSIBILITY OF A PARTICIPATORY READING OF 1 THESSALONIANS 1:1

Evidence Supporting a Participatory Interpretation of 1:1

The plausibility of reading 1 Thess 1:1 as a statement of participation is supported from grammar and the epistolary context. Beginning with

---

3. Adolf Deissmann, *Paul: A Study in Social and Religious History* (2nd ed.; trans. William E. Wilson; London: Hodder & Stoughton, 1926) 117–35.

grammar, it is a rare occurrence in Paul to find the Greek preposition "in" combined with a term for God. Occasionally, he employs this expression (1 Thess 2:2; Rom 2:17; 5:11), but it is typically interpreted in instrumental terms.

How, then, is the ἐν-clause of 1 Thess 1:1 to be interpreted? A few contemporary interpreters have taken it in a participatory way.[4] The majority of interpreters, however, go in a different direction, taking it in the instrumental sense. Interpreted instrumentally, the verse expresses that the Thessalonian church exists "by" or "through" God the Father.[5] Taken this way, the Thessalonian ἐκκλησία in 1:1 is "an assembly called into being by the Creator."[6] In addition, and cohering with the phrase's instrumental sense, there is an anti-imperial interpretation, stressing God's fatherhood against that of Caesar.[7]

Nonetheless, while these non-participatory interpretations of "in God the Father" are viable, they do not exclude a participatory reading; and here it should be recalled that the Greek preposition ἐν is fluid and polyvalent in its range of meanings.[8] Interpreters too often put a straightjacket on the Greek preposition "in" and limit its broad semantic range. Evidence for the participatory sense of "in God the Father" is suggested from the ensuing christological phrase, "and the Lord Jesus Christ." In grammatical terms, the use of the preposition "in" governs both phrases in 1 Thess 1:1, indicating that the church of the Thessalonians is not only "in" God the Father but also "in the Lord Jesus Christ." The christological phrase represents a variation of a more common christological expression of participation in Paul's letters: "in Christ" or "in the Lord."

---

4. Deissmann, *Paul*, 132. Raymond F. Collins, *Studies on the First Letter to the Thessalonians* (BETL 66; Leuven: Leuven University Press, 1984) 244. See also M. Eugene Boring, *I & II Thessalonians: A Commentary* (NTL; Louisville: Westminster John Knox, 2015) 46; and James W. Thompson, *The Church according to Paul: Rediscovering the Community Conformed to Christ* (Grand Rapids: Baker Academic, 2014) 54–56.

5. Ernest Best, *The First and Second Epistles to the Thessalonians* (BNTC; London: A & C Black, 1972; repr., New York: Continuum, 1986) 62–63; Victor Paul Furnish, *1 Thessalonians, 2 Thessalonians* (ANTC; Nashville: Abingdon, 2007) 68.

6. Abraham J. Malherbe, *The Letters to the Thessalonians: A New Translation with Introduction and Commentary* (AB 32B; New York: Doubleday, 2000) 103.

7. See, e.g., James R. Harrison, *Paul and the Imperial Authorities at Thessalonika and Rome: A Study in the Conflict of Ideology* (WUNT 273; Tübingen: Mohr Siebeck, 2011). Harrison reminds us that Thessalonica was a Roman imperial province.

8. M. Eugene Boring observes that, "contrary to English usage, Greek usage of this preposition does not necessitate a choice between 'in' and 'by'. . ." (*I & II Thessalonians*, 46). For a similar thought, see Constantine R. Campbell, *Paul and Union with Christ: An Exegetical and Theological Study* (Grand Rapids: Zondervan, 2012) 67–73.

These latter instances of the formulation "in Christ" express the believers' location or incorporation into Christ and yield a participatory sense (Rom 6:11; 8:1; 1 Cor 15:18; 2 Cor 5:17; Gal 3:28; Phil 3:8–9). For example, Paul speaks of those "in Christ" being a new creation (2 Cor 5:17); conversely, he also speaks of Christ being or living "in" believers (Gal 2:20; 4:19). In these instances, Paul envisions a view of Christ as a locus or sphere in which believers live, a locus that likely involved a communal or ecclesial dimension. As one scholar has observed, mystical participation in Christ "is inseparable from communion with fellow believers."[9]

The following observations offer additional support for a participatory reading "in the Lord Jesus Christ." First, in other epistolary prescripts Paul employs a similar formulation in a participatory sense, such as in Phil 1:1; 1 Cor 1:2; (cf. Col 1:1; and Eph 1:1). In Phil 1:1, for example, Paul writes "to all the holy ones *in Christ Jesus* who are in Philippi." One commentator observes that here "in Christ Jesus" points to a union of the Philippians with Christ and "Christ Jesus as the sphere in which the Christian lives and moves."[10]

A second observation offers even stronger support for a participatory reading of the formulation "in Christ" in 1 Thess 1:1. Throughout 1 Thessalonians, there are other participatory uses of the phrase "in Christ." A few occurrences are ambiguous and thus difficult to interpret, such as 4:1, which speaks of the Thessalonians being "in the Lord Jesus," and 5:12, in which Paul speaks of respecting those who are over you "in the Lord."[11] Other instances, however, are arguably or clearly locative. In 3:8, Paul urges the Thessalonians "to stand firm *in the Lord*."[12] In 5:18, he says "this is the will of God for you *in Christ Jesus*." Also widely accepted as locative is 1 Thess 2:14, in which Paul says that the Thessalonians "have become imitators of the churches of God that are in Judea *in Jesus Christ*."

Another intriguing instance of the formulation "in Christ" carrying participatory significance is 1 Thess 4:16. This verse is part of a wider hortatory unit, 4:13–18, in which Paul seeks to console the Thessalonians over some recent deaths in their community. He exhorts them through a hopeful vision of the parousia and future resurrection. In 4:16, Paul exhorts by saying that, at the parousia, Jesus, the Lord, will descend from

9. Thompson, *Church according to Paul*, 53.

10. Peter T. O'Brien, *The Epistle to the Philippians: A Commentary on the Greek Text* (NIGTC; Grand Rapids: Eerdmans, 1991) 46.

11. Thompson, *Church according to Paul*, 54. Interpreters tend to take these instances as modal or instrumental in force, rather than locative.

12. Teresa Morgan observes of 3:8 that "Paul is unlikely to be thinking instrumentally in this passage" (*Being 'in Christ' in the Letters of Paul: Saved through Christ and in His Hands* [WUNT 449; Tübingen: Mohr Siebeck, 2020] 43).

heaven "and the dead *in Christ* will rise first." Paul's reference to "the dead *in Christ*" is recognized as an instance of the believers' participatory union in Christ extending beyond death.[13] Teresa Morgan has noted the pastoral function of these words, saying that the participatory reading of 4:16 "makes good sense," given that the gentile Thessalonians had "belonged to a thought world in which the gods of heaven . . . had no authority in the underworld. After death, they had no power to help."[14] In 4:16, then, Paul was reassuring the gentile Thessalonians that, after death, they "are still in the hands of Christ: in his power and under his protection."[15] Further, Paul's exhortation also extends to assuring the Thessalonians that their future resurrection will follow from their participatory union with Christ. Those who have lived and died "in Christ" will also be raised from the dead.

These observations support the conclusion that the christological clause of 1 Thess 1:1 has a participatory (locative) significance, and, if this is so, then by implication the first clause also carries participatory significance. As Michael Gorman has observed of 1:1, "[T]here is no sharp dichotomy for Paul between being "in Christ" and being "in God the father; rather, existence in Christ is existence in God, and vice versa."[16] Further, given the fluidity and semantic range of the Greek preposition "in," this participatory reading of 1 Thess 1:1 does not entail excluding the instrumental interpretation. Paul here in 1:1 can be interpreted as saying that the Thessalonian church came into being through God the Father, but then it also continued to exist locatively "in" the reality and life of God. The cumulative weight of the previous observations suggests the plausibility of accepting a participatory interpretation of 1 Thess 1:1 and its expression of being found "in God the Father."

The Enigma of the Participatory Reading: What Could It Mean to Be "in God the Father"?

Even if it is plausible to interpret 1 Thess 1:1 in a participatory sense, a basic question arises. What would it mean to speak in a participatory sense of the Thessalonians as an ἐκκλησία in God and in the Lord Jesus

---

13. Campbell, *Paul and Union with Christ*, 119–20. See also Udo Schnelle, *Apostle Paul: His Life and Theology* (trans. M. Eugene Boring; Grand Rapids: Baker Academic, 2005), 482. James D. G. Dunn lists 1:1; 2:14; and 4:16 as subjective usages (*The Theology of Paul the Apostle* [Grand Rapids: Eerdmans, 1998] 398 n. 42).

14. Morgan, *Being 'in Christ'*, 44.

15. Ibid.

16. Michael J. Gorman, *Inhabiting the Cruciform God: Kenosis, Justification, and Theosis in Paul's Narrative Soteriology* (Grand Rapids: Eerdmans, 2009) 115. See also Best, *First and Second Epistles to the Thessalonians*, 62.

Christ? Presumably, such a participatory sense would have been familiar to the Thessalonians in the first century. This familiarity is suggested by the general manner in which Paul expresses participatory thought and expression throughout his letters, for example, 2 Cor 5:17; Gal 3:27; and Rom 6:3–8. Typically he expresses participation without clarifying it, and this suggests the familiarity of his first-century audiences with it. That is, it is something that Paul does not need to explain to his first-century audiences. Because of this familiarity of Paul's audience's with participation, Paul can thus leave his participatory expression unclarified, and he does so. This lack of clarification, however, leaves modern interpreters with the enigma of participation and the challenge of understanding it.

What could it mean, then, for believers to be "in God" in the locative sense? About a century ago, arguing for a Pauline God-mysticism, which was part of Paul's "pre-Christian mysticism, inspired by the Septuagint," Deissmann maintained that the formula "in Christ" was "the more vivid substitute" for the older formulation "in God," the latter of which is given classic expression in Paul's Areopagus speech in Athens, where he states, "In [God] we live and move and have our being" (Acts 17:28). [17] In response to this claim, however, most interpreters today are skeptical, viewing Acts 17:28 as expressive of Luke's thinking, but not Paul's.

Nonetheless, Deissmann's claim is worth reconsidering in relation to 1 Thess 1:1. In pursuing this claim in the following discussion, I will consider two questions: How do we unravel the enigma of the Thessalonian ἐκκλησία being "in God the Father" in a participatory sense? Further, how does this putative participatory significance of 1 Thess 1:1 serve Paul's wider pastoral aims in the letter? In addressing these questions, my approach will involve a general exploration into Paul's God-talk within the wider context of 1 Thessalonians. I adopt this approach because of the enigma of this putative participatory sense of being-in-God in 1 Thessalonians. My thought is that this sense would emerge in relation to Paul's more general presentation of God in the letter; and so an exploration into the general presentation of God in 1 Thessalonians would yield hints and clues on what being-in-God could mean in a locative sense in 1:1.

The following examination of Paul's God-talk in 1 Thessalonians thus seeks to shed potential new light on what it would have meant for the Thessalonians to participate in God as it can be inferred from the broader witness of Paul's theological stance in the letter. Here I seek to examine specific ways in which Paul speaks about God in 1 Thessalonians, both

---

17. Deissmann, *Paul*, 132.

explicitly and implicitly, in order to illuminate God's character as one in whom the Thessalonian church participated.

■ PAUL'S GOD-TALK IN 1 THESSALONIANS

The following discussion will examine Paul's God-talk, making use of earlier studies of God in 1 Thessalonians, such as are found, for example, in the work of Raymond Collins and Abraham Malherbe.[18] Building on these earlier studies, the following discussion will be organized into four sections, seeking to explore certain features of God, as Paul describes them in 1 Thessalonians. Key among the features discussed will be God's relational character to Jesus and to the Thessalonians as "Father," as well as God's living and active presence to the Thessalonians through the gospel and holy Spirit. The four sections are the following: (1) God's Relational Character: The Living God as "Father" of Jesus; (2) God's Relational Character: God and the Church of the Thessalonians; (3) The Gospel of God and Ecclesial Faith; and (4) The holy Spirit as a Mode of Divine Presence. Each of these sections will draw out and highlight aspects of God's character that will provide clues to what it would mean to participate in God.

God's Relational Character: The Living God as "Father" of Jesus

The first observation in exploring Paul's general presentation of God in 1 Thessalonians involves the transformation of the traditional notion of the God of Israel, whom Paul describes in 1:9–10 as the God who is "living and true."[19] It was this living God who had formed Israel into a covenantal people and was active in its history and "living" in its midst, sometimes exercising wrath but also delivering Israel in times of crisis.[20] In the Hellenistic era, Jews in the Greek-speaking diaspora adapted this traditional notion of an active living God into a polemic directed against the surrounding polytheistic culture, and particularly the gentile worship of

---

18. Raymond F. Collins, "The Theology of Paul's First Letter to the Thessalonians," in idem, *Studies on the First Letter to the Thessalonians*, 230–54. In addition, I will draw heavily upon Malherbe, *Paul and the Thessalonians*.

19. Mark J. Goodwin, *Paul, Apostle of the Living God: Kerygma and Conversion in 2 Corinthians* (Harrisburg, PA: Trinity Press International, 2001) passim.

20. In both biblical and Jewish sources, the epithet "living God" is associated with the Sinai covenant, the giving of the Decalogue, and worship in the Jerusalem temple; see, e.g., Deut 4:33 LXX; Deut 5:26 LXX/MT; 2 Macc 15:4; *Sib. Or.* 3:763; Philo, *Decal.* 67; 2 Kgs 19:4, 16; and Ps 41:3 LXX (42:2 MT); 83:3 LXX (84:2 MT).

idols that were "dead," not "living." Diaspora Jews promoted their living God as active not only in the life of Israel but also on the universal stage of history, as would be seen in a great day of judgment that was coming.

These traditional scriptural and Jewish notions of the living God were taken up and transformed in 1 Thess 1:9–10, two verses that fall within the initial thanksgiving period of the letter, 1 Thess 1:2–10. The two verses in 1:9–10 serve as the culmination of the thanksgiving period, presenting a summary of Paul's prior missionary preaching in Thessalonica.[21] In these verses, Paul says that the Thessalonians "turned from idols to serve a living and true God, and to await his Son from heaven, whom he raised from the dead, Jesus, who delivers us from the coming wrath." What is striking in these verses is the way in which the traditional notions of the living God are transformed into a new understanding of the living God as *the God of Jesus*. This new understanding is revealed through God's act of raising Jesus, the Son, from the dead (1:9–10), thus revealing "a uniquely Christian view of God" that "comes to expression in and through traditional Jewish language."[22]

Most significant in 1:9–10, for our purposes, is the way in which the living God's act of raising Jesus implies an identity as "father" in relation to Jesus. If God's act of raising Jesus is revelatory of Jesus's identity as God's "Son," then by implication this act also suggests God's identity in relation to Jesus as "Father." The syntax of 1:10 suggests that Paul's notion of God entails a christological dimension of God "who can also be defined relationally, as the God and Father of our Lord Jesus Christ (Rom 15:6; 2 Cor 1:3; Eph 1:3; variant forms in 2 Cor 11:31; Eph 1:17)."[23] Paul's manner of speaking about the living God in 1 Thess 1:10 thus expresses a view of God, whose identity is that of a "Father" in relation to a "Son," who is Jesus. This relational view of God as "Father" to Jesus likely supplies a clue to a participatory interpretation of 1 Thess 1:1 and its expression of the Thessalonians being "in God the Father and the Lord Jesus Christ."

The clue is Jesus's unity with the Father and his agency in acting on behalf of God. Jesus's agency in relation to the Father likely covers a broad range of actions, but in 1 Thess 1:10 this agency is specifically related to Jesus's eschatological role of delivering believers from coming wrath.

---

21. The majority of commentators today accept an unusually extensive thanksgiving in 1 Thessalonians that runs from 1:2 to 3:13 (Best, *First and Second Epistles to the Thessalonians*, 65; Malherbe, *Letters to the Thessalonians*, 103–5; and Furnish, *1 Thessalonians, 2 Thessalonians*, 39–40).

22. Francis Watson, "The Triune Divine Identity: Reflections on Pauline God-Language, in Disagreement with J. D. G. Dunn, *JSNT* 80 (2000) 99–124, here 103.

23. Ibid., 106.

Jesus, the Son, is he "who delivers us from the coming wrath." This role is given further expression in 1 Thess 4:14: "if we believe that Jesus died and rose, so too will God, *through Jesus*, bring with him those who have fallen asleep" (cf. 5:9). A further nuance of Jesus's role as eschatological deliverer may be implicit in the syntactical interrelation of clauses in 1:10, in which God's act of raising Jesus is closely bound up with Jesus's role of delivering from the coming wrath. Put another way, the syntax of 1 Thess 1:10 suggests that Jesus's role as agent of the Father at the parousia was based in God's act of raising Jesus from the dead, an act in which God revealed (and appointed?) the risen Jesus as agent-deliverer on the father's behalf.

Finally, Jesus's role as God's agent is likely encapuslated in the title of Lord, or κύριος, a title that Paul employs throughout the letter, for example, 1:1, 3, 6; 3:11, 13; 4:2, 15, 17; 5:12, 23. While κύριος is employed occasionally of God in 1 Thessalonians, the vast majority of uses are christological, stressing Jesus's identity as resurrected Lord who will return at the parousia.[24] Significantly, the christological title of κύριος, for Paul, was not primarily about equalizing Christ and God, but was more about expressing "a certain unity of action between God and his Christ," especially at the parousia.[25] This unity of action between Jesus as "Lord" and God as Father is expressed numerous times throughout the letter (2:14–15; 3:11, 13; 4:14, 15, 16; and 5:9, 18, 23).[26] The implications of this unity of action between God and the Son for 1 Thess 1:1 are intriguing and are addressed in the following summary of some significant points about the living God that emerge from this discussion.

In 1 Thess 1:9–10 and other verses, the living God is revealed as fundamentally relational in character, and this relational character is explicit in 1:9–10 in God's act of raising Jesus from the dead. This act revealed God as a divine "father" in relation to Jesus, the Son. Put another way, 1 Thess 1:9–10 illumines God as having a fundamental christological dimension. Through both Jesus's resurrection and the parousia, the living God is revealed as a "Father" who acts in concert with Jesus, who is "Son" and "Lord." God is the "Father" who "lives" and acts through a Son, who is also "Lord," serving as the Father's agent of salvation.

How, then, do these insights bear on 1 Thess 1:1? Whatever may be the exact participatory meaning of believers being "in God the Father,"

---

24. Collins notes that 1 Thess 5:2 represents an instance in which κύριος is applied to God ("Theology of Paul's First Letter," 247–48).

25. Ibid., 248.

26. Ibid., 234: "Paul's understanding of God cannot be separated from his appreciation of the Lord Jesus Christ."

the foregoing discussion suggests that it is closely aligned with a christo-logical dimension. That is, being in God is inextricably linked to believers being "in the Lord Jesus Christ." Put another way, 1 Thess 1:1's double reference to being "in God the Father and the *Lord* Jesus Christ" expresses a unity of action between God and Christ. This unity of action in 1:1 thus implies Christ's role as agent in mediating the experience of being in God to those who believe.

God's Relational Character: God and the Church of the Thessalonians

In 1 Thessalonians, the relational character of the living God as "Father" is expressed not only in relation to Jesus as Son but also in relation to the Thessalonians as an ἐκκλησία and a new family of God, and this is another important clue for interpreting the phrase "in God the Father" in 1:1. In the letter, the Thessalonians and Paul share a relationship with God, as is evident in the references to "our God" and "our Father" (1:2–3; 3:9, 13). The latter phrase, "our Father," is especially significant, occurring twice in the letter (1:2–3; 3:13). In 1:2–3, for instance, Paul says, "we give thanks to God always for you, remembering you in our prayers, unceasingly call-ing to mind your work of faith . . . *before our God and Father.*" Paul can also speak of his own relation to God in terms of his ministry that is "before *our* God" or "in the sight of God" (3:9; cf. 2:19).[27]

This relational understanding of God as Father to the Thessalonian church correlates to Paul's use of kinship language in the letter to describe the Thessalonians as a household or family. For example, Paul employs the kinship terms ἀδελφοί or ἀδελφός to designate members as brothers and sisters within the community (e.g., 2:17; 4:6, 10; 5:27). The begin-nings of this Thessalonian community as family involved a faith in God that Paul describes as a movement toward God away from idolatry. These beginnings are alluded to throughout the letter but are given significant expression in 1:9–10. In 1:9, Paul speaks of the Thessalonian conversion as a "turning" to God that consisted in two movements, the first of which was a turning away from the former life of idolatry, and the second involving a movement toward the one true God (πρὸς τὸν θεόν). This latter movement of "turning" to God was an acceptance of the living God in faith as divine Father.

Further, following the birth of this new family of God, the Thessalo-nians were bound to the living God in a new life of "service" oriented fundamentally toward God, which marked a particular relation of the

---

27. Best, *First and Second Epistles to the Thessalonians,* 70.

Thessalonians to God as Father. In 1:9, the Thessalonians turned from idols to "serve" (δουλεύειν) the living God. The verb δουλεύειν suggests a significant result of conversion as a new life of service rendered to God, a service in which doing God's will took precedence for all within the community.[28] In 1 Thessalonians it is clear that conversion entailed a total life-service rendered to God, involving all facets of the believer's life, including the moral life as a life of loving one another in the community (4:9). In this new life of service, Paul could therefore exhort the Thessalonians to walk worthily of God (2:12) and to lead lives that were "pleasing" to God (2:4; 2:15; 4:1). This new life of service rendered to the living God thus manifested how the Thessalonians stood in relation to "our God and father."

In addition, this relation of the church of the Thessalonians to its divine father also involved an affective aspect, expressed by Paul as an ecclesial love for one another (2:8), but also as a divine love directed to the Thessalonians, who were God's "beloved" (1:4). 1 Thessalonians 1:4 expresses the conversion of the Thessalonians and their beginnings not as a human act but as God's own initiative, which was the result of God's elective calling of the Thessalonians. In 1 Thess 1:3–4, Paul gives thanks to God, "calling to mind your work of faith and labor of love and endurance in hope of our Lord Jesus Christ, before our God and Father, knowing brothers and sisters beloved by God [ἀδελφοὶ ἠγαπημένοι ὑπό θεοῦ] how you were chosen." Then, 1:5 goes on to clarify this act of divine elective love (1:4) as manifested through Paul's preaching of the gospel. Viewed in these terms, Paul's preaching was ultimately a divine elective act.

Moreover, this divine elective act in 1 Thess 1:4, manifested through Paul's preaching, was also an experience of divine love to the Thessalonians, as Paul expresses it. The term used by Paul to speak of the Thessalonians as "beloved" in 1:4, ἠγαπημένοι, has a rich scriptural background, recalling God's covenantal relation with and love for Israel, a love associated with Israel's special status as God's chosen people.[29] Strikingly, then, in 1 Thess 1:4, Paul expresses a vision of the Thessalonian church as receiving the elective love of the divine father, a love that marked the

---

28. Collins, "Theology of Paul's First Letter," 245.

29. The participial phrase "beloved by God" has a biblical background in designating Israel as God's chosen people. In Deut 7:6–8, for example, God's love was the mysterious ground of Israel's election. Related to this latter passage is the use of the perfect passive participle "beloved" (Deut 32:15 LXX; 33:5, 26 LXX) to express the ongoing enduring quality of the divine love. See Malherbe, Letters to the Thessalonians, 65.

church as a family that served God. The Thessalonian status of being God's "beloved" thus offers some insight into the deeply personal character of the Thessalonians' relation to God as "our Father," one that transformed them into covenantal brothers and sisters (ἀδελφοί).

In sum, then, the foregoing discussion has uncovered further hints and clues to Paul's portrayal of the living God as a relational God, "in" whom the Thessalonians could have participated. This God was the divine "father" who was closely interrelated with the Thessalonian ἐκκλησία as the new family of God. Relational aspects of this God are seen in Paul's language addressing God as "our Father," a divine Father whom the Thessalonians "served" as the fundamental point of orientation in their ecclesial lives. Further, the personal character of this relationship between God as father and the Thessalonians was confirmed by 1 Thess 1:4 and its mention of divine love. In this verse, Paul speaks of God's "love" as directed to the Thessalonians, identified as God's "beloved." God was thus living to the Thessalonians in the sense of being a divine Father, characterized by a relation to beloved children who were specially chosen.

From these observations, a question thus arises. Does this relation of God as Father to the Thessalonians somehow presuppose the transformation of the Thessalonians into God's children, a status mediated to them by Christ? Put another way, is Jesus's identity as "Son" somehow shared or mediated to the Thessalonians, as part of their transformation into the family of God? Unfortunately, Paul does not clarify this point in the letter, although it would seem to be implied by Paul's kinship language and the language of God as father.

The Gospel of God and Ecclesial Faith

Other hints and clues of a participatory significance associated with 1 Thess 1:1's "in God the Father" are expressed in the letter's references to the gospel viewed as a divine power. One such hint emerges in Paul's phrase "the gospel of God" (2:2, 8, 9), which not only involved the beginnings of the Thessalonian community, manifested through Paul's preaching of the gospel, but also involved a mode of divine presence and the continuing faith relationship of the Thessalonians to God as Father. It will thus be helpful to explore this notion in the letter.

For Paul, the gospel preached by him in Thessalonica was "the gospel of God," signifying that the gospel had its source in God, but also that it had God as its object (a God-centered message). This "gospel of God" had its origins in God and was thus divine, but it was also Paul's proclamation about God. 1 Thessalonians expresses the divine origins of the gospel in various ways. In 1:5, for example, Paul's gospel did not come to Thessalonica in word alone but also "in power and in the holy Spirit" (cf. 1 Cor 2:4–5). As in Paul's other letters, 1 Thessalonians refers to the gospel as something that was more than human words and concepts; it was "a power of God for salvation" that was efficacious in transforming lives (cf. Rom 1:16; 1 Cor 1:18).

Further, Paul alludes to this "gospel of God" in 1 Thessalonians when he mentions the Thessalonian response of faith, leading to their turning to the living God in faith. In 1 Thess 1:8, Paul speaks of the Thessalonian "faith in God," referring to the Thessalonians' conversion as a faith response to the gospel of God, in which the living God became the basic point of orientation for their new ecclesial lives.[30] In 1:8, Paul commends the Thessalonians, saying that "in every place your faith in God [ἡ πίστις ὑμῶν ἡ πρὸς τὸν θεόν] has gone forth." The phrase "faith in God" is a *hapax legomenon* in Paul's letters, articulating God as the object of Thessalonian faith, as Paul proclaimed and taught. Further, it is also clear that this Thessalonian faith in God entailed a life of faith that was experienced ecclesially, that is, within the new family of faith. In 1 Thess 1:1, Paul calls this family of God the ἐκκλησία or, more specifically, "the church of the Thessalonians."

Moreover, Paul also suggests in 1 Thessalonians that this ecclesial "faith in God" was something ongoing within the ἐκκλησία, functioning as a kind of mode of divine presence in it. This thought is expressed in 1 Thess 2:13, in which Paul refers to the gospel as a continuing divine power at work in the lives of the Thessalonians. He says that the Thessalonians, "in receiving the word of God from hearing us," received not "a human word," but rather "the word of God, which is now at work *in you* who believe." In this verse, Paul recalls the preaching of the gospel (of God) in Thessalonica, as mentioned previously in 1:5–6, "the word of God," which the Thessalonians had received "with joy from the holy Spirit." Significant here is the thought of Paul's gospel as "the word of God" continuing to operate as a divine reality in the Thessalonians by virtue of their "believing."

What was this "word of God" that continued to operate in the Thessalonians by virtue of their believing? Paul leaves this question unclarified, but Thompson opines that it was "a divine energy which is the equivalent of the power (δύναμις) that was present in the first preaching of the gospel."[31] Further, since the holy Spirit, in addition to the gospel,

---

30. Malherbe, *Paul and the Thessalonians*, 30–32.
31. Thompson, *Church according to Paul*, 33. In Phil 2:13, Paul tells the Philippians that "it is God who *works* among you."

was also received by a "hearing" with faith (Gal 3:2), the "word of God" for Paul was also closely interrelated to the Spirit. Put another way, Paul, in 1 Thessalonians, does not make a clear distinction between the Spirit and "God's word," which both continued to work in the communities of faith.[32] For my purposes, however, the significant point is that for Paul, the gospel, as the word of God, was a divine reality that was ongoing and efficacious in the ecclesial life of the Thessalonians. Through its faith, the ἐκκλησία was energized through the presence of God's word in them.

Moreover, Paul speaks of this "word of God" as being "in" the Thessalonians who believed, suggesting a participatory mode of presence. But what could it mean that this word of God was present "in" the Thessalonians who believed? Can this presence be understood in a participatory sense? An affirmative answer is suggested subsequently in 1 Thess 2:14, which speaks of the Thessalonians as "imitators of the churches of God that are in Judea *in* Jesus Christ." In 2:14, the phrase "in Jesus Christ" carries a participatory significance, as previously discussed, and it stands logically connected to 2:13, as is clear from the γάρ ("for") at the beginning of 2:14: "For [γάρ] you, brothers and sisters, have become imitators of the churches of God that are in Judea *in* Jesus Christ." The inference here is that 2:14's participatory "in Jesus Christ" suggests a parallel participatory sense of 2:13's phrase, the word of God "at work *in you* who believe." Arguably, in 2:13 Paul is saying that the church of the Thessalonians, energized by the divine word, thus imitates the Judean churches through the latter's participation "in Jesus Christ."

In sum, then, the church of the Thessalonians received its beginnings through the divine initiative of "the gospel of God" that came through Paul's preaching. Accepting this preaching, the Thessalonians responded with their "faith in God," which engendered the ἐκκλησία of the Thessalonians. Further, this divine initiative, which engendered the church of the Thessalonians through the gospel, continued beyond the community's beginnings into its ongoing faith relationship with God as Father. In 2:13, the Thessalonian faith relation was sustained and energized by the continuing presence of the divine word, which continued to work "in" the Thessalonians who believed. Arguably, this word of God "in" the Thessalonians expressed a mode of God's presence among and in them.

Moreover, the idea of "in" can also be interpreted as representing a divine presence "in" which the Thessalonians participated. What it meant for the Thessalonians to have "the word of God at work in them" is arguably clarified by the reference in 2:14 to the churches of Judea being "in

---

32. Thompson, *Church according to Paul*, 25.

Jesus Christ." Reading 2:13 in the light of 2:14 enables the inference that the "word of God, which worked *in* you" in 2:13 involved an ecclesial participation in the divine reality of God's word. And if this interpretation is viable, new light is shed on 1 Thess 1:1 and its reference to "the church of the Thessalonians in God the Father." God's word, a divine reality closely related to the Spirit, represented a mode of divine presence in which the church could participate. We will return to this question in the conclusions.

The Holy Spirit as a Mode of Divine Presence

Finally, the Thessalonian ecclesial faith relation to God was also bound up with the presence of the holy Spirit in the community, as well as the cor-related expectation of a sanctified life. The Thessalonians' experience of the Spirit went back to their founding as a community (1:5, 6). 1 Thessa-lonians 1:5 links the Spirit's activity to the proclamation of the gospel and describes the Spirit's role in the founding of the community: "For our gospel did not come to you in word alone, but also in power and the holy Spirit and with much conviction." Here the holy Spirit is identified as the source of power behind Paul's gospel proclamation; and Paul's "Spirit-empowered preaching of the gospel" was closely associated with the Thessalonian conversion and their beginnings as an ἐκκλησία.[33]

Just as significant, however, was also the Spirit's ongoing presence and activity in the community following its beginnings. Paul expresses this in 4:3–8 and 5:19–20. In the latter, Paul exhorted the Thessalonians that they "not quench the Spirit" and "not despise prophetic utterances." No prophetic gift of the Spirit should be extinguished, as it is a sign of the Spirit's continued presence in the community. Along similar lines, 1 Thess 4:3–8 expresses the community's present experience of the Spirit as part of Paul's exhortations on sexual morality. At the conclusion of the unit, in 1 Thess 4:8, Paul says that it is God who "gives" (present tense) the holy Spirit to the Thessalonians. Using this present-tense verb, Paul expresses the presence of the holy Spirit as the result of God's present action of "giving."[34]

Further, the references to the Spirit in 4:3–8 also hint that the Spirit's presence functioned as a mode of God's being present in the ἐκκλησία. In 4:8, Paul says not only that God is the giver of the Spirit in the present but

---

33. Gordon D. Fee, *God's Empowering Presence: The Holy Spirit in the Letters of Paul* (1994; repr., Grand Rapids: Baker Academic, 2012) 43–44.

34. Malherbe, *Paul and the Thessalonians*, 29. See also Frank J. Matera, *God's Saving Grace: A Pauline Theology* (Grand Rapids: Eerdmans, 2012) 163.

also that the Spirit is God's Spirit; it is God's own holy Spirit that God gives to the Thessalonians. In speaking this way, of course, Paul did not give any precise articulation on how the Spirit was God's, or how the Spirit stood in relation to God (or Christ). Modern interpreters therefore should be wary of anachronistically reading later trinitarian categories back into the Pauline text (although a triadic interrelation of the Spirit with God does seem to be implicit in 4:8). My main point, however, is that the activity of the holy Spirit in the Thessalonian community functioned as a mode of God's self-revelation and presence to the Thessalonians. Put another way, God's giving of the Spirit to the Thessalonians provided them with some kind of experiential connection to God.

Taking this thought a step further, one could also argue that this Thessalonian connection to God, as mediated through the Spirit, involved a Thessalonian participation in the Spirit. This point is supported by an interpretation of the prepositional phrase "to you" in 4:8. In this verse, Paul says that God gives the Spirit "to you" (εἰς ὑμᾶς), that is, "to" the Thessalonians. However, the Greek phrase εἰς ὑμᾶς can also be translated as "into you," referring to an indwelling of the Spirit given "into" the Thessalonians. God gives the holy Spirit "into" the Thessalonians. This idea of the Spirit indwelling the Thessalonians is further supported from the likely allusion in 4:8 to a prophetic background, as seen in Ezek 36:27 and 37:6, 14. In 37:14, for example, God promised, "I will give my Spirit *into you* [εἰς ὑμᾶς]," expressing notions of an interior divine indwelling.

Against this background, then, 1 Thess 4:8 can be plausibly read as saying that the Spirit was given "into" the Thessalonians as an indwelling presence that was "set within them."[35] In Paul's other letters, there are similar mentions of the Spirit's interior dwelling (1 Cor 3:16–17; 6:19; 2 Cor 1:22; Gal 4:6), mentions in which he speaks of the Spirit as "given into [εἰς] your hearts."[36] The inference here is that 1 Thess 4:8 and its reference to the Spirit given "into you" can be read as expressing the Spirit's participatory indwelling in the hearts of the Thessalonians. The verse suggests that the Thessalonians experienced God's presence in the midst of their community through a participation in the holy Spirit. Arguably, such a notion is found in 1 Cor 3:16–17, in which Paul speaks about the church of the Corinthians being "God's temple" because of the Spirit's indwelling of the community.

Pushing this argument just a little further, the notion of 1 Thess 4:8 expressing a participation in the holy Spirit may also involve Paul's under-

35. Best, *First and Second Epistles to the Thessalonians*, 169.
36. Fee, *God's Empowering Presence*, 52.

standing of sanctification as a sharing in divine holiness (ὁ ἁγιασμός). The term ὁ ἁγιασμός can be translated as "holiness" or "sanctification," the latter indicating the transformation by which the church of the Thessalonians was becoming holy (cf. Rom 6:19), a transformation through an experiential sharing in divine holiness. In other words, it is not hard to imagine that, for Paul, the experience of participation in the Spirit involved a sharing in God's holiness, a holiness that was central in the future salvation of the Thessalonians. In 1 Thess 3:13, Paul prays for the Thessalonians, asking the Lord to make them abound in love and to strengthen their hearts, "to be blameless *in holiness* before our God and Father at the coming of our Lord Jesus with all the holy ones" (3:13).

In support of this reading are two observations from the text of 1 Thessalonians. First, there is in 4:3–8 Paul's repetition of the term "holiness" (or "sanctification" as becoming holy), which is mentioned three times in 4:3–8 (4:3, 4, and 7). For example, in 4:7 Paul says God "did not call us to impurity, but to holiness" (cf. 3:13; 5:26). Paul's hortatory stress on living in holiness has to be interpreted in connection with the specific reference in 4:8 to the *holy* Spirit (cf. 1:5, 6). It cannot be coincidental that in 4:3–7 Paul expresses exhortations on holiness (sanctification) and then in 4:8 describes the Spirit as the *holy* Spirit (4:8). This mention of the *holy* Spirit in 4:8 likely clinches the preceding exhortations on holiness (4:3, 6, 7), and it does so by reminding the Thessalonians of the holy Spirit's role in bringing about their sanctification and, more specifically, by identifying the Spirit as the mediating source of holiness.

The inference from these observations is that God gave the holy Spirit to the Thessalonians in order to forge a relationship with them that involved their sanctification, something that also involved a share in God's holiness. In other words, for Paul, the Spirit was the agent through which the Thessalonians came to share in divine holiness. Michael Gorman supports this view of the Spirit's role:

> Human holiness is participation in divine holiness. Holiness, therefore, is both the property and activity of the Father, Son, and Spirit. God not only sets people apart but also conveys to humans the very character of God. Human holiness is therefore not only a human imperative; it is a divine product or "fruit" (Gal 5:22).[37]

Ultimately, however, the most significant point from this discussion is that 1 Thess 4:3–8 suggests the Spirit's presence in the Thessalonian church as a mode of divine presence among them (cf. 1 Cor 3:16–17).

---

37. Gorman, *Inhabiting the Cruciform God*, 153.

■ CONCLUSIONS: A PARTICIPATORY INTERPRETATION
OF 1 THESSALONIANS 1:1

What, then, could it mean in the participatory sense for the Thessalonians to be an ἐκκλησία "in God the Father and the Lord Jesus Christ"? And if the text is so understood, how does the latter phrase in 1 Thess 1:1 function as part of Paul's wider pastoral aims in the letter? As we have seen, these questions are difficult to answer due to Paul's contingent epistolary discourse in 1 Thessalonians, a discourse that expresses participation in cursory and unclear terms. For example, Paul speaks of believers participating "in Christ," as in 2:14 and 4:16, but he never clarifies what this is, nor does he clarify the interrelated phrase of 1:1, in which the church of the Thessalonians was "in God the Father."

Nonetheless, from the foregoing discussion of God-talk in 1 Thessalonians, some hints and clues have emerged that are suggestive of what Paul's language in 1:1 could mean in a participatory sense. An important clue emerges in 1 Thess 1:9 and its discussion of a God who is "living." This living God of Israel was revealed with a new and distinctive Christian identity as the "Father" of Jesus, the Son, having raised him from the dead. This verse implies the living God's fundamental relational character as "Father," as well as suggesting an identity that involves a fundamental christological dimension. More specifically, this relational dimension of the living God as "Father" involves a unity of action with the Son through whom the living God acts. For Paul, then, the living God is living and active through Jesus, the Son of the living God, who will be God's agent of deliverance at the parousia.

These insights into the christological-relational dimension of the living God suggest a viable participatory interpretation of 1 Thess 1:1. The latter's assertion of the church being "in God the Father" was closely aligned with being "in the Lord Jesus Christ," and the latter was a reality that linked up with other participatory "in Christ" formulations in the letter, e.g., 2:14; 4:16. The suggestion, then, is that the Thessalonian community's participation "in God the Father" is best understood as something mediated through the agency of Jesus, the risen Son and Lord, whose salvific actions were done in unity with the divine Father. My claim of a Thessalonian participation in God, then, would necessarily involve a christological dimension, referring to an experience of believers being in Christ.

Another significant hint clarifying the nature of a Thessalonian participation in God involves the living God's relationship to the Thessalonians as "Father." The relationship of the Thessalonians to their divine Father was an *ecclesial* one mediated through Christ, and it also involved their faith response to the gospel (cf. 1:8, "faith in God"). The putative participatory reading of 1 Thess 1:1, in which the Thessalonians participated in God the Father, would have involved a fundamental ecclesial dimension linked to faith. This ecclesial dimension permeates the letter but is specifically evident, it will be recalled, from its beginning, in which the opening verse is addressed to "the church of the Thessalonians." The ecclesial dimension of participation involves a host of realities and experiences within the community, including Paul's proclamation of "the gospel of God" that resulted in the Thessalonian response of a "faith in God" and the creation of an ἐκκλησία, a familial community of brothers and sisters called into existence through a revelation of divine elective love (1:4). In this ecclesial context, the Thessalonians' "faith in God" was constitutive of their relationship to God as the divine Father, who became the fundamental point of orientation in their lives of faith, service, and holiness.

Moreover, and within the ecclesial context, there is another clue pointing toward the Thessalonian experience of participating in God. This clue involves Paul's repeated expressions of the living God as manifested and present in the Thessalonian ἐκκλησία. The living God, who had dwelled in Israel's midst, now "dwells" or "lives" in the church of the Thessalonians, providing the Thessalonians with a sense of divine presence. How so? As we have seen, God's presence, for Paul, was manifested through "the word of God" (2:13) and the holy Spirit (1:5–6; 4:3–8), both of which were closely interrelated realities and functioned as modes of divine presence to the Thessalonians. In 2:13, Paul's "gospel of God" was also the "word of God" present as an ongoing divine power at work "in" the believing Thessalonians. The presence of this ongoing divine word "in" the Thessalonian church was a kind of divine energy, manifesting God's "living" presence to the community.

In addition, and closely related to this continuing divine word as a mode of God's presence, was God's holy Spirit, present and active in the church of the Thessalonians. For Paul, the holy Spirit was from God and thus served to manifest God's presence to the Thessalonians. This holy Spirit was experienced by the Thessalonians at the founding of their community when the gospel came "in power and the holy Spirit" (1:5–6). Yet this founding experience of the Spirit did not end there but continued as an active presence in the Thessalonian community, as evident in both 5:19–20 and in 4:3–8. For example, in 1 Thess 4:8, the Spirit was an ongoing and present divine reality; the living God "gives" (present tense)

God's own holy Spirit to (into) the Thessalonians. The Spirit was a mode of God's living presence and self-revelation to the Thessalonians.

Moreover, the sense of 4:8 suggests the Spirit's presence as a participatory indwelling of the Thessalonians. In 4:8, Paul says that God gives the Spirit "to you" or, more literally, "into" you, likely referring to the Spirit's indwelling of the Thessalonians. This language of indwelling recalls the prophetic promises of Ezekiel, in which God would give the divine Spirit into the hearts of the future Israel. If this reading of 1 Thess 4:8 is sound, then the verse can plausibly be interpreted as expressing the participatory notion of the Spirit's indwelling, something familiar from Paul's other letters, for example, 1 Cor 3:16–17; 6:19. Taking these thoughts a step further, the Pauline notion of the Spirit's indwelling may also have involved a notion of the Thessalonians' participation in divine holiness. The continuing activity of the holy Spirit in Thessalonica enabled the Thessalonian experience of a connection to God through a sharing in God's holiness.

The main point in all of these latter reflections, however, is the basic idea that *God was experienced as present in the church of the Thessalonians through the indwelling of God's holy Spirit,* empowering a sense of a connection with God, a connection expressed in 1:1 as being "in God the Father."

In these different ways, then, 1 Thessalonians provides the hints and clues that can be developed and synthesized into a clearer picture of how the church of the Thessalonians could have experienced a participation "in God the Father." What specifically, therefore, could it mean for the Thessalonians to be "in God the Father" in a participatory or locative sense? For Paul, the living God was not simply an abstract concept or a remote reality to the Thessalonians, but a living presence among them, experienced ecclesially through faith by being "in Christ." This ecclesial experience of being in Christ served to mediate a living relationship with God as "our Father." This relationship to God as "our Father" was an experience of God's presence through the continuing reality of the divine gospel-word in the community, energized through faith, and through the Spirit's indwelling.

Expressed in participatory terms, Paul in 1 Thess 1:1 was saying that the Thessalonians experienced God as Father, as one whose divine presence was around them, with them, and in them, as mediated through Christ, the ongoing divine word, the Spirit, and membership in the new family of God. Being "in God the Father" involved an ecclesial life energized through divine love, the word of God, faith, and the holy Spirit. As one commentator expresses it, the church of the Thessalonians "is not alone in the world, but lives its life in the reality of the divine presence, by the help and power of God who calls it into being."[38] Participation "in God the Father" involved a powerful ecclesial experience of belonging to God as divine Father.

This participatory reading of 1 Thess 1:1 fits well into the letter's overall pastoral thrust. In a community of newly converted gentiles, still experiencing the growth pains of a new life of faith and the trauma of the death of some of its members, Paul's stress on the reality of God's presence and love could only strengthen and console them. In pastoral terms, Paul's opening assertion of their being "in God the Father" functioned as the ground of the letter's subsequent exhortations on the Thessalonian hope of a future resurrection of the dead, as well as comforting and encouraging them in the present life of faith. The living God was the divine Father who loved the Thessalonians, and who was not remote from them but "lived" in their midst through the mediation of Christ and the holy Spirit. And this was a God who, through the resurrected Jesus, would not abandon them to the nether world in death.

38. Boring, *I & II Thessalonians*, 46.

7

Mapping Paul's Rhetorical Discourse about God in Philemon

FERDINAND OKORIE

Several early Christian commentators placed the Letter to Philemon under scrutiny and judged it to be devoid of doctrine. The letter was dismissed as a very short missive with a mundane subject matter addressed to a single person. It was too personal for church matters, making no meaningful contribution to Paul's theology and gospel message as did the other letters that he wrote. For this reason, the letter was seldom mentioned alongside other Pauline letters by diverse early Christian commentators. While Philemon's abiding value and usefulness have received more attention in modern scholarship, what remains to be examined in an extensive manner, as in the other letters of Paul, is the image of God in Philemon, the letter's *theo*logical message.

As a result of God's revealing Jesus Christ to him and his being commissioned to proclaim Christ to the gentiles (Gal 1:15–16), Paul's view of God and the divine plan for the world inform his self-identity, vision, and ministry. It is in this context, therefore, that Paul's identity as "prisoner of Christ" finds its meaning (Phlm 1, 9): he is a prisoner in the hands of the Romans because of his conviction about God's plan for the world that he is commissioned to proclaim. The impact of this fundamental conviction about God's presence in his life and ministry is no less pervasive in Philemon than it is in his other letters. Like his other letters, Philemon is fashioned out of a matrix of God's image that undergirds Paul's ministry about God's presence in the world through Jesus Christ, a relationship with humankind that includes Philemon and Onesimus.

Two factors tend to marginalize a focus on God's relationship with humankind that includes Philemon and Onesimus: the issue of slavery and the use of the word "Father" to designate God. Regarding the former, the letter to Philemon has been a *magna carta* for divisive human relationships in the form of the indignity of slavery and its promotion and preservation in human society.[1] As to the latter, the interpretation of the *theo*logical messages of biblical texts like Philemon through a patriarchal lens has undermined the experience of women in their relationship with God; this interpretation is seen instead as promoting gender inequality and violence. My discussion of the fatherhood of God in Philemon as Paul conceives of it will include feminists' critique of the overbearing history of the exclusive interpretation of the male metaphors for God. In my exposition of Paul's language for God, therefore, I will address, on the one hand, the matter of the fatherhood of God in the only letter in the New Testament that mentions a woman in its opening section and, on the other hand, the inhumanity of slavery in a letter that at a first glance is surprisingly replete with the language of brotherhood and sisterhood.

As a consequence of these two factors, God's image and orientation in Philemon are starkly implicit: what Paul says about God in this letter is at best covert and hidden in the words of Paul's rhetorical persuasion that Philemon should welcome back Onesimus as a beloved brother. In fact, individuals and households who hear Paul's message about Jesus Christ consequently embrace the presence of God in this message. Because of his faith in Christ, therefore, Paul asks Philemon to welcome back Onesimus as a beloved brother. On this note, the absence of an explicit theology or language about God in Philemon, unlike in the other undisputed letters of Paul, is no longer enough reason to dismiss the letter's theological value. This is because Paul's letters, including Philemon, bear the emblem of the divine wisdom and presence that undergird his ministry (see 1 Cor 2:4). In what follows, I will examine the implications of Paul's several mentions of God in the letter under the four headings: (1) the providential God; (2) the benefaction of God; (3) the children of God; and (4) gratitude to God.

■ THE PROVIDENTIAL GOD

There is scarcely any ambiguity in Paul's letters about the divine power that is present in his life and ministry. The overarching trajectory of his

---

1. See Emerson B. Powery and Rodney S. Sadler Jr., *The Genesis of Liberation: Biblical Interpretation in the Antebellum Narratives of the Enslaved* (Louisville: Westminster John Knox, 2016) 130–36

experience of God, beginning with the divine call and the revelation of Jesus Christ to him in order that he might proclaim Christ to the gentiles, can easily be recognized in what he writes. Paul's divinely inspired ministry brings him face to face with, and places him in the lived experience (*das Erlebnis*) of, Onesimus and Philemon in the pernicious slave system of the Greco-Roman world. Paul's ministry to Philemon and Onesimus reveals several implicit theological tapestries of this letter.

Paul identifies himself as a "prisoner of Christ Jesus" (vv. 1, 9), making a bold claim that he is writing this letter from confinement at an undisclosed location. Both Rome and Ephesus have been strongly suggested in modern scholarship as the possible cities where Paul is held in confinement. Any excellent commentary on Philemon will provide evidence to support either of these cities, proposals that need not to be rehearsed in this essay.[2] He is indicted and imprisoned because of his ministry of proclaiming Jesus Christ to the gentiles, a divine mandate that has been given to him. Identifying himself as a "prisoner of Christ Jesus" reveals, on the one hand, Jesus's authoritative claim on Paul, and, on the other hand, Paul's unalloyed dedication to that claim and identity, which has been made possible by the grace of God's choice and appointment of Paul for his ministry to the gentiles.

Broadly speaking, Paul's calling and mandate from God have led not only to his experience of imprisonment but more so to hunger, nakedness, homelessness, sickness, shipwrecks, beatings, lashing, stoning, and sentence of death (1 Cor 4:9, 11; 2 Cor 11:23–30). These are the results of Paul's unqualified disposition and dedication to his ministry. Just as in his other letters, likewise in Philemon, God is the driving force and power in his ministry—a direct consequence of his God-driven life. In his confinement, Paul sees the hand of God and the plan of God at work in his life as he sits in a Roman prison because of the ministry God has handed to him (v. 13; see Phil 1:12–13). In this particular instance, the hand of God in Paul's life has brought him into direct confrontation with the system of slavery of the Greco-Roman world as he mediates between a slave-owner Philemon and his slave Onesimus.

In the letter, Paul himself suggests that Onesimus's separation from Philemon happens within the plan of God (v. 15). As scholars have noted, the evidence lies in the fact that Paul describes the separation of Onesimus from Philemon by employing the "theological or divine passive"

---

2. Bonnie B. Thurston, and Judith M. Ryan, *Philippians and Philemon* (SacPag 10; Collegeville, MN: Liturgical Press, 2005) 256. The commentary on Philippians is by Thurston, and that on Philemon is by Ryan.

(v. 15a: τάχα γὰρ διὰ τοῦτο ἐχωρίσθη πρὸς ὥραν, "Perhaps this is why he was away from you for a while" [NAB]). The value of the divine passive "lies in the emphasis on divine involvement" as is the case in most written materials from ancient times.[3] In biblical narratives, the pervasive custom of speaking about God's actions in periphrasis is palpable; and it is obvious that circumlocution is an acceptable way of describing God's presence and involvement in the world.[4] Therefore, the presence of the passive voice in certain instances of the biblical narrative with the clear absence of an identifiable subject *ipso facto* means that logically God is the subject.[5] Any individual or household that accepts Paul's gospel must be open to God's empowering presence and transformation, as this affects the individual's or household's interaction with the social order to which they belong. For Philemon and his household with slaves like Onesimus, the experience of God's empowering presence challenges their participation in the Greco-Roman social order of slavery. The evidence at our disposal, however, is insufficient to support an explicit conclusion of Philemon freeing Onesimus and the other household slaves. Nonetheless, the strength of this letter reveals that Philemon would have been hard-pressed to deny Onesimus the reception that Paul requested, as a brother in Christ (v. 16).

From these points, we can conclude further that the separation of Onesimus from Philemon is the result of God's presence in Philemon's household, upending the master–slave relationship, in order to transform its destructive penetration of the human person and instead rebuild human relationships into brothers and sisters in God's household. In fact, the commissioning of Paul to preach Jesus Christ is God's way of intervening in human affairs and relationships in order to accomplish God's plan for humankind. The effects of God's providential power in Philemon's household is at the center of the issue Paul is dealing with in the letter, which gives it an implicit theological undertone. As Paul sees it, what is presently happening in the household of Philemon is as God intended it, demanding that members of the ecclesial community desist from upholding the inhumanity of the slave society of the ancient world. Thus, it makes sense to conclude that v. 15a is an example of a divine passive that connotes "a language of destiny and of cause and effect." It

---

3. E. M. Sidebottom, "The So-Called Divine Passive in the Gospel Tradition," *ExpT* 87 (1976) 200–204. See also Todd Still, "Philemon among the Letters of Paul: Theological and Canonical Considerations," *ResQ* 47 (2005) 133–42, here 136.

4. Joachim Jeremias, *New Testament Theology: The Proclamation of Jesus* (New York: Scribner, 1971) 9.

5. Sidebottom, "So-Called Divine Passive," 202.

also "lends itself more readily to the description of the unfolding of events than to the personal and direct action of God."[6]

Paul expresses his conviction that Philemon will acquiesce to the demand to welcome back Onesimus as a beloved brother in Christ (v. 21, Πεποιθὼς τῇ ὑπακοῇ σου ἔγραψά σοι, "With trust in your compliance I write to you . . ." [NAB]). Earlier in the letter he appeals to Philemon to welcome back Onesimus on the basis of love rather than merely the obedience that derives from the authority of his apostolic commissioning (vv. 8–9). In this context, it seems sensible to interpret Paul's confidence in Philemon's obedience as conformity to how God is present, transforming and building the relationships between Philemon and members of his household, including Onesimus. Therefore, Philemon's obedience is to God, who has commissioned Paul to proclaim the brotherhood between Philemon and Onesimus in God's household. My interpretation of Paul's appeal for obedience from Philemon finds support in some of Paul's other letters. For instance, Paul praises Roman Christians for their obedience to the teaching of faith that has been handed on to them (Rom 6:17b: ὑπηκού–σατε δὲ ἐκ καρδίας εἰς ὃν παρεδόθητε τύπον διδαχῆς, "you have become obedient from the heart to the pattern of teaching to which you were entrusted" [NAB]). Furthermore, Paul speaks about believers' obedience to the message of God through Christ that is entrusted to him to proclaim to the gentiles (Rom 15:18–19; see 16:19). Obedience is to Christ alone; Paul has been commissioned by God to proclaim it, thereby securing gentiles' obedience to Christ (2 Cor 10:5–6). When Philemon welcomes back Onesimus as Paul requests, he too shows obedience to God's presence in his household through faith in Christ. All these instances express loving obedience to God by the believer through faithful relationship with Christ.

God will intervene in the future to bring about Paul's intended visit to Philemon and his household after his release from prison. Based on his experience of God's power in his life, Paul tells Philemon and the house church that he is looking forward to a reunion with them (v. 22). Expressing confidence about his impending visit, Paul asks Philemon to prepare the guest house for him; the confident assertion in his words strongly suggests that the visit will happen very soon.[7] In addition, Paul's statement in v. 22, "that I will be gifted to you through prayer" (ὅτι διὰ τῶν προσευχῶν ὑμῶν χαρισθήσομαι ὑμῖν) shares the same passive-voice con-

---

6. Ibid.
7. See Scot McKnight, *The Letter to Philemon* (NICNT; Grand Rapids: Eerdmans, 2017) 22–23; Carolyn Osiek, *Philippians, Philemon* (ANTC; Nashville: Abingdon, 2000) 142.

struction as in v. 15 above. To be specific, this construction is used here to "predict an event"; the emphasis is placed on an event that will doubt-lessly happen as long as Paul's request for prayer from the community is offered to God.[8] Just as in v. 15, here also the subject of the verb regarding who will offer Paul as a gracious favor (χαρίζομαι) to Philemon and the community remains unstated. Paul places his hope to visit Philemon and the house church on the community's prayer for him, thereby reiterating the role of prayer to God in view of attaining the desired result (v. 22: ἐλπίζω γὰρ ὅτι διὰ τῶν προσευχῶν ὑμῶν, "for I hope to be granted to you through your prayers" [NAB]). Just as Paul prays that Philemon's good deeds will become even more effective in the lives of the "holy ones," including Onesimus, likewise he asks the community to pray that his desire to visit Colossae and Philemon's home will come to fruition.

Obviously, Paul does not ask that prayer be directed to the Roman authorities holding him in prison and/or to the judge on whose decision his fate rests. Rather, God is the one to whom the community's prayer is to be directed, and it is God alone who can restore Paul to the commu-nity. Marion L. Soards makes an excellent observation that "Paul hopes God may graciously give him to the church in Philemon's house in rela-tion to that church's prayer to God for Paul."[9] Once more, we discern the profundity of God's presence in Paul's life and ministry, directing the events and outcomes of the apostle's experiences as one called and com-missioned by God.[10]

■ THE BENEFACTION OF GOD

Paul's customary greeting in his letters ("grace to you and peace from God our Father and Lord Jesus Christ") appears also in Philemon (Phlm 3; 1 Thess 1:1; 1 Cor 1:3; 2 Cor 1:2; Gal 1:3; Phil 1:2; Rom 1:7). Notwith-standing the Hellenistic and Semitic backgrounds to the terms "grace" and "peace," respectively, Paul modifies their meanings, imbuing them

---

8. Sidebottom, "So-Called Divine Passive," 202; see also Ryan, *Philemon*, 256.

9. Marion L. Soards, "Some Neglected Theological Dimensions of Paul's Letter to Philemon," *Perspectives in Religious Studies* 17 (1990) 209–20, here 218.

10. We read in the Letter to the Galatians Paul's defense of the ministry that he was commissioned by divine benefaction to proclaim to the gentiles. He describes himself as being entrusted by God with the gospel message of God's transforming presence in the world. See Ferdinand Okorie, *Favor and Gratitude: Reading Galatians in Its Greco-Roman Context* (Lanham, MD: Lexington Books/Fortress Academic, 2021) 40–41.

with a theological nuance and import. The term χάρις ("grace," "favor") is widespread in the letters in which Paul's authorship is not in any serious doubt: it appears twice in Philemon (vv. 3, 25); and in a compound in v. 4. In Philemon, an explicit and overt presence of God in the letter stems from the attribution of the origin of grace and peace to God (v. 3a). Paul uses the term here to invoke upon Philemon and the members of the house church the gratuitous and unbounded free gift of God for their well-being. God's favor is the activity of God through Jesus Christ that has reached Philemon and members of the house church through Paul's ministry. By and large, Philemon and the members of the house church will understand Paul's benediction as an invocation of the gratuitous gift of God's favor for their well-being and community unity.

Some scholars have observed that Paul's invocation of God's χάρις in the prescript of his letters functions as a prayer by which the apostle places the well-being of the community under divine power, blessing, and salvation.[11] The χάρις is the gift of God to humankind through Christ, which makes God the benefactor of the new beginning in the divine–human relationship. By invoking the grace of God in his other letters, as well as in Philemon, Paul reminds believers that their membership in the new creation divinely inaugurated through Christ is by God's gratuitous favor. God initiates this moment, making it possible for humankind to experience divine grace: God's favor is manifested in Christ, and Paul has been chosen to proclaim it. Certainly, Philemon and the members of the house church have embraced it. Through the outpouring of grace, God becomes also the patron of Philemon, Onesimus, and the community. The fatherhood of God that Paul invokes in the prescript (v. 3) lends credence to the patronal role of God in the divine household that includes Paul, Philemon, Appiah, Onesimus, all those who are named in the letter, and members of the house church.

The fatherhood of God is another obvious identification of God in Paul's message. The separation of Onesimus from Philemon is just one more reality in the life of Philemon to be transformed through the gratuitous gift of divine grace. The fatherhood of God, which Paul invokes in this letter, is clearly experienced in the gift of divine grace through Christ (v. 3). God's fatherhood is a common theme in the letters of Paul. For his part, when writing about the fatherhood of God, Paul describes God's relationship with believers as adoption. By adoption believers are made children of God's household, with the rights and privileges to call God "Abba

---

11. See, e.g., Raymond E. G. Burnish, "The Doctrine of Grace from Paul to Irenaeus" (dissertation, University of Glasgow, 1971) 35–36.

Father" (Gal 4:6; Rom 8:15). On this note, by reminding Philemon and the members of the house church about God's fatherhood (v. 3), Paul wants them to see one another as brothers and sisters of a divine adoption through their faith in Christ, who is the firstborn child of God's divine fatherhood (see Gal 3:19; 4:4–7).

Feminist scholars have called attention to the problematic features of the image of God as a father, especially when, like other male metaphors for God, this image is used literally and exclusively to present patriarchy as normative for human society and, by default, for the human relationship with the divine. It must be noted that the fatherhood of God, as a metaphor, is undoubtedly fraught with limitations and, therefore, should never be the sole designation for God. At the same time, since a metaphor is nonspecific, and indefinite, male metaphors for God should not be interpreted as a statement about God's gender or identity. Such language about God, however, is often taken literally, adopting the image of a male model of power and dominion, with the reult that God is identified with the authority of the Greco-Roman peterfamilias. Yet such metaphors as the fatherhood of God should be an affirmation of believers' experience of the love and the parental presence of God.[12] Even if Paul's image of God's fatherhood in Philemon comes from a context of male leadership within a patriarchal system, God, who is indeed divine, must never be reduced solely to male language or one single gender and identity.

With this in mind, Elizabeth A. Johnson warns about reducing the ineffability of God to exclusively male metaphors.[13] This warning must be heeded so that humankind might still experience the divine mystery of God in order for the encounter to inform an individual's self-knowledge in relationship with God. My reading of Paul's language of the fatherhood of God in Philemon reveals that this image indicates a relationship of benefaction, an experience of the gratuitous gift of divine favor to the believer, male and female alike, in a familial context. Therefore, the fatherhood of God in Philemon is a metaphor of personal relationship between God and members of the community that incudes Appiah and, in no small measure, recognizes Onesimus as a beneficiary of the same favorable relationship with God as are other members of the community. Suffice it here to say that Paul wishes that Philemon and the church that meets in his home might understand the fatherhood of God in this letter as the invitation to

---

12. See Dorothy Lee, "The Symbol of Divine Fatherhood," *Semeia* 85 (1999) 177–87.

13. Elizabeth A. Johnson, *She Who Is: The Mystery of God in Feminist Theological Discourse* (New York: Crossroad, 1992) 39; Mary L. Coloe, *John 1–10* (Wisdom Commentary 44A; Collegeville, MN: Liturgical Press, 2021) 61–64.

encounter a personal God who bestows divine favor on every believer. This point of view will become even clearer below when I treat the description of children of God in the letter. Identifying the fatherhood of God in Philemon in a literal and exclusive sense of the male gender denigrates the ineffability of God and of God's divine benefaction for believers.

■ THE CHILDREN OF GOD

In his letters, Paul appeals to both the literal and the metaphorical views of the relationship between a slave and a master. An example of the metaphorical sense appears when Paul expresses the link between the believer and sin in the language of a slave and a master (see Rom 6:5–23). The Letter to Philemon, however, is an example of the literal sense of the relationship between a slave and a master. It is clear in Philemon that Paul does not engage the Greco-Roman law on manumission, and he never requests in clear terms that Philemon should manumit Onesimus. In other words, Paul ignores in this letter the social and legal regulations that define the relationship between slaves and their masters in the Greco-Roman world, especially when separation resulted from a strained relationship between a master and a slave. This makes Paul's view of the master–slave relationship in the Greco-Roman world a complex interpretive issue in modern scholarship. The Roman Empire of Paul's day was a society of class and status: slaves, who composed an estimated 35 percent of the entire population, were at the lowest cadre of the Greco-Roman pyramid of social class. The city of Rome, to cite one particularly significant example, depended on slave labor for commerce and the social development of the polis. Slaves in the Roman Empire who were manumitted or otherwise gained their freedom nonetheless remained in total dependency and loyalty to their former masters.[14]

Thus, in the modern sense of the word, Paul is no abolitionist; he did not demonstrate against slavery in the agora, in council buildings, at civic or religious festivals, and so on, demanding the end to slavery or calling attention to its inhumanity. Perhaps Paul's eschatological belief that the end of the world was imminent (Rom 13:11) and that the beginning of the eschatological age would soon break out in the Christian community (see 1 Thess 5:5, 8–9) influenced his view on most aspects of his ministry,

---

14. On manumission of slaves in the Roman Empire, see McKnight, *Letter to Philemon*, 12–15.

including slavery and manumission, particularly in the literal sense. The evidence shows that Paul strongly proclaims that believers are presently living as freed children of God while anticipating the full consummation of that experience in the future (see Gal 2:4b–5; 3:27–29; 5:1). For these reasons, Paul avoids open and public condemnation of Roman slave society. The text of 1 Cor 7:21–24 reveals that Paul's attitude toward slavery in the empire is far from activism. Although Paul encourages believers who are slaves not to be troubled by that identity and social status (v. 21a), he states that anyone who is able to secure freedom should pursue it without hesitation (v. 21b). This reveals that Paul's position about slavery is informed by his conviction that those who have been called by God and have faith in Christ belong to a new identity and relationship that are not encumbered by any dehumanizing social institutions like slavery. Therefore, Paul concludes that a slave is a freeperson in Christ (1 Cor 7:22a).[15]

Before I go any further with illustrating how oneness in Christ transforms the master and slave relationship between Philemon and Onesimus into brothers in Christ as Paul presents it, I must explore the ethical and social questions that have had a greater bearing in the history of the interpretation of Philemon. The letter has exerted enormous authority and support in justifying the institution of slavery, codifying for slaveholding societies the treatment of slaves who flee from the household of their masters. The proslavery interpretive history of Philemon dates back to the homiletic reconstruction of this letter by John Chrysostom. His reading of the letter as Paul's appeal on behalf of the *salvus fugitivus* (runaway slave) Onesimus, provided authoritative support for the servile relationship between a master and a slave among early Christians, and in modern times, the slave system of the U.S. antebellum South.[16]

The evidence shows that the preaching of this letter in the slaveholding communities of the U.S. antebellum South is an example of how the interpretation of the letter is completely devoid of the theological enterprise that I have mapped out in this essay as Paul might have conceived of the characteristics of the relationship between God and the children of God beyond gender, class, status, and creed (see Gal 3:28). In fact,

---

15. Dale B. Martin, *Slavery as Salvation: The Metaphor of Slavery in Pauline Christianity* (New Haven: Yale University Press, 1990) 64–65; Okorie, *Favor and Gratitude*, 42–43.

16. James W. Perkinson, "Enslaved by the Text: The Uses of Philemon," in *Onesimus Our Brother: Reading Religion, Race, and Culture in Philemon* (ed. Matthew V. Johnson, James A. Noel, and Demetrius K. Williams; Paul in Critical Contexts; Minneapolis: Fortress, 2012) 121–41, here 123–24; Mary Ann Beavis, *The First Christian Slave: Onesimus in Context* (Eugene, OR: Cascade, 2021).

Philemon was used in both political and ecclesial contexts to provide support for the claim on the bodies of Black people who experienced the power of the letter in confinements, beatings, whippings, and other atrocities to which they were subjected.

An atypical and oft-cited example is the sermon of the white slave-holding preacher Charles Colcock Jones, which he delivered to a Black congregation.[17] The use of Philemon in his sermon reveals that the first *opposition* to this ideological interpretation of Philemon by the slavehold-ing Christian communities emerged among the uneducated Black slaves who voiced their disapproval with the letter and its apparent status as a handbook for slaveholders. They were convinced that the letter to Phile-mon was not part of the Bible, but rather was a text of the master. Find-ing, therefore, the Letter to Philemon "and its interpretation incompatible with their experience of God and their quests for human dignity and socio-political liberation," the Black slaves rejected the letter, calling into question its biblical authority and divine inspiration.[18] Increasingly, the interpretation of biblical texts, particularly the Letter to Philemon in African American scholarship, has been nurtured by the hermeneutic of suspicion and rejection. To this end, African American hermeneutical perspectives take their place alongside other approaches, sharing a liber-ationist stance that seeks to unmask racism and oppression in the history of reading and interpreting biblical texts in both the dominant and pro-slavery societies. This effort embraces a conscious strategy of contextual reading of the Black experience as the starting point of the exercise in biblical interpretation.[19] On this note, this effort has transformed the interpretation and preaching of Philemon today, as both scholars and preachers read in Philemon as in the other Pauline letters the saving plan of God for humankind.

I surmise, on the strength of what we know about Paul's attitude toward slavery, that he avoids asking Philemon to manumit Onesimus according to Roman law but rather asks Philemon to welcome back Onesi-mus as a beloved brother according to the law of Christ that has trans-formed and governed his life since his experience of coming to faith in

17. For the full texts and commentary on Colcock Jones's homily, see Demetrius K. Williams, "'No Longer as a Slave': Reading the Interpretation History of Paul's Epistle to Philemon," in Johnson, Noel, and Williams, *Onesimus Our Brother*, 11–45, here 36; Perkinson, "Enslaved by the Text," 124–26; Albert J. Raboteau, *Slave Religion: The "Invisible Institution" in the Antebellum South* (Oxford: Oxford University Press, 2004) 294.

18. Williams, "No Longer as a Slave," 36.

19. Ibid., 37–42.

Christ. The brother and sister relationship of the children of God that Paul envisions transcends the constraint of social or political systems of relationships. It is in this context that returning Onesimus to Philemon (v. 12a) after a brief separation (v. 15a), so that Philemon might have him back forever (v. 15b), no longer as a slave (v. 16a) but rather as a beloved brother both in the flesh and in the Lord (v. 16b), must be understood and appreciated. The brief separation of Onesimus from Philemon and their reunion as brothers in the household of God are indeed the divine transformation of the relationship among those who have come to faith in Christ.

The same kind of relationship that Paul conceives between Philemon and Onesimus runs throughout his other letters. Believers are children in the household of God, with Jesus Christ as the firstborn (see Gal 4:4–7). Paul leaves no ambiguity that would suggest that his understanding of the brother and sister relationship of God's children is a human initiative; rather, its origin and character are from God. It is important to note that Paul does not say that Onesimus is filled with remorse and that he is returning to Philemon's house to seek forgiveness, expressing regrets for his actions and pledging to regain trust through obedience. Furthermore, the letter does not mention that Philemon is to forgive Onesimus.[20] Although Paul knows the law and the social practices regarding reuniting a separated slave with the master, yet the apostle chooses to urge a different kind of relationship between Philemon and Onesimus, one resulting from God's transformation of relationships beyond the social norms of the empire.

Paul's experience of God in Jesus Christ (Gal 1:15–16), and the overpowering impact of that experience in his life, informed his conviction that Philemon should welcome back Onesimus as a beloved brother in the Lord. Paul sees his request for a familial relationship between Philemon and Onesimus as defined and ultimately determined by Philemon's experience of familial relationship with God. God is "our Father" (v. 3) and we are brothers and sisters. The only identity marker for believers in this present age manifests itself in their sharing with one another that same love with which God has loved them.[21] Their identity as children of God marks them off from the larger Greco-Roman society as the "holy ones" (Phlm 5), implicitly linking their holiness with God's (see Lev 19:2; Phil 2:5; 1 Pet 1:16). There is no gainsaying that recent African

20. Soards, "Some Neglected Theological Dimensions," 216.
21. Pieter G. R. De Villiers, "Love in the Letter to Philemon," in *Philemon in Perspective: Interpreting a Pauline Letter* (ed. D. Francois Tolmie; BZNW 169; Berlin: de Gruyter, 2010) 181–203.

American interpretations of Philemon have insisted on reading the letter to emphasize the *philadelphia* of Philemon and Onesimus in Christ. Onesimus knows that Paul's intervention in his situation with Philemon brings him a certain degree of hope, hope born out of his choice to become a Christian in order to enjoy "Christian brotherhood" and an experience of freedom.[22]

The children of God in Philemon are connected by familial and ministerial bonds. Paul shares the ministerial bond of co-workers with Timothy, Philemon (v. 1), Mark, Aristarchus, Demas, and Luke (v. 24). The ministerial bond Paul shares with Epaphras has led to their experience of Roman imprisonment (vv. 1, 9, 23); Paul and Archippus are fellow soldiers (v. 2); Paul and Philemon are partners and dear friends (v. 1, 17). Paul, Timothy, Philemon, and Onesimus are brothers, and Appiah is a sister (vv. 1, 2); Onesimus is a child who is begotten by Paul in his imprisonment (v. 10), making Paul a father. Paul identifies himself as a father to Onesimus (v. 10), thereby assuming the social role of a paterfamilias, just as many members of the early church are patresfamilias to their households. Nevertheless, the fatherhood of God (v. 3) over every member of the community including Paul is the central theme of the family imagery in Paul's theology in this letter. Paul addresses Philemon as beloved (v. 1), asking him to take Onesimus as a beloved brother, too (v. 16); in addition to being addressed as a sister, some manuscripts describe Appiah as beloved sister (D[2], Ψ, M [syp, sa[mss]]).

The above analysis strengthens the point of view that Onesimus experiences a change in status as a believer, as is the case with the other members of the community. For example, Appiah, who is the only woman named as an addressee in the New Testament, is a matriarch of the community; and she will experience God's immutable presence in the familial relationships that Paul suggests beyond the constraints of male metaphors for God (the fatherhood of God). In other words, the theological message of Philemon reveals the inherent dignity of every child of God, which outweighs the ideological interpretations of slavery and patriarchy.

On the basis of the foregoing, Paul's view of the early church is that of a community of brothers and sisters based on the firm belief that God alone is a parent over them. As fellow workers, soldiers, prisoners, partners, sisters, and brothers, they are living, sharing, and doing the work of God their father. Differently said, together as one household, they are doing the work of God in order to bring to fulfillment the divine plan to

---

22. Esau McCaulley, *Reading while Black: African American Biblical Interpretation as an Exercise in Hope* (Downers Grove, IL: IVP Academic, 2020) 155–56.

redeem the world. As brothers and sisters, they are already presently living the values of the kingdom of God, whose fulfillment they await. In this kinship image with God as a parent, Paul also introduces an eschatological image of his gospel message. Indeed, if Philemon welcomes back Onesimus into the brotherhood of God's children, as Paul demands, then he has embraced the transformative power of God through Christ. Seen through the lens of Paul's scheme of thought, the community of believers living in unity with one another inspires gratitude to God, whose divine plan is the backdrop against which their fellowship rests.

▪ GRATITUDE TO GOD

It remains only to discuss the customary thanksgiving section at the beginning of Paul's letters, which expresses and reveals the theological enterprise of the entire letter. It formally introduces issues about God, Jesus Christ, and the Christian life that are relevant to the occasions for writing which Paul then develops more extensively in the body of the letters. This is in fact the case also in Philemon. In prayer Paul remembers Philemon, thanking God for Philemon's love and faith (vv. 4–5). Paul's thanksgiving to God is another obvious and explicit naming of God in the letter. Paul reveals that what he has heard about Philemon's love for the "holy ones" and his faith in Christ makes up the intention of his prayer. In the letter, Paul does not simply write, "I thank my God . . . ," as he does in his other letters (see Rom 1:8; 1 Cor 1:4; Phil 1:3; 1 Thess 1:2), but instead writes, "as I remember you . . ." (v. 4). Philemon is the only undisputed letter of Paul where the apostle describes his prayer as a remembrance, a ritual that has its background in the apostle's Jewish roots. Scot McKnight observes, "Remembrance involves the mentioning of a person's name in God's presence, the history of that person or event, and the importance of intercession in solidarity with God's mission."[23] Paul's remembrance of Philemon in the context of prayer places him in the presence of God; and the thanksgiving that accompanies the prayer celebrates Philemon's faith in Christ that has led to his love of the "holy ones."

In Paul's letters, God is always the sole recipient of thanksgiving (see 1 Cor 14:18; 15:57; 2 Cor 4:15). The same is true in Philemon, as Paul shows appreciation through prayer for the divine blessings given to Philemon. His thanksgiving to God focuses solely on Philemon's attitude toward the "holy ones," an example of the in-breaking of God's plan in

---

23. McKnight, *Letter to Philemon*, 64.

the lives of believers. By mentioning Philemon's faith in Christ and his love for the members of the community in the context of prayer, Paul expresses his conviction that God is responsible for the transformation that has taken place in Philemon's life. Hence, when Paul claims ownership of Philemon's life, that claim should be understood in the context of Philemon's life of faith in Christ and his love for the members of the community, both virtues that Philemon practices as a result of his encounter with Paul and his acceptance of the gospel that Paul preaches. Accordingly, there is a triadic relationship that involves thanksgiving to God, who has sent Paul to the gentile world with a mandate and an expectation that the mandate will produce the intended result in the life of believers.

In Paul's short missive, God's gift of divine grace leads to Philemon's faith in Christ, which is the believer's proper response to God's offer of relationship through Christ. Biblical faith, like Abraham's faith, is an experience of a trusting and intimate relationship with God, which also inexorably affects the believer's relationship with others in the community.[24] The grace of God and faith in Christ are the basis of Philemon's love for all the "holy ones" because the grace of God makes Philemon's faith experience possible, moving him to enter into fellowship with the community, a communion that manifests itself in his love for them. Evidently, when he writes ὅπως ἡ κοινωνία τῆς πίστεώς σου ("that the sharing of your faith," v. 6a) to Philemon, Paul denotes the Christian's lifestyle of sharing with others the fruit of one's faith in Christ. The next phrase, παντὸς ἀγαθοῦ τοῦ ἐν ἡμῖν εἰς Χριστόν ("all the good in us for Christ," v. 6b), links Christian unity with union in Christ; Paul explicitly underscores that the believer's union in Christ (vv. 6, 8, 20, ἐν Χριστῷ), in the Lord (vv. 16, 20, ἐν κυρίῳ), and in Christ Jesus (v. 23, ἐν Χριστῷ Ἰησοῦ) is deepened by mutual fellowship with one another.

The example of Philemon's life of faith in Christ reveals that faith in Christ is not a passive response to God's gift of divine grace but an active presence through love for the community of believers. Bonnie Thurston rightly observes that Paul understands faith as the seed out of which the Christian life grows, the finest fruit of which is love.[25] The apparent chiastic sequence of love–faith–love in vv. 5–7 is Pauline (see 1 Thess 1:3; 3:6; 5:8; 1 Cor 13:13; 16:13; 2 Cor 8:7; Gal 5:6), attesting to the apostle's understanding of faith and love in the life of the believer.

---

24. See Okorie, *Favor and Gratitude*, 54–56.

25. Bonnie Thurston, "The New Testament in Christian Spirituality," in *The Blackwell Companion to Christian Spirituality* (ed. Arthur Holder; Oxford: Blackwell, 2008) 55–70.

There are two ways, therefore, that Paul speaks in his letters about the love of God for believers. First, Paul speaks about God's love for the believer in the subjective sense, mirroring the quality of God's love (see 2 Cor 13:13): God loves humankind (see 2 Cor 13:13; Rom 5:5, 8); Paul calls believers God's beloved (see 1 Thess 1:4; Rom 1:7), and he identifies God as our Father (Phlm 3), thereby linking God with familial love. Second, Paul describes God's love in an objective sense of believers' response to that love (see 1 Cor 1:9; 8:3). The objective sense of the believers' response to God's love is what Paul proclaims in Philemon. Paul praises Philemon's love of the "holy ones" and entreats him to welcome back Onesimus as a beloved brother (v. 16) because of the fundamental Christian moral principle: God provides the incentives for Christians to love one another and to be in fellowship with one another.

By and large, love is a central feature of the message that Paul has been called to proclaim when he declares that obedience to divine law manifests itself in mutual relationship between believers (see 1 Thess 1:3; 5:8; 1 Corinthians 13; Gal 5:6, 13, 22). In the thanksgiving section of Philemon, therefore, Paul gives thanks to God and publicly praises Philemon for practicing the gospel value that God has called and commissioned him to proclaim. Paul implicitly underscores the divine nature and origin of love by linking it with faith. He gives gratitude to God for Philemon's love and declares his own feeling of joy for Philemon's love. In this letter, therefore, Paul describes Christian behavior in two virtues, which he deliberately links together in an apparent dyadic relationship: relationship with God, which is inexorably linked with relationship with one another.[26]

■ CONCLUSION

Among Paul's letters, Philemon is unique for dealing with only a single issue, the relationship between a master and his slave in the Greco-Roman world. The letter lacks the theological enterprise for which Romans and Galatians are known. Further, the moral exhortations so ubiquitous in Philippians, 1 Thessalonians, and the Corinthian correspondence are completely missing in Philemon. Although the letter contains the names of several people connected with Paul and purports to include all the members of the house church as addressees, it is nonetheless addressed to a single individual on how he should relate to his slave. I would be remiss,

26. See Michael Wolter, "The Letter to Philemon as Ethical Counterpart of Paul's Doctrine of Justification," in Tolmie, *Philemon in Perspective*, 169–79.

however, to dismiss the letter as lacking, if only implicitly, in the *theologi-cal* framework that undergirds Paul ministry and message.

In this essay, I have examined how Paul articulates the role of God in the lives of believers who have come to faith in Christ. In the letter, Paul persuades Philemon that welcoming back Onesimus is a testament of his faith in God's plan through Christ. Therefore, Paul frames the letter to convince Philemon that the request to welcome back Onesimus is driven by God; God is the one working out the liberation of humanity through Jesus Christ from the experiences of inhumanity manifesting itself in myriad ways, specifically in this instance through the scourge of Greco-Roman slave society and the patriarchal system that undermines the equal place of women in the relationship between God and humanity. God's liberating power is manifested in Onesimus's experience of freedom as he returns to his master's house with a letter requesting a status trans-formation from a slave to a beloved brother. It is important as well not to minimize the significance of mentioning Appiah in the opening section of the letter; she takes her place like everyone else in the community as a child of God far beyond gender disparity. For his part, Philemon expe-riences God's liberating power in Paul's persuasively emphatic words requesting that he free himself from complicity in a social system that dehumanizes others. For Philemon and Onesimus to accept the gift of God's grace through Jesus Christ means that they have opened them-selves up to the liberating presence of God's transforming power in their lives, and they have embraced their new identity as beloved brothers in God's household.

8

God and New Creation in Galatians
2 Corinthians, and Romans

NAJEEB T. HADDAD

The concept of new creation finds its importance among Jewish prophetic literature.[1] Most prominently, it is found in the writings of Jeremiah, Ezekiel, and Isaiah. New Testament scholars would readily recognize the promise of the new covenant in Jer 31:31–34. Here Yhwh announces a new covenant, not according to the previous one that was outwardly expressed as written laws but one inscribed upon the hearts of believers. In a similar way, in the Book of Ezekiel God promises to refashion the people by placing within them a new heart and a new spirit (Ezek 36:26–27; cf. 11:19–20; 18:31). In Deutero-Isaiah, Yhwh is described as creator, redeemer, and savior. Here, Yhwh promises the looming return from exile as a new exodus. Moreover, this redemptive act is not only a renewal of Israel but also a renewal of all of God's creation (Isa 43:15–21). The former things will be replaced by the new. In Trito-Isaiah, the promises move beyond a renewal of creation to the cosmic level with the promise of a new heaven and a new earth (Isa 65:17–18; 66:22).

A cursory examination of these prophetic texts should give one a rudimentary understanding that Paul's language of *new creation* is not a novel one. Though Paul coins the phrase "new creation" (Gal 6:15; 2 Cor 5:17; καινὴ κτίσις), he is very much dependent on these, and other, Second

---

1. See the work of Ulrich Mell, *Neue Schöpfung: Eine traditionsgeschichtliche und exegetische Studie zu einem soteriologischen Grundsatz paulinischer Theologie* (BZNW 56; Berlin: de Gruyter, 1989); Moyer V. Hubbard, *New Creation in Paul's Letters and Thought* (SNTSMS 119; Cambridge: Cambridge University Press, 2004) 11–76.

Temple writings. Much has been written on Paul's Christocentric understanding of new creation.[2] In this essay, I focus on the role of God in Paul's understanding of new creation, especially in Galatians, 2 Corinthians, and Romans. Of central importance is transformation "in Christ." It is through Christ's passion, death, and resurrection that a new creation is inaugurated. However, God is the primary agent of this transformation "in Christ." God is the author of humanity's and creation's renewal. The cross of Christ is God's will, and it is at the center of Paul's theology of new creation.

■ GOD AND NEW CREATION IN GALATIANS

In the closing of the Letter to the Galatians (6:11–18), Paul not only revisits some of the key themes of this letter but includes one of only two mentions of the Pauline phrase καινὴ κτίσις (Gal 6:15; cf. 2 Cor 5:17).[3] Paul says, "For neither circumcision nor uncircumcision is anything, rather [a] new creation [καινὴ κτίσις]."[4] This new creation is qualified by the cross of Christ. Whereas the opponents boast in the flesh (6:12–13), Paul boasts only in the cross of Christ, "through which [δι᾿ οὗ] the world has been crucified [ἐσταύρωται] to me and I to the world" (6:14b). The use of the preposition διά with the genitive of the relative pronoun ὅς indicates the means *through* which life has radically changed for Paul.[5] Because of the cross of Christ, a new creation has dawned on all believers. In the new creation, the world with all its perversions has been and continues to be crucified to Paul and, ultimately, to all Christ-believers. If the letter's conclusion highlights some of its key themes, then with regard to the new creation two central elements are present: liberation from the "world" and the transformation of the believer.

2. See Mell, *Neue Schöpfung*; Hubbard, *New Creation*; Jeff Hubing, *Crucifixion and the New Creation: The Strategic Purpose of Galatians 6.11–17* (LNTS 508; London: Bloomsbury T&T Clark, 2015).

3. Most commentators consider Gal 6:11–18 as the postscript, *conclusio*, of the letter. See, e.g., Hans Dieter Betz, *Galatians: A Commentary on Paul's Letter to the Churches in Galatia* (Hermeneia; Philadelphia: Fortress, 1979) 312–28. Jeff Hubing, however, identifies Gal 6:11–17 as the closing of the letter *body* (*Crucifixion and New Creation*, 43–84).

4. All translations are mine, unless otherwise noted. The Greek text is from the NA[28].

5. The pronoun ὅς can refer either to "our Lord Jesus Christ," likely based on the immediate context of Gal 6:14, or to the person of Christ. Betz, however, notes that either understanding "is of no consequence, since for Paul 'Christ' is always the crucified redeemer Christ" (*Galatians*, 318).

Christ's cosmic role in God's economy of salvation is central to Paul's eschatological soteriology. Paul understands the sending of Christ as God's promise to redeem humanity. This redemption has been fulfilled because humanity has entered the fullness of time (τὸ πλήρωμα τοῦ χρόνου, Gal 4:4; cf. 2 Cor 6:2). But this creates a paradox for the believer. Even though he says the fullness of time has come, Paul asserts that God has sent the divine Son in order that Christ may rescue humanity from "the present evil age" (ὅπως ἐξέληται ἡμᾶς ἐκ τοῦ αἰῶνος τοῦ ἐνεστῶτος πονηροῦ, Gal 1:4b). In other words, although redeemed, the believer still lives in an unredeemed age (αἰών).

The Synoptic Gospels, the Pauline letters, and Hebrews all adopt the Jewish apocalyptic notion of two ages.[6] In this apocalyptic framework, the present age is identical with the time of the world, which is linear. The future age, however, is the time after the end, which can be represented symbolically as the kingdom of God, or the "new creation" (Gal 6:15; 2 Cor 5:17; cf. Rom 8:18–21). Paul never speaks of the "age to come" because the new age has already dawned on believers by Christ's death and resurrection. He does, however, speak of "this age." In the undisputed Pauline letters the phrase ὁ αἰὼν οὗτος ("this age") appears seven times (Rom 12:2; 1 Cor 1:20; 2:6–8 [2x]; 2:8; 3:18; 2 Cor 4:4), and the phrase ὁ αἰὼν ὁ ἐνεστὼς πονηρός ("the present evil age") appears once (Gal 1:4). In each instance where it appears, ὁ αἰὼν οὗτος connotes negativity and can be associated with foolishness, sin, and death.

In close parallel to Paul's use of αἰών is the term κόσμος ("world," "universe"). In several passages where Paul uses this word (e.g., Rom 3:6; 1 Cor 1:20–21; 2:12; 4:13; 11:32; 2 Cor 7:10; Phil 2:15), κόσμος reflects the ethical notions of ὁ αἰὼν οὗτος. Though αἰών has to do with time, κόσμος is the world that reflects this present evil age. In the Letter to the Galatians, both the "flesh" and the "law" are cosmic powers warring with the Spirit of God (Gal 3:23–25; 4:4–6; cf. 1:4; 6:14).[7] Paul suggests that the κόσμος, exemplified by the sins of the σάρξ ("flesh"), has come under judgment because of the Christ-event (Gal 6:14). However, as Paul states in the very beginning of Galatians, the liberation of humankind from "this present evil age" is occurring because of the will of "our God and Father" (Gal 1:4). Yet believers live in the world and therefore cannot transcend the world unless they have been transformed.

Being transformed into an angelic nature was one of the ways Second Temple Judaism characterized its eschatological hope.[8] Moreover, writing

6. Herman Sasse, "αἰών, αἰώνιος," *TDNT* 1:197–209, esp. 205–7.

7. Rodrigo J. Morales, *The Spirit and the Restoration of Israel: New Exodus and New Creation Motifs in Galatians* (WUNT 2/282; Tübingen: Mohr Siebeck, 2010) 143.

8. E.g., Dan 12:3; Sir 45:2; Mark 12:25; 2 *Bar.* 51:3, 10–12.

in the second century C.E. about the goddess Isis and her mysteries in his *Metamorphoses* (11.23–25), Apuleius describes how an initiate is transformed into a godlike being.[9] For Paul, a similar transformation must occur for the believer to enter a new creation. This transformation is very much emphasized in Galatians, as James D. G. Dunn notes on transformation: "Paul in effect agrees that something as radical as personal transformation is essential if the enervating power of the flesh's weakness is to be successfully countered. But for him the template and goal of Christian transformation is Christ."[10] Again, Dunn among others notes that a believer is transformed "in Christ/in the Lord."[11] Though the focus is rightly on transformation "in Christ," God remains the primary agent of such transformation.

To better understand Paul's notion of transformation *in Christ* in Galatians, one must begin with the proposition (*propositio*) of the letter (2:15–21).[12] Paul not only "lives to God" (θεῷ ζήσω), but this living to God includes having been crucified with Christ (χριστῷ συνεσταύρωμαι, 2:19). For Paul, to "live to God" is to have "Christ live in me" (ζῇ δὲ ἐν ἐμοὶ χριστός, 2:20). Notice that this transformation in Paul's life occurs only by means of the cross of Christ. Not only was Christ crucified, but Paul has been, and continues to be, crucified with him. The verb συνεσταύ-ρωμαι ("have been crucified with") is in the perfect passive indicative, which expresses a determinate action, accessed only by memory.[13] In addition, Troy W. Martin notes, "[S]uch actions occur in the past, while their indeterminate effects and consequences or resultative states belong to the present and are accessible to the senses."[14] Paul's crucifixion with Christ happened at a specific point in the past, yet he continues to experience its effects and consequences—his transformation in Christ is

9. Likewise, Plutarch, *Is. Os.* 352B. See the discussion in Betz, *Galatians*, 188.

10. James D. G. Dunn, *The Theology of Paul's Letter to the Galatians* (Cambridge: Cambridge University Press, 1993) 118–20; quotation from 118.

11. Ibid., 118–20. See also James D. G. Dunn, *The Theology of Paul the Apostle* (Grand Rapids: Eerdmans, 1998) 396–401.

12. The *propositio*, rhetorically, concludes the narrative of facts and introduces the basic proposition of a letter. In the remainder of the letter, specifically Gal 3:1–4:31, Paul will substantiate his proposition using six specific proofs. See Thomas H. Tobin, *Paul's Rhetoric in Its Contexts: The Argument of Romans* (Peabody, MA: Hendrickson, 2004) 64–65; Betz, *Galatians*, 113–14.

13. See Herbert Weir Smyth, *Greek Grammar*, revised by Gordon M. Messing (Cambridge, MA: Harvard University Press, 1980) §§1945–51.

14. Troy W. Martin, "Perceived Reality and the Tenses of the Greek Verb" (paper presented at the Annual Meeting of the Midwest Region of the Society of Biblical Literature, South Bend, Indiana, February 10, 2019) 6. Cf. Smyth, *Greek Grammar*, §§1945–51.

ongoing. To be crucified with Christ not only releases him from bondage to the Mosaic law but also allows him to live outside this age, outside this world.

Transformational language is in Paul's discussion of baptism in Gal 3:26—4:11. At baptism a believer is transformed into Christ. Paul writes, "for you all are children [υἱοί] of God through the faith in Christ Jesus; for as many as have been baptized in Christ have clothed yourselves in Christ" (3:26–27). To be clothed in Christ is no simple metaphor for Paul, for the one who believes now shares in death with Jesus. It is an initiation into the Christ-event, a metaphysical transformation becoming like Christ. Just as one shares in his death, one now receives a share in his inheritance by the Spirit and through adoption (υἱοθεσία) (cf. Rom 6:1–6). In Gal 3:2 Paul asks a rhetorical question to which the answer would have been obvious. Did they receive the Spirit by the observance of the law or by the hearing of faith? More specifically, when did they receive the Spirit? The obvious answer would have been "at baptism." This is consistent with Paul's ethical exhortations to walk and be led by the Spirit (Gal 5:16; 6:7–10, respectively). God has sent Christ not only to redeem but to adopt, so that humanity may be able to share in Abraham's promise fulfilled in Christ (Gal 3:15–18). To be a child of God, to call on God as *Abba*, is to join God's family. As a result of this divine adoption, believers participate in a new creation whereby the identity markers of the world and its major divisions are abolished. Where the spirit of God is, there one will find freedom. For in the new creation "there exists neither Jew nor Greek, there exists neither slave nor free-person, there does not exist male and female; for you all are one in Christ Jesus" (Gal 3:28).

For Paul, it would seem, a new creation is brought about by God's sending of Jesus Christ. To live in God is to be transformed into Christ crucified. New creation begins by the will of God, who willed Christ to be crucified, and willed that through baptism believers are clothed with Christ. To live in a new creation, however, believers must realize that they live in a renewed community. In three of the four occurrences of the verb "crucify" in Galatians, Paul uses the perfect tense (2:19; 3:1; 6:14).[15] The reason may have to do with Paul's beliefs that one's spiritual transformation, one's having been crucified with Christ, has continuing indeterminate effects. "Crucified" appears in the aorist in 5:24; the action of being crucified also has definiteness and determinate actions in the past. So those that are of Christ have "crucified [ἐσταύρωσαν] the flesh with its passions and desires."

---

15. In Gal 5:24 Paul wants to point to a specific moment in the life of the believer.

The flesh as a cosmic power can arouse the passions and desires which Paul warns may exclude one from the kingdom of God (Gal 5:19–21). Victory, however, has been achieved by God through Christ crucified. In this new reality, the "elemental spirits of the world" (στοιχεῖα τοῦ κόσμου) have been overcome by Christ's crucifixion and resurrection (4:8–11; cf. Col 2:13–15). It is a victory accomplished in the past with ongoing effects. The Galatians are struggling with their new transformative life in Christ, which Paul highlights by saying in anguish, "My children, for whom I again suffer birth-pangs until Christ is formed [μορφωθῇ] in you" (4:19). For in belonging to Christ, one has crucified the flesh. As J. Louis Martyn observes, "Just as their baptism into Christ gave them a new Lord, so it involved a decisive separation from the Flesh, a separation so radical as to amount to the death of the Flesh, whose effects are pictured in 5:19–21a."[16] To live in a renewed creation is to live according to God's Spirit that dwells within each believer (4:6). To "live by the Spirit" (5:16) is to recognize that believers live in God, and in effect Christ lives in them (2:20; cf. 4:19). God has deigned for Christ to be crucified so that God may refashion and renew the entire creation. To be a new creation means conformity with, and transformation in, Christ. It is a death to the "world" (cf. 1 Cor 15:31; Phil 1:20–21), a rising with Christ out of sin, and the eschatological hope of believers physically rising from the dead (1 Cor 15:50–57). In Galatians, the world is not simply crucified in the mind of Paul. Rather, Christ's death and resurrection bring about the overthrowing the "elemental spirits of the world," stripping them of their power. This renewed life, however, is possible since everything has occurred according to the will of God (Gal 1:4).

■ GOD AND NEW CREATION IN 2 CORINTHIANS

The phrase καινὴ κτίσις ("new creation") appears in 2 Cor 5:17. It is part of the larger exhortation in 5:11–6:10, where Paul emphasizes that Christ-believers are known by God as a result of the Christ-event. In 2 Cor 5:16–17 Paul explains,

> Wherefore, we now know no one according to the flesh; even if we have known Christ according to the flesh, yet now we know him so no longer. Then if any person be in Christ, there is a new creation. The old things have passed away, behold all things have become new.

16. J. Louis Martyn, *Galatians: A New Translation with Introduction and Commentary* (AB 33A; New York: Doubleday, 1997) 501.

The theocentric aspect of new creation can often be overlooked. Here, as in Galatians, Paul links new creation with God, who is the author of this major anthropological and cosmological shift. Paul continues in 2 Cor 5:18–19:

> But all things are from God who has reconciled us to himself through Christ and has given us the ministry of reconciliation; that is, God was in Christ reconciling the world to himself, not reckoning their trespasses to them and placing in us the message of reconciliation.

God has sought to reconcile humanity to God's-self and therefore is the primary agent behind the new creation.

As with the idea of new creation in Galatians, in 2 Corinthians Paul is focusing on the transformation of both the believer and the created order, although the emphasis here seems to be anthropological. This transformation occurs through the ministry of reconciliation, which God has bestowed on humanity through Christ. First, in 2 Cor 5:11–13, Paul contrasts himself with the external boasting of the opponents, comparable to Paul's "boasting" in Gal 6:11–16. Paul's boasting is found in the "heart" (καρδία, 2 Cor 5:12). As emphasized in Galatians, so too here in 2 Corinthians: "old things have passed away, behold all things have become new" (2 Cor 5:17). In 2 Cor 5:14–15 Paul reiterates the central tenets of the faith, namely, that Christ's death was for all. Therefore, the life now lived should be lived for Christ, who died and rose from the dead for the sake of the faithful. Worldly standards, κατὰ σάρκα ("according to the flesh"), no longer have a place in the community of believers. Rather, believers must know each other "in Christ" by means of God's reconciling creation to God's-self. As Martyn observes, the former lives of the Corinthian believers are categorized by knowledge κατὰ σάρκα. It is the "old-age of knowledge" that centers on a life in the flesh (cf. Gal 5:16–21). The new age, however, is categorized by knowledge κατὰ σταυρόν ("according to the cross"). Martyn comments, "*Christ* defines the difference between the two ways of knowing, doing that precisely in his cross. The cross of Christ means that the marks of the new age are at present hidden *in* the old age (2 Cor 6:3–10)."[17] At the heart of Paul's understanding of new creation is transformation "in Christ."

In his appeal to the Corinthian believers in 2 Cor 5:18, Paul insists that "all things are from God." Although this appeal has much to do with

---

17. See J. Louis Martyn, "Epistemology at the Turn of the Ages," in idem, *Theological Issues in the Letters of Paul* (London: T&T Clark, 1997) 89–110, here 110 (italics original).

his apostleship, it also reveals God's relationship with the new creation.[18] Paul emphasizes three important features of this theology in 2 Cor 5:18–19: (1) God reconciles the world to God's-self; (2) God brought about this reconciliation through Christ; and (3) reconciliation means not charging trespassers with their trespasses. Reconciliation is the restoration of a broken relationship. Often, those who are guilty will seek to be reconciled with the party they have injured. For Paul, however, God is seeking reconciliation with guilty humanity. This "ministry of reconciliation" is the life-giving "ministry" of the new covenant (cf. 2 Cor 3:6–9; 4:3).[19] This ministry of reconciliation is given not only to the apostle but to all Christ-believers.[20] According to Victor Paul Furnish, "[Paul's] reference to *the ministry of reconciliation* helps to define the responsibility laid upon the whole community of faith as it is reconciled to God and drawn under the rule of Christ's love."[21] Because they are now part of a new creation, believers have been reconciled with God. However, the fullness of the new creation has not yet been achieved, for the ministry of reconciliation is made available only to those who are now in Christ.

In the background of the discussion of transformation in 2 Corinthians is Paul's understanding of baptism in 1 Cor 12:12–13. It is worth noting the similarities between this passage and Gal 3:26–28, in which believers are conformed into Christ by being baptized "into Christ." By clothing themselves with Christ, they shed the identity markers the world places on humanity—"Jews or Greeks," "slave or free," "male and female"—for now all are "one in Christ." Similarly, in 1 Cor 12:12–13 Paul points out that "we all were baptized into one body" (εἰς ἓν σῶμα). With 1 Cor 12:13 suggesting that this baptism destroys the identity markers of

---

18. Some scholars note that the structure of 2 Cor 2:14–7:4 is Paul's *apologia* for his apostolic ministry. Scholars have attempted to divide this section of the letter based on the literary and rhetorical devices employed. For an examination of Paul's *apologia*, see, e.g., Jan Lambrecht, *Second Corinthians* (SacPag 8; Collegeville, MN: Liturgical Press, 1999) 43–44; Jens Schröter, *Der versöhnte Versöhner: Paulus als unentbehrlicher Mittler im Heilsvorgang zwischen Gott und Gemeinde nach 2 Kor 2,14–7,14* (TANZ 10; Tübingen: Francke, 1993) passim.

19. Craig S. Keener, *1–2 Corinthians* (NCBC; Cambridge: Cambridge University Press, 2005) 185.

20. Victor Paul Furnish, *II Corinthians* (AB 32A; Garden City, NY: Doubleday, 1995) 336. For an in-depth study of Paul's use of the "reconciliation" word group, see John T. Fitzgerald, "Paul and Paradigm Shifts: Reconciliation and Its Linkage Group," in *Paul beyond the Judaism/Hellenism Divide* (ed. Troels Engberg-Pedersen; Louisville: Westminster John Knox, 2001) 241–42.

21. Furnish, *II Corinthians*, 336 (italics original).

the world, to be baptized "into one body" is an alternate formula to being baptized "in Christ."[22]

Paul's concept of transformation in 2 Corinthians is best seen in 3:1–18. In this passage, Paul speaks about an intimate encounter with God that allows the believer to be transformed into Christ.[23] Here, Paul contrasts the veiled ministry of Moses with the unveiled, life-giving ministry of Christ. The new covenant brings about an internal transformation, as opposed to Moses's external revelation (2 Cor 3:3; 4:6, 16–18). In 2 Cor 3:12–18 Paul emphasizes this internal transformation: "But all of us, with unveiled faces, gazing at the glory of the Lord as in a mirror, are transformed into the same image from [one degree of] glory into [another degree of] glory, just as from the Lord who is the Spirit" (2 Cor 3:18).[24] For Paul, the life of faith is often described in language of birth or adoption (e.g., Rom 8:15, 23; 9:4; Gal 4:5), or in language of "turning toward/conversion" (e.g., Gal 4:9). The Christ-event is now made manifest in the life of believers (2 Cor 4:7–15), and they must live according to their new identity. Though they live in a new creation, the fullness of it is not yet realized. Therefore, just as Paul was transformed by the power of God in Christ to preach the gospel and live according to the new covenant of God in Christ (2 Cor 4:1), so too are the Corinthian believers called to live in this new creation, this new reality. But once again, one must notice that God is the primary author of this eschatological reality. It is God who seeks to reconcile the world to God's-self and does this through the sending of Christ. By being baptized "into one body," believers enter a new creation wherein they live in a manner worthy of the gospel of God in Christ.

■ GOD AND CREATION'S TRANSFORMATION IN ROMANS

Though the phrase "new creation" does not appear in Paul's letter to the Romans, the word "creation" (κτίσις) does. In the undisputed letters, the stand-alone noun occurs only in Romans (1:20, 25; 8:19–22 [4x], 39; cf. Col 1:15, 23). Of interest is Rom 8:18–22, since the freedom of the κτίσις is dependent on the future glory of the "children of God" (v. 21). In Romans 8, Paul is building on the eschatological framework of the "already" and "not yet." Believers received the Spirit and are "alive to

22. Tobin, *Paul's Rhetoric*, 201
23. See a similar discussion on transformation in Christ by Michael J. Gorman, "Paul and the Cruciform Way of God in Christ," *JMT* 2 (2013) 64–83.
24. See Murray J. Harris, *The Second Epistle to the Corinthians: A Commentary on the Greek Text* (NIGTC; Grand Rapids: Eerdmans, 2005) 313–19.

God in Christ Jesus" (6:11) but have not yet inherited the resurrection from the dead (cf. 6:1–11). They have received the Spirit of adoption (8:15) but have not yet received the fullness of that adoption (8:23). Creation has been subjected to futility, and its freedom from bondage to decay rests on the future glory of the children of God (8:22). Though we have focused thus far on the anthropological implications of the new creation, there are also cosmological implications. At the center of the cosmological implications of new creation in Romans is God. God not only is described as the creator of all things in 1:20, but also is the one who gives life to the dead (4:19–25; 6:3–4; 8:11 [2x], 34; 10:9).

Creation's renewal rests on the transformation of humanity, on the final resurrection of believers. It is in Rom 6:1–14 where Paul speaks about believers' transformation, their "newness of life" (καινότητι ζωῆς, v. 4). By being baptized into Christ's death (v. 3), believers are not to allow sin to rule over them (v. 6). Paul's version of being baptized into Christ's *death* is the first appearance of this interpretation in early Christian literature.[25] Just as he emphasized in Gal 3:26–4:11 and 1 Cor 12:12–13, there are ethical implications to one's baptism.[26] To be baptized "into Christ" is to be united with Christ.[27] Paul says in Rom 6:6 that "our old self [ἄνθρωπος] was crucified with him [συνεσταυρώθη] in order that the body of sin may be abolished, so that we are no longer to be slaves to sin." In baptism, believers conform to Christ in all ways: they are dead to sin and alive to God (Rom 6:11). In his death, Christ fulfilled his obligations and ministry to humankind, according to the will of God (cf. Gal 1:4). Since his death, Christ's orientation has been toward God.[28] Believers too must have a theocentric way of life. As Robert Jewett observes, "In their quests for honor and sustenance, guidance, and comfort, believers share a directionality 'to God' that replaces their former orientation 'to sin.'"[29]

25. Ulrich Wilckens, *Der Brief an die Römer* (3 vols.; EKKNT 6; Zurich: Benziger; Neukirchen-Vluyn: Neukirchener Verlag, 1978–1982) 2:250. See Tobin, who rightly comments, "Paul himself is reinterpreting baptism as a baptism into Christ's death, and this reinterpretation emphasizes the ethical implications of baptism" (*Paul's Rhetoric*, 198).

26. Paul's description of baptism dramatically changes from Galatians and 1 Corinthians to Romans. See Tobin, *Paul's Rhetoric*, 198–208.

27. See, e.g., James D. G. Dunn, *Romans 1–8* (WBC 38A; Dallas: Word, 1988) 311; Douglas J. Moo, *The Letter to the Romans* (2nd ed.; NICNT; Grand Rapids: Eerdmans, 2018) 379–80. To be "baptized into Christ" is not the same as being "baptized into the name of Christ." See Tobin, *Paul's Rhetoric*, 203; contra Thomas R. Schreiner, *Romans* (2nd ed.; BECNT; Grand Rapids: Baker Academic, 2018) 309.

28. Ben Witherington III, *Paul's Letter to the Romans: A Socio-Rhetorical Commentary* (Grand Rapids: Eerdmans, 2004) 162.

29. Robert Jewett, *Romans: A Commentary on the Letter to the Romans* (Hermeneia; Minneapolis: Fortress, 2007) 408. Also, Dunn, *Romans 1–8*, 324.

To be "in Christ" and "to live" in Christ is ultimately to live for God (cf. Gal 2:19).

The new creation was promised to Israel (Isa 65:17–18; 66:22) and inaugurated by Christ. It includes the promise of renewal for humanity but also for God's nonhuman creation. In Romans, Paul employs creation imagery in 1:18–25 and advances his argument toward creation's restoration in 8:18–30.[30] Preston M. Sprinkle shows the literary connections between these passages:[31]

Romans 1:18–25	Romans 8:18–30
κτίσεως κόσμου/τῇ κτίσει (1:20, 25) "the creation of the world"/"the creature"	ἡ κτίσις/τῆς κτίσεως (8:19, 20, 21, 22) "the creation"/"the creation"
ἐδόξαν/τὴν δόξαν (1:21, 23) "they (did not) honor"/"glory"	δόξαν/ἐδόξαν (8:17, 18, 21, 30) "glory"/"he glorified"
ἐματαιώθησαν (1:21) "they became futile"	ματαιότητι (8:20) "futility"
εἰκόνος (1:23) "images"	τῆς εἰκόνος (8:29) "the image"
ἀφθάρτου/φθαρτοῦ (1:23) "immortal"/"mortal"	τῆς φθορᾶς (8:21) "decay"
τὰ σώματα αὐτῶν (1:24) "their bodies"	τοῦ σώματος ἡμῶν (8:23) "our body"

These commonalties reveal that in both 1:18–25 and 8:1–39 Paul is alluding to the creation accounts in Genesis 1–3. Sprinkle notes that Rom 8:18–23 is a call for the renewal of the created order, a reversal and restoration of humanity's fall depicted in 1:19–23.[32] However, Paul is describing not merely creation's renewal but its complete transformation.[33]

30. Peter Stuhlmacher, *Paul's Letter to the Romans: A Commentary* (trans. Scott J. Hafemann; Louisville: Westminster John Knox, 1994) 133–35; John Bolt, "The Relation between Creation and Redemption in Romans 8:8–27," *Calvin Theological Journal* 30 (1995) 34–51.

31. Preston M. Sprinkle, "The Afterlife in Romans: Understanding Paul's Glory Motif in the Apocalypse of Moses and 2 Baruch," in *Lebendige Hoffnung, ewiger Tod?! Jenseitsvorstellungen im Hellenismus, Judentum und Christentum* (ed. Michael Labahn and Manfred Lang; Arbeiten zur Bibel und ihrer Geschichte 24; Leipzig: Evangelische Verlagsanstalt, 2007) 201–33, here 221.

32. Ibid.

33. As far back as the patristic period, debate has surrounded the referent for κτίσις in Rom 8:18–22. I will not rehearse this debate here. For an analysis of the debate and for the meaning of κτίσις in Romans 8, see Harry Alan Hahne, *The Corruption and Redemption of Creation: Nature in Romans 8.19–22 and Jewish Apocalyptic Literature*

In 8:18 Paul begins a new phase of his exposition on the Spirit with the verb λογίζομαι ("I consider"). In the context of Romans 8, this verb takes on a more serious connotation than οἴδαμεν ("we know," vv. 22, 28). As Dunn notes, "There is a *gravitas* here" based on Paul's reception of the Spirit.[34] An expanded translation may read "I am firmly of the opinion that . . ." or "it is my settled conviction that. . . ." Paul believes that the pathway to glory is by means of suffering: a believer transformed into Christ is crucified with Christ. To endure suffering with Christ (συμπάσχω, v. 17) is not only to be co-crucified with Jesus (συνεσταυρώθη, 6:6) but also to inherit a resurrection like his at the eschaton (6:4). Therefore, the sufferings of the present cannot compare to the "glory" (δόξα) that is to be revealed at the end. Paul often uses the term "glory" to describe the eschatological inheritance of believers (Rom 2:7, 10; 5:2; 2 Cor 4:17; Phil 3:21; 1 Thess 2:12; cf. Col 3:4; 2 Tim 2:10).[35] This glory will be revealed "to us" (εἰς ἡμᾶς), shown to and manifested within the believer.[36]

In Rom 8:19–22, Paul ties the renewal and transformation of God's creation with humanity's eschatological hope in resurrection. He writes that "creation anxiously longs for the revelation of the children [υἱῶν] of God" (v. 19). Creation personified awaits the final resurrection so that it may fulfill its original purpose.[37] Creation has been subjected to futility (ματαιότης), not because it has sinned against God. Rather, God subjected creation to futility because of Adam's sin (v. 20). Creation is "frustrated" (ματαιότης) because it is ineffective in reaching its intended goal. As Harry Hahne observes, "the created world wants to act as God designed, but it is restricted due to the damage of human sin."[38]

Undertones of Genesis 3 in Rom 8:19–22 are suggested not only by the links to Adam in Rom 5:12–21 but also by the use of the aorist passive

---

(LNTS 336; New York: T&T Clark, 2006) 176–81. See also Jonathan Moo, "Romans 8.19–22 and Isaiah's Cosmic Covenant," *NTS* 54 (2008) 74–89, here 75–77. A growing consensus of scholars, in keeping with the usual meaning of κτίσις in biblical literature and in the context of 8:18–22, rightly suggests that "creation" refers to the nonhuman creation. According to Hahne, "Since angels, demons, humanity, and heaven are excluded [in the immediate context of Rom 8:19–22], this suggests that κτίσις means the subhuman material creation, roughly equivalent to the modern term 'nature.' The LXX uses κτίσις in this sense both collectively (Wis 2:6; 16:24; 19:6) and of individual creatures of the natural world (Tob 8:15; Sir 43:25). Πᾶσα ἡ κτίσις sometimes refers to all nature (Tob 8:15; Wis 19:6; Sir 43:25)" (*Corruption and Redemption of Nature*, 180).

34. Dunn, *Romans 1–8*, 468.

35. Ibid.; cf. Schreiner, *Romans*, 425.

36. Compare 2 Cor 4:17, which says, "for the momentary light affliction of ours is achieving for us an eternal weight of glory surpassing all measure."

37. Creation is also personified in Wis 2:6; 5:17; 16:24; 19:6.

38. Hahne, *Corruption and Redemption of Nature*, 189.

of ὑποτάσσω ("to subject"), ὑπετάγη ("was subjected," 8:20) and the future passive of ἐλευθερόω ("to free"), ἐλευθερωθήσεται ("will be set free," v. 21). These verbs are divine passives.[39] The God who subjected creation to futility because of Adam's sin (Rom 5:12; cf. Gen 3:17–19) is the same God who will free it from bondage to decay as a result of Christ's resurrection. Because humanity was given dominion over nonhuman creation in Gen 1:26–28, Adam's sin has caused creation to lose its purpose. The return of creation to its purpose, however, is coupled with the "freedom of the children of God" (Rom 8:21). The current state of creation's "slavery" is a contingent slavery because "it remains at the mercy of the effects of ongoing human sin and divine judgment."[40] Just as God transformed believers through their baptisms into Christ's death and granted them the hope of resurrection, so too is this hope of transformation extended to creation.

■ CONCLUSION

In light of these observations, we can draw several conclusions about Paul's theocentric understanding of new creation. It is important to consider that Paul draws from the eschatological hopes of Second Temple Judaism.[41] In these writings, God not only promises to transform humanity but will also transform creation. Paul adopts this tradition and believes that God has inaugurated this new creation, according to God's will, in Christ's death and resurrection. Yet the new creation is both "already" and "not yet." God transforms believers at the moment of their baptism, in their present, by sending the Spirit into their hearts, adopting them as children. Transformation by baptism allows believers to enter a new creation where they are obliged to walk by the Spirit. Through baptism, they are united by the Spirit of God: the same Spirit that raised Christ from the dead also destroys the identity markers of the world, even though believers still live in *this age*. Believers, however, have not yet inherited the

---

39. So Schreiner, *Romans*, 427; C. E. B. Cranfield, *A Critical and Exegetical Commentary on the Epistle to the Romans: Introduction and Commentary on Romans* (2 vols.; ICC; Edinburgh: T&T Clark, 1975–1979) 1:413; Dunn, *Romans*, 1:470; J. Moo, "Romans 8.19–22," 538.

40. J. Moo makes a convincing case that Isaiah 24–27 lies as a backdrop for Paul's understanding of creation's slavery to decay ("Romans 8.19–22," passim, here 89).

41. The concept of new creation became especially important in Jewish literature of the Second Temple period, particularly from the third century B.C.E. to the first century C.E.; see, e.g., *Jub.* 1:29; 4:26; *1 En.* 72:1; 91:14–16; *4 Ezra* 6:13–25; 7:30–32, 75; *2 Bar.* 32:6; 44:12–15; 57:2.

future resurrection from the dead. Moreover, creation also suffers as a consequence of Adam's sin. Because God has subjected it to futility, creation is unable to fulfill its *telos*. As God promised in Isa 43:15–21, God will transform creation. Therefore, creation waits in eager longing for the revealing of the glory to the children of God. Only then will creation be transformed into something greater, just as the children of God are being transformed into something greater. The promises of God have begun to be fulfilled through Christ. Yet the fullness of that promise, the new creation, will not be manifested to the entirety of creation until the last day.

9

God's Gospel for All People in Romans

MARY T. BRIEN

A key part of Paul's letters involves God's universal sovereignty over all levels of creation and all peoples. Aspects of God's limitless domain are found often in the Old Testament Scriptures, yet Paul expands the privileges of God's grace and adoption to the elect from all nations, without partiality—to the Jews first and then to the Greeks (Rom 1:16; 2:9). Although the gentiles had neither a genealogical connection to Abraham or Israel nor knowledge of the law, God's wisdom crafted for them a pathway to righteousness and glory through Christ's act on the cross (Gal 2:15). Joined to Christ's death, they were washed and redeemed (1 Cor 1:26–31; 6:11). They had access to adoption and grace (Rom 8:12–17; Gal 3:23–29). And this was on account of their faith and of their maintaining that faithfulness in proper living (e.g., Rom 12:1–21; Phil 3:12–21; 1 Thess 4:1). Yet the most substantial and systematic of Paul's explanations about God's character and sovereignty over all peoples is arguably found in his Letter to the Romans. For this reason, the present contribution will evaluate how Paul describes the character of God and what God has done in Christ for Jews and gentiles alike, with a focus on Romans.

There are as many readings of Romans as there are commentaries. Yet each valid reading of the letter says something about God and about Paul's portrayal of God. It may be said that Romans is more about God than it is about Christ, even though at times the actions of God and of Christ are indistinguishable.[1] God, *God's own self*, is particularly prominent in Romans. Leon Morris writes, "No other book in the NT has this

---

1. For example, "what proves that *God* loves us is that *Christ* died for us" (5:8). See also 3:24; 5:1–2. English translations of biblical passages in this study are taken from the New Jerusalem Bible (NJB).

143

same concentration on the God-theme."[2] God's name appears 153 times in Romans.[3] This is not surprising, given that the introductory verse offers an important clue, unique among introductory verses in the Pauline corpus. This opening verse announces the Good News of God, or God's Good News. With this rather astounding introduction, the reader (or hearer) is alerted to a vital interpretive key for unlocking an important facet of Paul's message. I will argue that Paul's message to Jesus-believers in Rome is encapsulated in the phrase εὐαγγέλιον θεοῦ ("the Good News, or gospel, of God").[4]

■ Defining the Problem

But what precisely is this Good News of God, or God's Good News?[5] Is Paul announcing something new about God or from God to these Jesus-followers in Rome? From both the prologue of Romans (1:1–15) and the epilogue (including 15:14–33, the "apostolic parousia," and 16:1–27) it is apparent that the addressees of this letter are not neophytes. In fact, according to Paul, and allowing for his tendency to flatter his audience, these addressees seem to be capable of being his instructors and mentors. Their faith is acclaimed "all over the world" (1:8). Paul hopes to "find encouragement" among them from their "common faith" (1:11). He is "quite certain" that they are "full of good intentions" and "well-instructed and able to advise each other" (15:14–15). Paul states, almost apologetically, that his reason for writing is none other than to "refresh their mem-

2. Leon Morris, "The Theme of Romans," in *Apostolic History and the Gospel: Biblical and Historical Essays Presented to F. F. Bruce on His 60th Birthday* (ed. W. Ward Gasque and Ralph P. Martin; Exeter: Paternoster, 1970), 249–63, here 263.

3. Ibid., 249. God, in Romans, is described as creator (1:20), immortal (1:23), judge (2:2–3), kind/patient (2:4), impartial (2:11), faithful (3:3), eternal (6:23), loving (8:35–39), inscrutable (11:33), sovereign (11:36), merciful (12:1), and wise (16:27).

4. I follow John M. G. Barclay (*Pauline Churches and Diaspora Jews* [2011; repr., Grand Rapids: Eerdmans, 2016] 4–6) in designating the recipients of Romans as "Jesus-believers" or "Jesus-followers" rather than "Christians" or "Christian communities."

5. The exact meaning of the phrase εὐαγγέλιον τοῦ θεοῦ is much debated. Is the genitive θεοῦ to be understood in the subjective/possessive sense, referring to an attribute of God, for example, God's goodness announced? Or should it be understood in an objective genitive sense, referring to a quality or gift of God which is good news for human beings? Paul is quite capable of ambiguously holding both meanings in tension and at the service of his pastoral concerns. According to Morna D. Hooker, "What Paul understood by 'the gospel of God' was not simply something to be proclaimed but something to be lived" (*Paul: A Short Introduction* [Oxford: Oneworld, 2003] 54).

ories" (15:15). Is Romans therefore no more than a lengthy and complex refresher of memories? If so, memories of what, one may ask, or of what teaching already delivered? Paul does not specify. Since he has not already visited these Jesus-followers in Rome or issued letters to them (1:13; 15:23), one must assume that he speaks of refreshing those teachings delivered by someone else, or of his own teachings previously transmitted by means unknown to us.

Even though it may seem that Paul's reasons for writing the letter are given in 1:11–15, they are so general as to be applicable to any missionary letter. Allowing for other factors, such as the desirability of Rome as a stepping-stone to a Pauline mission in Spain (15:24), and a hope that, through contact with Jesus-followers in Rome, he "may escape the unbelievers in Judea" as he delivers "a generous contribution to the poor in Jerusalem" (15:27–31), problems persist about the need for such a lengthy and complex "letter-essay."[6] Does the charge of redundancy hang over it?

Lastly and importantly, since Romans does not easily fit into the category of a circumstantial letter in the mode of most of Paul's other letters available to us, what issue or issues among Jesus-followers in Rome provoked it? Apart from a reference in Rom 14:10 to problems in the Roman community around observance of food laws, "passing judgment" and "treating a brother with contempt," and hints about the need for "mutual tolerance" (15:5) among the "weak" and the "strong" (14:1–15:13), there is no evidence in the text of pressing problems, scandal, or division such as those claiming Paul's attention in Thessalonica, Philippi, or Corinth. So why this hefty, theological letter-essay about "the Good News of God" visited on a community or an audience that, seemingly, did not provoke or invite it? Could it be a kind of proverbial sledgehammer engaged in cracking a nut? These seem to be fair, reasonable, and basic questions. In one way or another they have occupied scholars over the centuries, generating solutions as wide-ranging and varied as can be imagined.

---

6. I am following Joseph A. Fitzmyer, Raymond E. Brown, and Martin L. Stirewalt in categorizing Romans as a "letter-essay." See Joseph A. Fitzmyer, *Romans: A New Translation with Introduction and Commentary* (AB 33; New York: Doubleday, 1993) 9; also Fitzmyer, "The Letter to the Romans," in *The New Jerome Biblical Commentary* (ed. Raymond E. Brown, S.S., Joseph A. Fitzmyer, S.J., and Roland E. Murphy, O.Carm.; Englewood Cliffs, NJ: Prentice Hall, 1990) 830–68, here 830; Raymond E. Brown, *Introduction to the New Testament* (New York: Doubleday, 1997) 564 n. 12; and Martin L. Stirewalt, *Paul, the Letter Writer* (Grand Rapids: Eerdmans, 2003) 10. David E. Aune and Richard N. Longenecker opt for the category of "protreptic message within a letter framework." See Aune, "Romans as a *Logos Protreptikos*," in *The Romans Debate* (ed. Karl P. Donfried; 1977; repr., Grand Rapids: Baker Academic, 1991) 278–96.

*Proposal: An Exploration of Literary Structure
as Hermeneutical Key*

What is proposed here is the exploration of a promising route to a possibly comprehensive answer to these questions. It will involve bypassing the twists and turns of well-worn paths in favor of a direct approach, along literary and rhetorical lines, toward one satisfactory reading of Romans—a reading that, in addressing the concerns of some Jesus-followers in Rome, has God, and what God has done in Christ, at the center.

Without claiming this interpretation to be the definitive or even the best possible reading of Paul's most challenging letter, this approach will respect all the data in the sixteen-chapter document that is the Letter to the Romans as well as the complexity and richness of Paul's argumentation. Within the hermeneutical circle, I will engage less with the finer exegetical details of individual "problem texts"—although these will be encountered along the way—and more with that moment in the hermeneutical circle that focuses on the entirety of the letter. I will attempt to "read Romans whole" in the hope of clarifying, to some degree, what Paul means by "the Good News of God" (or Good News about/of God).[7] In doing so, I will also say some important things about God, the One whom Paul calls "my God" (1:8), the creator God (1:20) "from whom comes all that exists" (11:36), God who is "our Father" (1:7) and "Father of Our Lord Jesus Christ" (15:6), "the only wise God" (16:27), who is just (3:25–26) and merciful (9:14–18), the God of Jew and gentile.

The Interpretive Project: Identifying Literary Cues

In any analysis of a literary work, structure emerges as one privileged key to meaning. Biblical literary studies in recent decades have appropriated many of the insights arising from structural literary criticism in non-biblical fields and have used these to advantage in providing avenues to the inner structures of biblical writings, because "the meaning is in the structure."[8] The inner supporting structures in any literary work, whether in prose or poetry, provide a key to the flow and functioning of image, line of argument, or sequence of thought, as well as the rhetorical process.

---

7. To translate εὐαγγέλιον θεοῦ into English as "the Good News of God" comes close, in ordinary usage and meaning, to "the Good News about God" and also includes that notion.

8. Dean B. Deppe, *All Roads Lead to the Text: Eight Methods of Inquiry into the Bible; A Template for Model Exegesis with Exegetical Examples Employing Logos Bible Software* (Grand Rapids: Eerdmans, 2011) 90.

Consequently, these structures offer avenues to interpretation. The task of identifying important inner structures (of which there may be several in any given literary work) is a vital element in the interpretive project. This involves a search for literary cues. "Literary cues are surer guides to the structure of Romans than theologically-oriented topics," writes Thomas H. Tobin.[9] In following a limited selection of key literary cues, I will focus on five rhetorical questions (see below)—"deep" questions, all interrelated, the answers to which surface intermittently throughout the letter, thus giving Paul the occasion to say some important things about God and about εὐαγγέλιον θεοῦ, the Good News of God for all people.

Methodology: Identifying Rhetorical Questions as Literary Cues

A close reading of the text of Romans will uncover a distribution of some thirty rhetorical questions, any or all of which, contextualized, may prove significant in the search for a satisfactory reading of the letter.[10] Among other literary cues, rhetorical questions emerge as particularly valuable because they point to the "Common Ground" of underlying problems and assumptions common to speaker and addressee.[11] Consequently, they

---

9. Thomas H. Tobin, *Paul's Rhetoric in Its Contexts: The Argument of Romans* (Peabody, MA: Hendrickson, 2004) 3.

10. My list of rhetorical questions includes 2:3–4, 17–22, 26; 3:1–2, 3–4, 9, 27, 28, 31; 4:9; 5:9, 10; 6:1, 2, 15, 20; 7:7, 13, 24; 8:31, 32, 33; 9:14, 20, 32; 10:18, 19; 11:1, 11.

11. According to current linguistic theory, rhetorical questions typically have the structure of a question but the force of an assertion. They are generally dependent on the notion of "Common Ground" between the speaker and the addressee. Defined as questions that neither seek information nor elicit a direct answer, they challenge the addressee's commitment to an implicit recognition of the implicit answer's obviousness and validity. For the basics of Common Ground Theory, see Robert Stalnaker, "Common Ground," *Linguistics and Philosophy* 25.5–6 (2002) 701–21; Hannah Rohde, "Rhetorical Questions as Redundant Interrogatives," *San Diego Linguistic Papers* 2 (2006) 134–68; Robert van Rooy, "Negative Polarity Items in Questions: Strength as Relevance," *Journal of Semantics* 20 (2004) 239–73.

Stalnaker's definition of Common Ground as "the union of participants' public belief" serves our purpose here. A study of current developments in the field of Applied Linguistics, such as Relevance Theory and the Cognitive Principle of Relevance, will yield pathways to interpretation similar to those generated by Common Ground Theory. The speaker presumes an appropriate set of contextual assumptions, which the hearer must also supply. According to Graham Bird, "The central claim of relevance theory is that the expectations of relevance raised by an utterance are precise enough, and predictable enough, to guide the hearer towards the speaker's meaning" ("Relevance Theory and Speech Acts," in *Foundations of Speech Act Theory: Philosophical and Linguistic Perspectives* [ed. Savas L. Tsohatzidis; London: Routledge, 1994] 292–311, here 292). See also Diane Blakemore, "Echo Questions: A Pragmatic Account," *Lingua* 4 (1994) 197–211, here 197.

may be regarded as just as important a matter for the exegete as they would have been for those who first heard Paul's letter delivered orally, whether in Cenchreae, Corinth, or Rome.[12] Since it will not be possible in the space of this brief study to deal with the entire spectrum of such questions in Romans, a limited selection of five rhetorical questions (two functioning as dyads) will be chosen as exemplars. These are chosen because they are structural in the letter and they are typical rhetorical questions. They are structural because they have a common referent, namely, God and God's relationship to Israel/gentiles, and because the implied answers are widespread and recurrent throughout the letter. They are typical rhetorical questions in that they presume an unambiguous response from the audience. Furthermore, I will argue here that these rhetorical questions act as cues, as pointers to the Common Ground that Paul shares with the community of Jesus-followers in Rome.[13] Sarah H. Casson contends that textual signposts can be reliable indicators of "the possible perspectives of the first audience" and of "the overlapping cognitive environment between communicator and addresees."[14] It is hoped that the limited sample of five rhetorical questions will prove sufficient to illustrate the thesis presented here, which may be summarized as follows: Romans, in its entirety, is an answer to important questions about God and about the implications for Jew and gentile of what God has done in Christ. It is an extended exposé of εὐαγγέλιον θεοῦ—the Good News of God.

12. Since Phoebe is named as the courier and probable deliverer and interpreter of Romans (16:1–2), it is likely that the letter was first read to a Corinthian assembly, or perhaps to the church that met in Cenchreae, where Phoebe was deacon. See Anthony C. Thiselton, *Discovering Romans: Content, Interpretation, Reception* (Discovering Biblical Texts; Grand Rapids: Eerdmans, 2016) 254–55. For another perspective on the first hearers of the letter, see Douglas A. Campbell, *Framing Paul: An Epistolary Biography* (Grand Rapids: Eerdmans, 2014) 53.

13. Since all rhetorical questions presume Common Ground between speaker and addressee, any study of any combination of rhetorical questions will lead to valuable outcomes. The present study is intended only as an exemplar for one such limited exploration.

14. Sarah H. Casson, *Textual Signposts in the Argument of Romans: A Relevance-Theory Approach* (Early Christianity and Its Literature 25; Atlanta: SBL Press, 2019) 42.

In the field of linguistics, Relevance Theory functions in much the same way as Common Ground Theory. It relies on textual signposts as pointers to a shared cognitive environment between communicator and addressees. In this way it provides possible pathways to interpretation.

■ FIVE SAMPLE RHETORICAL QUESTIONS AS LITERARY CUES[15]

This way of reading Romans will not lay claim to offering a detailed exegesis of each of the five rhetorical questions chosen and/or of associated answers. Its focus will be on identifying some structural and interlocking features in Paul's rhetorical strategy. In a word, it will trace a limited number of Paul's approaches to the five questions chosen and to the presumed underlying dilemmas. In pointing out examples of the widespread reverberations throughout the letter of Paul's often convoluted responses, responses involving diatribe and some apparent contradictions, I hope, in this reading of Romans, to uncover core concerns that are structural in the letter—concerns constellated around God and God's Good News.[16]

- 3:1: Is a Jew any better off? Is there any advantage in being circumcised?
- 3:3: What if some of them [i.e., Jews] were unfaithful? Will their lack of fidelity cancel out God's fidelity?
- 3:29: Is God the God of Jews alone and not the God of gentiles too?
- 9:14: Does it follow that God is unjust?
- 11:1: Is it possible that God has rejected [God's] people?

I will address each of these in turn.

First Literary Cue: "Is a Jew any better off? Is there any advantage in being circumcised?" (3:1)

In the context of a conversation with an imaginary interlocutor, Paul encounters a typical question that a Jewish opponent might ask: Since Jews observe the law of Moses, abstain from certain foods, and observe certain festivals, they have an entitlement to a special relationship with God. Jewish males are circumcised as a sign of the covenant between God and Abraham. It would seem that Paul's law-free gospel disregards Jewish tradition.

---

15. Two of the rhetorical questions chosen here (the first and second) take the form of dyads.

16. Questions about God and about Paul's reading of the Hebrew Scriptures were current in synagogue debates at the time. Inclusivism and particularism (relating to Jewish–gentile relations) as expounded in the Isaiah Targums were live issues. See Delio DelRio, *Paul and the Synagogue: Romans and the Isaiah Targum* (Eugene, OR: Pickwick, 2013) 70–98.

Gentiles are now inheriting without cost what Jews have long guarded as uniquely theirs. The questioner may rightly ask if there is any advantage in being a Jew, since the benefits that Jews considered to be theirs are now widely available, outside the law, to non-Jews.

Paul's answer to this rhetorical question is an extended one with multiple ramifications. In 3:2–4 he will argue that Jews are the people "to whom God's message was entrusted." The law is spiritual (7:14). The law is sacred, and what the law commands is sacred, just, and good (7:12). The Jews are those who were adopted as children, and to them was given "the glory and the covenants, the Law and the ritual" (9:4). They are descended from the patriarchs, and "from their flesh and blood came Christ, who is above all. God be forever blessed!" (9:5). All of this confirms the continuity between what Paul is preaching as his gospel with "what God promised long ago through the prophets in the scriptures" (1:2). For Paul, there is no disconnect.

To the repeated question "Are we any better off?" (3:1, 9), Paul claims the Common Ground and identifies himself with his Jewish interrogator. He gives an answer that seems to contradict his previous stance: "Not at all. As we said before, Jews and Greeks are all under sin's dominion" (3:9b). This is supported by a catena of scriptural references (3:10–18), showing Jew and gentile to be equally under sin's dominion. This prepares the way for a lengthy defense of the righteousness of God (δικαιοσύνη θεοῦ). Here the catena works as part of Paul's strategy for establishing the true advantage in being a Jew (3:21–31). The righteousness of God, once revealed through the law and the prophets, has now been revealed "apart from the law" (v. 21), but this is no reason for boasting, since it is the same divine righteousness that is revealed within and outside the law (3:27).

To this topic Paul will return in 11:1–36 when he identifies personally with his own Jewish origins: he is an Israelite, descended from Abraham "through the tribe of Benjamin." He is, in the language of current scholarship, "a New Covenant Jew."[17] The Jews are still God's chosen people. But Paul has been sent as apostle to the gentiles so that his own people will be "provoked to jealousy" (11:14) and thereby ultimately be saved. The jealous love of God as portrayed in Deut 32:20–21 will embrace both Jew and gentile.[18] Christ is ἱλαστήριον—the mercy seat or sacred meeting

---

17. Brant Pitre, Michael P. Barber, and John A. Kincaid, *Paul, A New Covenant Jew: Rethinking Pauline Theology* (Grand Rapids: Eerdmans, 2019).

18. See Richard H. Bell, *Provoked to Jealousy: The Origin and Purpose of the Jealousy Motif in Romans 9–11* (WUNT 2/63; Tübingen: Mohr Siebeck, 1994). Also John G. Gager, *Reinventing Paul* (Oxford: Oxford University Press, 2002) 101–49; James W.

place (3:25). The word ἱλαστήριον occurs in the New Testament only here and in Heb 9:5. While scholarly debate continues today around the exact meaning of the term, a first-century audience would surely make links with the ark of the covenant and with God's promise to Moses: "There I will meet you" (Exod 25:22; Lev 16:2).[19] The notion of mercy elaborated in Rom 3:25 will find fuller expression later in 15:7–13.[20]

Paul argues that "Christ became a servant of circumcised Jews" so that God could carry out the promises once made to the patriarchs. But some Jews failed to recognize "the righteousness that comes from God," replacing it with their own idea of righteousness (10:1–21). They have been misguided because they failed to see that "the law has come to an end with Christ, the end (or goal) of the law" (τέλος νόμου, 10:4).

On the question of circumcision, "Is there any value in being circumcised?," Paul takes the debate to a deeper level with a reminder that true circumcision is more than a physical operation. It is about interior disposition: "The true Jew is the one who is inwardly a Jew" and genuine circumcision is "circumcision of the heart" (2:29)—circumcision that is linked to faith (περιτομὴν ἐκ πίστεως, "circumcision through faith," 3:30). This is a Jew's true identity marker and the real meaning of circumcision. The redefined Israel of God can now embrace an extended family—"Jews first, but Greeks as well" (1:16; 2:9–19; cf. 3:10). Paul's God is God of Jew and gentile alike.

Paul's gospel affirms the value of being a Jew, of being a member of God's chosen people, of circumcision understood as "circumcision of the heart" (2:29). God has not revoked the original choice of Israel. God's promises still hold. The law finds its completion and its end in Christ, who became a "servant of the circumcision" so that all could be saved.

Second Literary Cue: "What if some of them [i.e., Jews] were unfaithful? Will their lack of fidelity cancel out God's fidelity?" (3:3)

Paul answers this question summarily in 3:4, even though a more complete answer follows in 10:1–21. In 3:4 the question is dismissed as absurd because "God will always be true (faithful), even though everyone else

---

Aageson, "Typology, Correspondence and the Application of Scripture in Romans 9–11," *JSNT* 10 (1987) 51–72.

19. For a detailed exposition of ἱλαστήριον as "the place of sacrifice," see Hooker, *Paul*, 77–79.

20. J. R. Daniel Kirk, *Unlocking Romans: Resurrection and the Justification of God* (Grand Rapids: Eerdmans, 2008) 49.

proves to be unfaithful" (Ps 116:11). Here the argument seems to get lost in the wider argument about Jews and gentiles being under sin's dominion (1:18–3:20). Yet it belongs here as part of Paul's answer to the question about Jewish infidelity. All human beings (whether Jew or gentile) have been unfaithful because all are under sin's dominion. While it may appear that Paul is contradicting his former statements about the advantage of being a Jew, he is really arguing in another arena. In the general context of human proclivity to sin, being a Jew is not an advantage (3:9). This is supported by a catena of quotations from the Psalter (Pss 5:9; 10:7; 14:1–2; 36:1; 53:1–2; 140:3), as well as from Isa 59:7–8.

As if reading the meaning of "unfaithful" in the narrow sense of failing to keep the law, Paul engages with a range of questions about the efficacy of the law, ending with a quotation from Ps 143:2: "No one can be justified in the sight of God by keeping the law" (3:20). This leads him to an exploration of God's justice (δικαιοσύνη θεοῦ) and fidelity, a topic that will occupy a great portion of chaps. 3–8. It is a complex notion, but one that carries a good measure of the weight of Paul's argument about God. The phrase itself, the equivalent of ṣedeq ʾElōhîm in Hebrew, does not exist in the Old Testament.

There are approximations in Deut 33:21 (ṣidqat Yhwh, "justice of Yhwh") and in Judg 5:11 (ṣidqat Yhwh). The exact Hebrew equivalent of δικαιοσύνη θεοῦ occurs in the Dead Sea Scrolls in the *War Scroll*, 1QM 4.6 (ṣedeq ʾEl, "justice of God"), and in the *Community Rule*, 1QS 10.25 and 11.12 (ṣidqat ʾEl, "the righteousness [or justice] of God"). This represents a significant clue to the use of the phrase in Romans because the meaning of the Hebrew ṣĕdāqâ (constuct ṣidqat), referring to God's uprightness or righteousness, had taken on a nuanced meaning in postexilic times. It assumed an extra semantic dimension, "the quality whereby God acquits his people, manifesting towards them a gracious, salvific power in a just judgment."[21]

So how does Paul deal with the question of God's fidelity to Israel? He engages in a lengthy and complicated discussion about God's justice, righteousness, trustworthiness, compassion, and mercy. He is resorting to a rich theological vein when he employs the term δικαιοσύνη θεοῦ in Romans. Whether or not he is aware of the Qumran document 1QS 11.9–15, he employs in Romans a complex and comprehensive theology of God's righteousness that is close to that source, and to understandings of

21. Joseph A. Fitzmyer, "Justification by Faith in Pauline Thought: A Catholic Perspective," in *Rereading Paul Together: Protestant and Catholic Perspectives on Justification* (ed. Davie E. Aune; Grand Rapids: Baker Academic, 2006) 77–94, here 80.

ṣedeq in the late first century B.C.E.[22] Paul's rich and multifaceted exegesis of δικαιοσύνη θεοῦ becomes a most important statement about God and about God's dealings with humankind. God is both just and merciful. God's loving-kindness (Hebrew ḥesed) is not time-bound. It finds its greatest expression in what God has done in Christ.

Paul's manner of dealing with the issue of Jewish infidelity and God's fidelity is complex in the extreme, yet it is structural and ultimately coherent. His argument begins with an elaboration of humanity's need for justification, supported by a catena of scriptural references (3:10–18) from the Psalter and Isaiah, followed by one of the richest passages in Romans about faith and God's faithfulness (righteousness/trustworthiness). Once revealed through the law and the prophets, God's faithfulness has now been revealed through Christ to everyone, Jew and Greek alike (3:22).

Third Literary Cue: "Is God the God of Jews alone and not the God of gentiles too?" (3:29)

This is a question about God, about God's unchanging nature and the extent of God's dominion. Paul's argument here is that, since there is only one God (3:30), Jews may not claim this God as theirs alone. God's reach is more extensive than Paul's audience can imagine. It is great and wide enough to include the gentiles too. For Jews and others, this could be read not as good news but as a denial of that special relationship between God and Israel on which their faith was founded.[23] The subtext here is Deuteronomy 32, and it raises a related question: Has God changed? In other words, if Paul is right in asserting that gentiles can now lay claim to the promises once made through the law and the prophets to Israel only, what is the implied message about God? To observant Jews, Paul seems to be preaching a gospel about a God who has changed course, a God who is no longer a trustworthy God. Jewish faith over centuries, based on Scripture, had given the certainty that Israel was set apart to be God's chosen people: "If the Lord set his heart on you and chose you, it was not because you outnumbered other peoples . . ." (cf. Deut 7:7). The implication is that Paul has been reading that sacred text from Deuteronomy and

---

22. 1QS 11:9–15 reads, "If I stagger, God's grace is my salvation forever. . . . In his righteous fidelity [δικαιοσύνη] he has judged me; in his bounteous goodness, he has expiated all my iniquities" (cited in Fitzmyer, "Justification by Faith," 80–81).
23. "The obedience of the nations," a live topic in synagogue debate, reemerges here. See n. 16 above.

other precious texts as well (e.g., Exod 19:5; Deut 7:7–8; 14:2) in a way that challenges the special status of the Jews. Those outside the law have been given free entry to Israel's privileged position. Understandably, some Jews may feel discommoded, with the very foundations of their special status before God under threat.

Paul addresses this topic many times and in multiple ways in Romans. The first hint appears in 1:1. Here Paul is preaching "the Good News that God promised long ago through the prophets in the Scriptures." His preaching is in continuity with the ancient promises of God. Paul is "not ashamed of the Good News"; it is "the power of God saving all who have faith—Jews first, but Gentiles as well" (1:16). Both Jew and gentile can incur God's wrath (1:18–3:20).[24] God makes no distinction between peoples. "He will repay each one as his works deserve" (2:6). God has no favorites (2:11). God will justly reward everyone, "Jews first but Greeks as well." The phrase is repeated twice (2:9–10). "Jews and Greeks are all under sin's dominion" (3:9). And δικαιοσύνη θεοῦ—the perceived Common Ground question emerges: "Has God changed or changed course?" In other words, "Is God steadfast and trustworthy?"

Romans in its entirety may be read as Paul's focused response to that rhetorical question. Examples abound. "God will always be true even though everyone else proves to be false" (3:4); "God's righteousness that was made known through the law and the prophets has now been revealed outside the law" (3:21). The law has not been abrogated. Paul is giving the law its true value (3:31). The God of Abraham is the God of those who walk in faith, since Abraham believed God before he was circumcised (4:10–11). Circumcision as a physical procedure is not the badge of faith. Righteousness comes through Jesus Christ (5:21), whom Adam prefigured (5:14). It does not follow that God is unfair (9:14). God is sovereign and will show mercy to those to whom God wills (9:15).

There is one God, who wants all to be saved (10:2). God will ultimately save the Jews, even if human wisdom cannot say how. God has not changed, but God's plan of salvation is wider, deeper, and more expansive than can be imagined. God is great enough to be God of Jews and of gentiles, too.

---

24. Brendan Byrne argues convincingly that Paul, in this section (1:18–20) is not addressing the community of believers in Rome. Instead he is allowing them to "overhear" his conversion with a fictive partner (*Paul and the Economy of Salvation* [Grand Rapids: Baker Academic, 2021] 76–77).

Fourth Literary Cue: "Does this mean that God has failed to keep [God's] promise?" (9:6)

The question pervades the letter, and internal responses often overlap. In 9:3–6, the Jews are those "who were given the glory and the covenants; the Law and the ritual were drawn up for them, and the promises were made to them. They are descended from the patriarchs." To the questioner, it now seems that God (by extending Jewish privilege to gentiles) may be accused of being unfaithful to those promises and, therefore, unfair. Paul's defense takes the form of a redefinition of Israel and of what constitutes the true Israel of God. For Paul, this can be none other than Christ-believing Israel.

The argument progresses along Wisdom lines, asserting God's sovereign right to choose as God wills. Paul will develop the issue further in 9:14–18, appealing to the text of Exod 33:19: "I have mercy on whom I will, and I show pity to whom I please" (9:15). God is free to be merciful. Human beings have no right to cross-examine God. The image of the potter from Isa 29:16 is invoked, "The pot has no right to say to the potter: Why did you make me this shape?" (9:21). While some scholars argue that this is the weakest of all of Paul's arguments in Romans, it serves Paul's purpose here.[25] God is sovereign. God's ways are not to be questioned. The new Israel is not defined by ethnicity or physical descent. "Not all who descend from Israel are Israel. Not all the descendants of Abraham are his true children" (9:6–7). For Paul, it is only "the children of the promise" who will count as true descendants of Abraham. Jacob, and not Esau, is God's chosen child of promise. God's promises have been fulfilled for the true Israel. It follows that God is trustworthy. God is not unfair. By making a distinction between "Abraham's children" and "his true descendants," Paul redefines the Israel of God, the true heir to God's promises.

The entire section 9:6–13 recounts the Old Testament version of Israel's election. Narratives involving Abraham, Isaac, Rebekah, and Jacob all give testimony to God's promises fulfilled and to the ineffable nature of God's purposes. In dealing with the issue of God's fairness, Paul is presuming Common Ground between himself and his addressees. It is simply unthinkable that God could be unjust or unfair (v. 14). The analogy of the potter and the clay (9:20–21) serves Paul's purpose in upholding God's sovereign right to choose. God is not answerable to humankind. God is

---

25. C. H. Dodd calls it "the weakest point in the whole epistle" (*The Epistle of Paul to the Romans* [MNTC; London: Hodder & Stoughton, 1932] 158–59).

great. God is sovereign. God's purposes are inclusivist. God is just. God is utterly trustworthy.

Fifth Literary Cue: "Is it possible that God has rejected [God's] people?" (11:1)

In dealing with this question, Paul begins with a definitive μὴ γένοιτο! ("By no means!"). Then he proceeds, during the course of some thirty verses (11:2–32), to explain why Israel has not been rejected by God. Through "a seemingly endless stream of exegetical conundrums" he develops a three-pronged approach to the issue.[26] First, he emphasizes again that he is an Israelite, a descendant of Abraham, of the tribe of Benjamin. As such, he could not possibly agree that God has rejected [God's] people (11:2).

Second, relying on arguments already presented, he returns to the notion of the true Israel of God, which he now describes as God's chosen remnant, "selected by grace" (11:5). By means of this remnant, in God's mysterious ways, all Israel will be saved. This corresponds to a pattern in Israel's sacred history, exemplified in the life of Elijah (1 Kgs 19:10, 14).[27] A small number of the faithful will be instrumental in the saving of the whole, and all will be saved by grace. Citing Isa 29:10 and Ps 69:22 (a psalm that was understood christologically among early Christians),[28] Paul turns the argument around: rejection has not been on God's side, but on the side of unbelieving Israel. Yet God always finds a way to work with a chosen remnant. In a clever appropriation of Psalm 69, Paul argues along another line: the Jews have not "fallen"; they have merely "stumbled."

Paul's third approach to the question involves what has become known as "the jealousy motif" (11:14). The argument is as follows: Israel will be saved eventually by being made envious of the grace given to gentiles. The "hardening" of Israel has meant grace and blessings for gentiles. In turn, the grace given to gentiles will be the occasion of Israel's envy and, by means of this, "All Israel" will be saved.

---

26. Kirk, *Unlocking Romans*, 181.

27. Interestingly, this is the only reference in the Pauline corpus to the Book of Kings.

28. Callia Rulmu writes, "In Romans 15:3 Paul cites verbatim Psalm 69:9b and assumes that Christ is the subject of the utterance. Since he does not feel the need to explain his hermeneutics, we can assume that such a Christological reading of the psalms was already accepted by his audience" ("The Use of Psalm 69:9 in Romans 15:3: Shame as Sacrifice," *BTB* 40.4 [2010] 227–33, here 230).

There are three distinct but complementary references to jealousy in Romans 9–11. The first occurs in 10:9 in a context where Paul is searching for answers to the question, Why is it that his fellow Jews, privileged people of the covenant, have failed to recognize in Jesus the Messiah foretold in their own sacred Scriptures? First, he deals with an implied objection that they have not heard the message (10:18) and concludes that they have no excuse, because, in the words of Ps 19:4, "the message has reached the ends of the earth."

A second question follows: Is it possible that Israel did not understand? Moses gives an answer, not immediately intelligible: "I will make you jealous of those who are not a nation" (Deut 32:21). Then comes an explanation: In the text of Deuteronomy there is dual jealousy. A "perverse generation" is portrayed as provoking God to jealousy. God, in turn, will provoke this perverse generation to become jealous of gentile neighbors. Jews will want to possess what gentiles enjoy. But why should Israel be jealous of gentiles? The answer is not given directly by Paul, but it may be deduced from the context: Israel will be "provoked to jealousy" by the extension of Israel's covenantal status to gentiles. The privileged position of Israel has been usurped by the heathen nations (Paul's gospel being responsible). This provokes jealousy among Jews.

The third and final occurrence of the jealousy motif is linked in a personal and emotionally charged manner to Paul's own ministry as apostle to the gentiles (Rom 11:14). The link with Moses in Exodus 32 is inescapable. Just as Moses is willing to be "blotted out" of the book of the Lord, for the sake of his people (Exod 32:32), so Paul has protested his willingness to be "cursed" and "cut off" from Christ for the sake of his own people, his own flesh (Rom 9:3). A similarly charged emotional outburst accompanies his reference to jealousy in 11:14. Paul's ministry as apostle to the gentiles is described in terms of provoking his own people (Israel) to jealousy, so that some of them may be saved. From this, it appears that Paul views his apostolic ministry among gentiles as reflective of that of Moses in Exodus 32 and Deuteronomy 32 and as allied with God's initiative of "provoking to jealousy" those whose hearts have been "hardened" (Rom 11:11), so that ultimately some Israelites will be saved.

Romans 11:14 reads: "The purpose of it is to make my own people jealous and thus save some of them." This is an extraordinary statement about Paul and his apostleship. It occurs only in Romans. It is also a pointer to the significance of the jealousy motif in God's salvific plan as understood by Paul. It is his ultimate answer to those who argue that God has rejected God's people.

The motif of jealousy is pivotal not only to Paul's response to the questioner in 11:1 but to the entire theological argument in Romans 9–11 and to the soteriology of the letter. Furthermore, as 11:14 shows, it is entwined in a vital manner with Paul's mission strategy as he understands it, and is foundational for an understanding of God's plan of salvation for all humankind—beginning with Israel. This motif provides a unique insight into Paul's own understanding of his ministry to gentile and Jew.

Paul is emphatic: God has not rejected [God's] people. As a Jew of the tribe of Benjamin, Paul could not entertain such a thought. God's plan involves a faithful remnant in the salvation of the whole. Invoking Scripture and, especially, the jealousy motif, he argues that Israel will be "provoked to jealousy" on seeing the gentiles' acceptance of the good news. Eventually God's merciful plan for the salvation of humankind will be realized. Rejection has not been on God's side but on the side of Israel, or rather, on a section of it. But by God's mercy, this has been the occasion for the salvation of the gentiles. In turn, this will provoke a remnant of Israel to jealousy, as Scripture has foretold, which will lead to Israel's return and the salvation of all. God has not changed course. God's plan has been unfolding over centuries, as the Scriptures confirm and as Rom 1:2–3 announces. Paul's God is a faithful God who is at once both just and merciful.

■ SUMMARY OF FINDINGS AND CONCLUDING REMARKS

This brief study of the Common Ground between Paul and Christians in Rome, seen through the lens of a sample of five rhetorical questions and Paul's manner of addressing them, reveals a significant amount of information about God in Romans. It also provides reasonably satisfactory answers to the questions posed at the beginning of this study—questions about the integrity and purpose of the letter and about its relevance to Jesus-believers and God-fearers in first-century Rome. Paul's "answers" to the sample rhetorical questions chosen here are revelatory of εὐαγγέλιον θεοῦ—the Good News of God—announced in 1:1 and summarized in 1:3–7. Paul's responses to the Common Ground questions about God's trustworthiness and the place of Jew and gentile in God's plan are consistent, multifaceted, and recurrent. They are structural in Romans. The corollary Common Ground issue is also structural: How can Paul's law-free gospel be plausibly received in Rome or elsewhere as "the Good News of God"?

God's great plan of salvation, "promised long ago through the prophets in the Scriptures," announced in the prologue (1:1–7), involves a call "to Jews first, but Greeks as well" (1:16). The Good News of God is the power of God, saving all who have faith. The righteousness of God (δικαιοσύνη θεοῦ), once revealed through the law and the prophets, has now been revealed "apart from the law" (3:21). God is steadfast and true to the promises made in the Scriptures. God has not changed. Neither has God rejected God's people. God's great plan of salvation has been unfolding in history. God will even take the circuitous route of working through human obstinacy and disobedience to bring people to "the obedience of faith" (ὑπακοὴν πίστεως), a phrase that, significantly, bookends the entire letter (1:5 and 16:26). The reverse side of δικαιοσύνη θεοῦ has been revealed through what God has done in Christ. It is called the mercy or compassion of God (ἐλέους θεοῦ). It was promised long ago to the ancestors of Israel (1:1–2; 15:9) and now gives gentiles reason to glorify God (15:9–12). This is "the Good News of God" that Paul announces to Jesus-followers in Rome.

10

Knowledge of God in Paul's Letters

ELLIOTT C. MALONEY, OSB

When Paul speaks of God, it is most frequently in terms of God's activity toward humans through Christ. This is because acceptance of God's self-revelation in the Christ-event is crucial for the believer's proper response to God for salvation. This is Paul's gospel, the center of his missionary effort. Right thinking is the key to the meaningful communal life that God wants for all of humanity, Jew and gentile alike. Thus Paul advocates: "Be transformed by the renewal of your mind, that you may discern what is the will of God" (Rom 12:2), and "think in harmony with one another . . . so that with one accord you may with one voice glorify God" (Rom 15:5–6).

This question of right knowledge of God is at the center of some very significant problems that Paul faced in his communities. Among them were the dispute over law observance for gentiles in Galatians, the necessity of Christ for the salvation of Jew and gentile alike in Romans, and several outcomes of the factionalism and individualism at Corinth. In this study I will concentrate on the participatory dimension of knowledge of God in order to address the seeming contradiction in 1 Corinthians that "the world did not come to know the will of God through wisdom" (1 Cor 1:21), when in Rom 1:18 Paul says that "what can be known about God is evident to [human beings] because God made it evident to them."

■ KNOWLEDGE OF GOD IN PAUL'S LETTERS

Romans and 2 Corinthians

In the Letter to the Romans, Paul teaches that the truth about God's existence should be obvious to every human being who observes creation

160

(1:20), but that sin, brought to all humanity by Adam (5:12), "darkened their senseless minds" so that they did not make the proper response, "for although they knew God they did not accord him glory as God or give him thanks" (1:21). The result was the further dis-enlightenment of their lives and their turning to ever greater degradation in idolatry and in their relationships to others (1:22–32).

Paul goes on in Romans to explain that a fuller understanding of God came to humanity through the direct revelation of God to the Jews, but that that knowledge alone did not produce righteousness in Israel. No, Paul says, those enlightened by the teaching of the law do not, in fact, do the good they want to do because of "the sin that dwells in [one]" (7:17).[1] He elsewhere makes the point negatively, by stating that "if a law had been given that could bring life, then righteousness would in reality come from the law" (Gal 3:21). But it doesn't! In fact, sin is so powerful that it can work evil even *through* the good law (Rom 7:13). Because of this Paul perceives that the law can even have a negative influence in one's moral life.[2] This is how Paul argues that the salvation wrought by God in Jesus Christ is necessary for Jew and gentile alike, for "all are under [the power] of sin" (3:9).

Paul avows that, although "theirs are the covenants, the law, and the promises" (9:4), "Israel, who pursued righteousness that is based on the law, did not succeed in fulfilling that law" (9:31). He gives the reason for this: "although they have zeal for God, it is without real knowledge [οὐ κατ᾽ ἐπίγνωσιν]" (10:2). What is lacking to them is the understanding of God's raising of Jesus Christ from the dead as God's definitive self-identification as God-who-saves. As Paul says, "If you confess with your mouth that Jesus is Lord and believe in your heart that God raised him from the dead, you will be saved" (10:9).[3] Without the Christ-event we

---

1. Paul points out that sin was able to undermine the guidance of the law by deceiving a person, enticing him or her with the knowledge given in the divine commandments, just as the serpent was able to deceive Adam and Eve about the forbidden fruit. As a result, like Adam and Eve the sinner is consigned to the dominion of death (Rom 7:7–11). So, the Jews do have true knowledge of right and wrong from God from the law, but they are unable to choose and execute right actions because of the presence of sin in their flesh. On this, see Joseph A. Fitzmyer, *Romans: A New Translation with Introduction and Commentary* (AB 33; New York: Doubleday, 1992) 468–69.

2. "For all its intrinsic holiness (Rom 7:12), the impotence of the law to deal with sin led to its becoming a negative rather than a positive factor in the quest for salvation" (Brendan Byrne, *Paul and the Economy of Salvation: Reading from the Perspective of the Last Judgment* [Grand Rapids: Baker Academic, 2021] 228).

3. On this identification of God as the God who raised Jesus, see the excellent discussion of Francis Watson in "The Triune Divine Identity: Reflections on Pauline God-Language, in Disagreement with J. D. G. Dunn," *JSNT* 80 (2000) 99–124.

lack full knowledge of who God is and are thus unable to make a full commitment to God in faith. This more complete knowledge would inform nonbelieving Jews that "Christ is the end of the law for the justification of *everyone* who has faith" (10:4), with a double meaning for "end" (τέλος), namely, that in God's greater plan the law has Christ as its *goal* and thus Christ marks the *termination* of the era of the law as God's definitive act of salvation.[4]

Paul explains Israel's lack of knowledge in another way when he speaks of the spiritual dullness of those who follow the law, using the metaphor of Moses's veil by which "their thoughts were rendered dull" (2 Cor 3:14). This situation can be remedied, "because through Christ the veil is taken away," in the transformation of the Christian by the Spirit (2 Cor 3:16–18). Thus, enlightenment by participation in the Spirit is necessary for the fullness of spiritual life.

Galatians, Philippians, and 1 Thessalonians

To address the question of whether gentiles must follow the Torah, Paul calls for correct knowledge when he reminds the Galatians that "at a time when you did not know [εἰδότες] God, you were enslaved to beings that by nature are not gods" (Gal 4:8). Knowledge of God is central to Paul's two admonitions to these new believers: first, now that "they have come to know [γνόντες] God," they should "not turn back again to the weak and destitute elemental powers" (4:9). Second, even though newly converted to faith in Christ, they should not undergo circumcision and try to live the law like a Jew for the simple reason, as Paul reminds Peter, that Christians "know [εἰδότες] that a person is not justified by works of the law but through the faith of Jesus Christ" (2:16).

Paul clarifies this point when he makes a rhetorical "mistake" here in the Letter to Galatians. He corrects his statement "now that you have come to know God" but immediately reversing it, "rather to be known by God" (Gal 4:8–9).[5] He does this in order to contradict his opponents, the

---

4. Thomas Tobin explains that here Paul means "that the *present* situation of his fellow Jews is due to their failure to recognize that this new era has dawned, that Christ is the goal of the law for everyone who *has faith*" (*Paul's Rhetoric in Its Contexts: The Argument of Romans* [Peabody, MA: Hendrickson, 2004] 347; italics original).

5. See Shane Berg's interesting disclaimer on using one letter of Paul to explain a text in another. He says that without "assuming that all the authentic letters are theologically coherent" they do not need "to be treated in hermetic isolation from one another" ("Sin's Corruption of the Knowledge of God and the Law in Romans 1–4," in *The Unrelenting God: God's Action in Scripture; Essays in Honor of Beverly Roberts Gaventa* [ed. David J. Downs and Matthew L. Skinner; Grand Rapids: Eerdmans, 2013] 119–38, here 132).

false "teachers" in Galatia. They were apparently proclaiming that gentile converts could come to a true knowledge of God only if they should reach a state of perfection that comes from a life of law observance. Paul "corrects" the teachers' avowal that believers "come to know God" in this way by saying that they need, first of all, "rather to be known by God" (4:9b). The foundation of true knowledge comes only in a relationship that responds to God's initiative "in Christ," not in the law or any other religious distinctions.[6] So far we have seen that Paul deals with the wrong response to knowledge of God by non-Christians, both Jew and gentile, in their lack of true wisdom. Yet Paul also experienced that even baptized Christians, who have received the Spirit of knowledge, can have their right understanding blocked by sin. Furthermore, the incomplete and erroneous wisdom of this age can hinder even a believer from making the appropriate response to God's will.

Believers can come to true knowledge of God and make the proper response, Paul avers, only by revelation from God when God knows them in a deeply personal sense. Then God's love elects them, chooses them for a covenant relationship as adopted sons and daughters (Gal 4:5; also 1 Thess 1:4).[7] Then only may they respond in love to the covenant invitation from God, as Paul says elsewhere, "God foreknew them (those who love God) and predestined them to be conformed to the image of God's Son so that he might be the firstborn among many brothers" (Rom 8:29). When they respond to God's love and do God's will they can understand "the supreme good of knowing Christ" and "know him and the power of his resurrection" (Phil 3:8, 10), to further their praxis of the will of God as empowered by their adoption by God who "sent the Spirit of God's Son into our hearts" (Gal 4:6).[8]

Paul confirms the Christian reality of selfless response to God that leads to true knowledge of salvation (the indicative), which in turn leads to the dynamic of the cross (imperative). When he begins the ethical section of Romans, he designates Christian living as an oblation of the whole

---

6. J. Louis Martyn, *Galatians: A New Translation with Introduction and Commentary* (AB 33A; New York: Doubleday, 1997) 413.

7. For Martyn this correction "encapsulates much of the [Galatian] letter's thrust," namely, that "the antidote to ignorance of God does not lie in our acquiring knowledge of God (religion)," but in the love of God who knows us "not as Jews and Gentiles, but rather apart from all religious distinctions" (*Galatians*, 411). God's salvation is not the result of any act on the believer's part, but solely from God's new way of incorporating us into Christ, whose saving grace we share gratuitously. See the full discussion in his *Galatians*, 411–18.

8. Paul indicates this truth elsewhere, by simply saying "whoever loves God is known by God" (1 Cor 8:3) and noting that only in the eschaton "shall I know fully even as I am fully known (by God)" (1 Cor 13:12).

self, "I urge you . . . to offer your bodies as a living sacrifice, holy and pleasing to God, your spiritual worship" (12:1). Then he ties it in closely with the importance of right knowledge in the very next verse, "that you may discern what is the will of God" (12:2). In a terse conclusion to this verse, Beverly Gaventa says, "Paul does not talk simply about having the right understanding of God. Instead, he talks about standing right before God, not just about thought but about worship."[9]

For this reason Paul insists in his first letter to the Corinthians that believers as a community share fellowship and follow a common understanding of the truth, one that is based on "the mind of Christ" (2:16). For the rest of this study I will concentrate on this divine knowledge of Christian faith as Paul explains it in 1 Corinthians.

■ KNOWLEDGE OF GOD IN 1 CORINTHIANS

Key Vocabulary in the Discussion of Knowledge in 1 Corinthians

For the action of "knowing" Paul uses two main verbs, οἶδα and γινώσκω. Quite frequent in the nondisputed letters are forms of οἶδα, which is the perfect tense of εἶδον, meaning literally "I have seen." The word has come, however, to be used for the simple possession of knowledge in a present tense, "I know this; we know that; do you not know something?" (some twenty-five times in 1 Corinthians). The second verb for knowing is γινώσκω, sometimes used in parallel with οἶδα, as, for example, "For what human being knows [οἶδεν] what is truly human except the human spirit that is within? So also no one knows [ἔγνωσεν] what is truly God's except the Spirit of God" (1 Cor 2:11; see also Rom 7:7; 2 Cor 5:16). Yet γινώσκω (sixteen times in 1 Corinthians) usually has the nuance of "coming to knowledge, recognizing," or involves the actual "understanding" of something, "I hope you will come to know [γνώσεσθε] that we are not failures" (2 Cor 13:6); "Realize [γινώσκετε] that those who have faith are children of Abraham" (Gal 3:7). This verb sometimes expresses a close relationship, as often in the Old Testament, a sense of personal involvement as, for example, "If one loves God, one is known by God" (1 Cor 8:3; Gal 4:9; with another human being 2 Cor 2:4, 9).

---

9. Beverly Roberts Gaventa, *When in Romans: An Invitation to Linger with the Gospel according to Paul* (Theological Explorations for the Church Catholic; Grand Rapids: Baker Academic, 2016) 93.

To complete the picture, I note that in 1 Corinthians Paul uses a few derivative verbs: σύνοιδα ("be conscious of," 4:4) and ἐπιγινώσκω ("recognize," 14:37; 16:18). Ἐπιγινώσκω is used in 1 Cor 13:12, "I know fully" in contrast to γινώσκω ἐκ μέρους, "I know partially." Paul also uses three verbs "to make known" in this letter, γνωρίζω (12:3; 15:1), δηλόω (1:11; 3:13), and φανερόω (1:45). The usual substantive for "knowledge" is γνῶσις, used some nineteen times in nondisputed Paul, along with its derivative ἐπίγνωσις, occurring five times, with the added nuance of "real knowledge, recognition of the truth." The word "learn" (μανθάνω) turns up three times (4:6; 14:31, 35), all referring to knowledge that comes through community members.

Finally, the key factor in the evaluation of correct knowledge for Paul is "wisdom" (σοφία), an idea that is concentrated in some twenty-six occurrences in 1 Corinthians 1–3.[10] For Paul, real wisdom can be attained only after the deep-seated vices of the flesh are discerned and rooted out by the power of the Spirit. Only with this elevation of one's inner life by contact with what is transcendent to it can one be reoriented to fully embrace the truth about salvation, as Paul says, "Do not be conformed to this world, but be transformed by the renewal of your mind, so that you may discern what is the will of God—what is good and acceptable and perfect" (Rom 12:2). This "new creation" allows the recognition of the only rationally coherent manner of reevaluating life and dealing with evil in the new framework of the gospel.[11]

Paul says that true wisdom, God's wisdom, is "mysterious, hidden . . . revealed to us through the Spirit" (1 Cor 2:7, 10). It is opposed to "the wisdom of the world" (1:20), "the wisdom of this age" (2:6), which is based on "human eloquence" (lit., "the wisdom of speech" in 1:17; cf. 2:1, 4) and vanity (3:20). It is not human reason as such that is problematic for Paul, but a "worldly wisdom" that is shot through with "moral weakness," that vitiates "human standards of evaluation."[12] On the contrary, Paul defines godly wisdom as knowledge that leads to correct judgment and action that we access in following Christ, "who became for us the wisdom of God" (1:30; cf. 1:24). We receive this divine wisdom from the Spirit, for "who knows what pertains to God [τὰ τοῦ θεοῦ, lit., "the things of God"] except the Spirit that is from God?" (2:11).

---

10. In undisputed Paul the total usage of noun σοφία is eighteen times and of the adjective σοφός fourteen times.

11. Ian W. Scott, *Paul's Way of Knowing: Story, Experience, and the Spirit* (Grand Rapids: Baker Academic, 2006) 48.

12. Ibid., 38.

Knowledge of God in 1 Corinthians 1:10–25

Paul makes clear that proper knowledge is an important concern in his opening words of thanks in 1 Corinthians. Here he singles out discourse (λόγος) and knowledge (γνῶσις) as the top two spiritual gifts that had enriched the Corinthians in their acceptance of the gospel (1:5). While he encourages their goodwill by these compliments, we note a certain irony when he begins immediately to criticize first their "unspiritual" knowledge, and then later to chide them on the vacuity of the tongues discourse they prize so highly.

One of the very first problems Paul encounters in his European mission is the factionalism that formed in the community at Corinth, a splintering of that group based on a false understanding of belonging. For the ancient Mediterranean person, the coalition or clique was an informal yet basic social institution formed inside a larger social structure to give the group identity and cohesiveness for a common interest. At Corinth these coalitions evidently had formed into factions dedicated toward specific purposes. Members were loyal to their founder far more than to the rest of the community.[13] This may have resulted from an idea, prevalent in the mystery religions popular at that time, that those who joined a new religion or cult inherited the prestige and spiritual gifts of their human sponsor, their "father" in the rites, along with the blessings of the god. The inductees of the most prominent cult members then vied for power in leadership of the whole group.[14]

As usual, Paul starts with the teaching of Scripture, where God says, "I will destroy the wisdom of the wise, and the learning of the learned I will set aside" (the context of this Isaian text is God's hidden plan for the restoration of Jerusalem in Isa 29:14, cited by Paul in 1 Cor 1:19). In this Paul is defending his own type of apostolic preaching, considered weak by some as "without eloquent wisdom" (1:17). He explains that the true nature of God and God's plan for salvation is not known from any such worldly wisdom, "since, in the wisdom of God, the world did not know God through wisdom" (1:21). The reason for this decision on God's part ("in the wisdom of God") was because God wanted such knowledge and the proper reaction to it to be a matter of faith, carried out in faithful commitment in imitation of the faith of Jesus Christ. Otherwise, humans would be *compelled* by their reason to submit to God's "eternal power and

---

13. On such cliques and factions, see Bruce J. Malina and John J. Pilch, *Social-Science Commentary on the Letters of Paul* (Minneapolis: Fortress, 2006) 342–43.

14. On this idea, see Craig S. Keener, *1–2 Corinthians* (NCBC; Cambridge: Cambridge University Press, 2005) 26.

divinity" (Rom 1:20), whereas now they can live the obedience of faith in complete freedom, for "where the Spirit of the Lord is, there is freedom (2 Cor 3:17).

Paul recognizes the Corinthians' false thinking and starts his counter-argument with three rhetorical questions in 1:13. He demands unity in the community because of the indivisibility of Christ through whom God offers salvation in Christ's unique accomplishment. Paul insists that incorporation into that community, which he later calls the "body of Christ" (1 Cor 12:27; Rom 12:5), comes from one's faith-filled attachment to Christ in baptism, and not because of the intervention of a sponsor of any kind, even himself. He has emphasized this unity with Christ already in the greeting of the letter: the whole "church of God that is in Corinth ... has been sanctified in Christ Jesus" along with "all those everywhere who call on the name of our Lord Jesus Christ" (1:2), for "by God you were called into fellowship with God's Son" (1:9).

Paul elaborates on his response to their disunity by tackling the root problem of the divisions, as he saw it, namely, that they were based on an exaggerated importance of what we would today call *personality*. He laments the results of such "rivalries," in which "each of you is saying, 'I belong to Paul,' or 'I belong to Apollos,' or 'I belong to Cephas,' or 'I belong to Christ'" (1:12). In his estimation, believers who are unaware of their fundamental unity in Christ can only be described as "unspiritual" (Greek ψύχικος, "pertaining to this life only" 2:14). By using this word Paul means that they were making their judgments not from inspired wisdom from God, as they thought, but on the mundane canons of human respect, embedded as they were in the secular culture of the Roman Empire.[15] Their mistake was in thinking that worldly wisdom gave them prestige like the rich and powerful. Paul mocks them by exaggerating their self-opinion: "Already you have grown rich; you have become kings without us!" (4:8).

Paul shows that there is no point in singling out any spiritual leader as one's own since the Spirit of God dwells in the believer, who thus "belongs to God." The Spirit restores human beings to the pristine state of Adam and Eve, created in God's image and given dominion over all creation (Gen 1:26–28; cf. Ps 8:6–8). It is in this sense that Paul can quote a Stoic proverb and give its true Christian meaning in these lapidary words: "'all things belong to you' [the wise person], whether Paul or

15. In his earlier life Paul himself had been guilty of a false way of evaluating people, basing all judgment of character on an unspiritual interpretation of the law as a Pharisee. This he admits in another context, "even though we once knew Christ from a human point of view, we know him no longer in that way" (2 Cor 5:16).

Apollos or Cephas or the world or life or death or the present or the future—all belong to you, and you belong to Christ, and Christ belongs to God" (1 Cor 3:21–22).[16]

As long as the "jealousy and rivalry" of human respect were driving the community, they were acting as if they were still "of the flesh and behaving in an ordinary human way" (κατὰ ἄνθρωπον, 1 Cor 3:3), and not as "spiritual people" (πνευμάτικοι, 3:1). Paul points out how he shared authority with Apollos, with both as "stewards of the mysteries of God" (4:1), "so that you may learn through us . . . so that none of you will be inflated with pride in favor of one person over against another" (4:6). On this last kind of preferential thinking that relies only on "worldly wisdom," Paul points out that "knowledge inflates with pride, but love builds up" (8:1; cf. 4:18).

The proper response of the community to God's grace would be, of course, to interact among themselves in a Christlike way, with the righteousness of true wisdom. But such a profound understanding of human interaction can be known only by the revelation of what God accomplished in the cross and resurrection of Christ, the content of Paul's gospel. Indeed, salvation came not through worldly wisdom, but through "Christ Jesus who became for us wisdom from God" (1:30). Thus, the only way for the whole community to "be united in the same mind and in the same purpose" (1:10) is to "have the mind of Christ" (2:16), to participate together in sharing the teaching and imitating the conduct of Christ, "with words taught by the Spirit, describing spiritual realities in spiritual terms" (2:13).

To sum up, in the first chapter of 1 Corinthians Paul shows that "worldly wisdom" is not a problem of human reason itself, but that if one's knowledge is not based on God's revelation in Christ it will never attain "the wisdom of God" (1 Cor 1:21) and will inevitably lead to the wrong conclusions. For Paul, the key to the proper response to God's overtures toward humanity for salvation is the true wisdom given by God's Spirit for the proper understanding of knowledge. The "rulers of this age" do not have it (2:8). Whether a particular bit of knowledge comes from experience or is possible only through God's revelation, the power needed to make the proper response to the truth comes from God. After quoting Isa 64:3 on the inscrutability of God's wisdom (2:9), Paul emphatically adds that "God has revealed this (wisdom) to us through the Spirit" (2:10).

16. On this passage, see Joseph A. Fitzmyer, *First Corinthians: A New Translation with Introduction and Commentary* (AYB 32; New Haven: Yale University Press, 2008) 208.

True Knowledge and the Love of God: 1 Corinthians 2:6–16

After considering the effectiveness of his own ministry as an imitation of the cross of Christ, he characterizes it as "a demonstration of the Spirit and of power . . . , the power of God" (1 Cor 2:4–5). He insists again that natural knowledge, "the wisdom of this age" (v. 6) is inadequate for comprehension of the transcendent God. In what Berg calls "a mini-treatise on religious epistemology,"[17] Paul contrasts the "wisdom of this age" to "God's wisdom," which is "concealed in mystery, established by God before time for our glory, and which none of the rulers of this age knew" (vv. 7–8). Here is how this revelation works: citing Isaiah (rather loosely), "What eye has not seen . . . God has prepared for those who love God" (Isa 64:4). Paul claims that this text speaks of God revealing the riches of divine wisdom in the community of believers, "those who love God." So here we see the connection between the believer's love of God and God's sharing of knowledge. God does this, of course, "through the Spirit" (v. 10), because the Spirit of God knows (ἔγνωκεν) the "depths of God" just as "the spirit of the person that is within . . . knows [οἶδεν] what pertains to a person" (v. 11). This knowledge enables the believer to "understand [εἴδωμεν] the things freely given us by God" (v. 12), what simply cannot be understood apart from the grace of God.[18] This grace also enables the apostle "to speak about [the mysteries of God] not with words taught by human wisdom but with words taught by the Spirit" (v. 13). This is the reason why Paul is so confident about his grasp of God's truth, "even if I am untrained in speech, I am not so in knowledge" (2 Cor 11:6).

Now the ψύχικος person cannot understand (γνῶναι) what is taught by the Spirit of God as described by Paul, namely, "spiritual realities" (πνευματικά) in "spiritual terms" (πνευματικοῖς), because these things can be "judged spiritually" (πνευματικῶς) only by the "spiritual [πνευμα-τικός] person" (2:13–15). It is the spiritual person alone who can judge everything because, as Paul says, "we have the mind of Christ" (2:16).

Other Texts on Knowledge and God in 1 Corinthians

Throughout the length of 1 Corinthians Paul throws out the rhetorical question "Do you not know . . ." (οὐκ οἴδατε, 3:16; 5:6; 6:2, 3, 9, 15, 16, 19; 9:13, 24), or he presumes that "we know" (8:1, 4) or "you know" (11:3; 12:2; 15:58; 16:15). These texts indicate that, for Paul, certain knowledge belongs only to the enlightened believer in the gospel, that is, in what

---

17. Berg, "Sin's Corruption," 135.

18. Cf. Gal 2:9, where God's grace in Paul enables "the pillars" of the Jerusalem church to recognize [γνόντες] and accept Paul.

God has revealed in Christ. Thus, rather than passing on new information, Paul feels he has only to remind the Corinthians of the truth they already should be living. The indicative of the faith-filled knowledge dictates the imperative of proper conduct.

In the context of his teaching on meat offered to idols in 1 Corinthians 8, Paul points out that the validity of the believer's knowledge depends on the use made of it. Certain kinds of information, when not understood according to the will of God, that is, in a communitarian sense and for the benefit of all, may be used for individualistic actions that are actually false, not because they might not be true in principle, but because they do not result in the "building up" (οἰκοδομῇ, 3:9; 14:3, 5, 12, 26; the verb form occurs in 8:1, 10; 10:23; 14:4 [bis], 17) of the community. Such "knowledge inflates with pride" (8:1), and such persons "do not yet know as they ought to know" (8:2). For example, protection of "ignorant" recent converts from reverting to idol worship is much more important than the "liberty" of one who "supposes he knows something" (8:2). The latter may know that there is no such thing as an idol, but one is not free to eat meat if it would scandalize the weak. Here is the way Paul explains it: "that person's conscience, weak as it is, may then be 'built up' [οἰκοδομηθήσεται] to eat the meat sacrificed to idols" (8:10). This "sin against your brothers [will] wound their consciences" and is actually "sinning against Christ" (8:12). Participation in the freedom of Christ means acknowledging the value and importance of one's brothers and sisters in community.

Paul brings to an end his poetic vision on the excellence of love in chap. 13 with a picturesque statement on the eschatological nature of human knowledge. He compares our present incomplete understanding to the fullness we will have at the end-time. For all the advantage that faith brings in the Spirit's sharing of divine wisdom with believers, there is still greater knowledge to come. As Paul says, "At present I know partially; then I shall know fully, even as I am known" (13:12). The divine passive at the end of this statement portends our God-promised destiny with a surpassing awareness of all things.

Knowledge Based on the Truth of the Cross

Now what is the true nature of this spiritual wisdom of which Paul speaks? It is the true knowledge of God, "the message of the cross," that alone can begin the saving process and end a lifestyle of fearful servitude to sin and death (1 Cor 1:18). The true nature of God must be understood in the faith of the believer—it cannot be proved by human reason—from the selfless action of the life and death of Jesus Christ. Paul says that in Christ God has lifted the darkness that sin brought, this God "who has shone in our hearts to give the light of the knowledge of the glory of God in the face of Jesus Christ" (2 Cor 4:6). So this is the paradox of the cross, that God is to be known preeminently through an event that can only be considered "foolishness" to those without faith (1:18), so counterintuitive to the unredeemed mind is the real nature of God and the wisdom to discern it.

But what is this true knowledge of God? What can this truth be that confounds all human wisdom? It is what Christ so perfectly reveals in his suffering, namely, that at the center of God's being-toward-us is *kenōsis*, the emptying of self to be and to act for the sake of others. So Paul asks, "What if God, desiring to show his wrath and to make known his power, has endured with much patience the objects of wrath that are made for destruction?" (Rom 9:22). Even God has suffered with much patience in the life and death of "Christ Jesus, who became for us wisdom from God, and righteousness and sanctification and redemption" (1 Cor 1:30). This means that in saving us God self-reveals perfectly in Christ. Michael Gorman puts it very strongly: "God's actions are self-revelatory, the expression of God's essence or character."[19] For God does not eliminate "natural" evil or inhibit the actions of sinful people who harm others. No, the effects of Adam's sin continue in this in-between time before the parousia, even for believers. Paul's frequent rebukes needed by the community here in Corinth attest to that. The present age with its sin and evil has not yet been totally overcome, but God shows us that its death grip has been broken. In imitation of Christ we can deal with evil and so live a righteous and holy life, led by the Spirit in freedom as redeemed from sin.

The paradox of the cross, the reason why it is so counterintuitive and thus impossible for human wisdom alone to uncover, is this stark truth: evil can be overcome only by one who relies on the transcendent God and embraces the evildoer in cruciform love. This is "the cross of Christ through which the world has been crucified to me and I to the world" (Gal 6:14). The answer to evil is not counterviolence with oppression or harm to the perpetrator of the evil. Such a response just perpetuates evil. Evil can be disarmed and dissipated only by active engagement, even though the loving action may cost the life of the

---

19. Michael J. Gorman, *Inhabiting the Cruciform God: Kenosis, Justification, and Theosis in Paul's Narrative Soteriology* (Grand Rapids: Eerdmans, 2009) 119.

believer, as it did in the case of Jesus himself. The one who is Christlike (and therefore Godlike) actually nullifies evil, neutralizes its poison, not by repelling it but by absorbing it, consuming it, as Paul says, "Death is swallowed up in victory" (1 Cor 15:54), and "what is mortal may be swallowed up by life" (2 Cor 5:4). For "to know [γνῶναι] Christ and the power of his resurrection" comes about through "the sharing of his sufferings by being conformed to his death, if somehow [= at some future time] I may attain the resurrection from the dead" (Phil 3:10–11; cf. 2 Cor 4:11; Gal 5:24; 6:14).

This does not mean that evil should ever be accepted as inevitable or as "deserved," but, by Paul's concrete metaphor, we can begin to understand what God reveals in the cross of Christ: evil, which is not from God, must be dealt with by absorbing it in love.[20] Today we might even extend Paul's image of "swallowing what is mortal" to the natural process of metabolism in which something harmful that is consumed may be broken down, its poison neutralized, and its substance even changed into life-giving nourishment. This is a powerful way to understand what happened on the cross: the evil intentions and actions of those who hated Jesus Christ were borne by him with love for them and for all. When Jesus died, it was the end of that hate, and his enemies' evil action toward him stopped. It disappeared. It was consumed. Out of this ugly event on the part of humans God was able to manifest the triumph of goodness by means of the resurrection, the proof that love is stronger even than death.

God's wisdom in all of this seems foolish, but it is "wiser than human wisdom" (1 Cor 1:25) because it is effective, unlike any other solution to evil. That is why Paul changes the metaphor from foolishness/wisdom to weakness/power when he says, "The message of the cross is foolishness to those who are perishing, but to us who are being saved it is the power of God" (1:18). This seemingly foolish plan of God, revealed in the apparent weakness of Christ on the cross, was powerfully effective in Paul's preaching. Just look, Paul says, at the success of his ministry in Corinth, where the community "has been enriched in Christ Jesus, in speech and knowledge of every kind!" (1:5). Yet in that community "not many were wise by human standards, not many were powerful" (1:26), but "God chose what is foolish in the world to shame the wise, what is weak in the world to shame the strong" (1:27).

---

20. I first developed this image in my *Saint Paul, Master of the Spiritual Life "in Christ"* (Collegeville, MN: Liturgical Press, 2014) 178–79.

■ CONCLUSION

In his descriptions of humanity's interactions with God, Paul shows a gradual revelation by God of the truth about God's own self and the plan for the salvation of all men and women. Although all people were blessed to be able to know God's "eternal power and divinity" in "the creation of the world" (Rom 1:19–20), the sin of Adam obfuscated God's place in human lives so that people did not respond properly to God. Sin quickly spread and further "darkened their minds" (1:21) with the result that their instinct to worship was now foolishly given over to idolatry and their humanity succumbed to "every form of wickedness" (1:29).

With great love God acted in righteousness to save humanity by forming a chosen people to witness to the world. God gave them an instruction, the law (Torah), which clearly delineated how God expected humans to live in order for them to become great in response to the graciousness shown to them. Thus, Paul presents law-abiding Jews as not confused about evil (as the gentiles might be), yet severely hindered in their ability to act rightly, for in their flesh they bear the legacy of sin: like all of humanity, they are still "under sin" (Rom 3:9). Since the law could not give the life that was needed to overcome the spiritual death of sin (Gal 3:21), the sad fact is that even the former "law-observant" Saul (Phil 3:5–6) must say, "the commandment that was for life turned out to be death for me" (Rom 7:10).

Finally, however, in the fullness of time God sent God's Son to enable a righteous union with God that brings with it the Spirit of understanding so as to know the great secret to the human dilemma: the power of sin can be broken. However, it is only when God's effective power breaches human time that the evil of sin and death can be halted by Christ's absorption of it in love. The understanding of this bedrock of gospel redemption comes only in the revelation of God through the cross of Jesus Christ; it cannot be grasped by the "unspiritual" (the merely ψυχικός) person.

Unfortunately, even Christians can sometimes be fooled by worldly wisdom into wrongful behavior and the abrogation of their duties as the Body of Christ, for "knowledge puffs up, but love builds up" (1 Cor 8:1). Indeed, the truth about life can be known only by God's revelation in the cross and resurrection of Jesus Christ through reception of the Spirit. Unlike the nonbeliever, those who confess that Jesus is the Lord whom God raised from the dead and share their Lord's Spirit are able both to see God's glory in creation and glorify God for it (cf. Rom 1:20–21). They fulfill the whole law by their love for one another (Gal 5:14), when they "have the mind of Christ" (1 Cor 2:16), namely, "each one looking out not for his own interests but everyone for those of others" (Phil 2:4). Thus, redemption in Christ brings about the restoration of the person to a righteous covenant relationship with God, in a new life in the Spirit as a member of God's own family, to the final goal of the glorification of God.[21]

The saving truth about God is spiritual; that is, it comes from God's Spirit to engage, to inspire, to quicken the human spirit for effective knowledge in life. Now the Spirit of God that knows "the depths of God" (1 Cor 1:10) is also the Spirit of Christ, "but we have the mind of Christ" (1:16). Thus, Paul teaches a complete process of revelation with the circle of true knowledge of God's existence coming through creation, as made clear in the first chapter of Romans. That knowledge is made explicit for the Jews in the law, but the law cannot bring life (Gal 3:21), for the law is "weakened by the flesh . . . , powerless to . . . condemn sin in the flesh, so that the righteous decree of the law could be fulfilled in us" (Rom 8:3–4). It is in 1 Corinthians, however, where Paul shows us just how the power to "live according to the Spirit" can be acted out in the daily lives of those who are united to God in imitation of the cross of Christ, empowered by the Spirit. Their commitment enables them to be transformed to know what is right and to have the ability to carry it out (Rom 12:2). They will employ the "power of the resurrection" to absorb life's evils and "to live to God" in unity with each other for the building up of the Body of Christ as ambassadors for Christ in a veritable ministry of reconciliation for the whole world.

---

21. See Richard B. Hays, "The God of Mercy Who Rescues Us from the Present Evil Age: Romans and Galatians," in *The Forgotten God: Perspectives in Biblical Theology; Essays in Honor of Paul J. Achtemeier on the Occasion of His Seventy-Fifth Birthday* (ed. A. Andrew Das and Frank Matera; Louisville: Westminster John Knox, 2002) 123–43, here 131.

Conclusion: *Quo Vadis?* Moving Pauline Theology Forward

Ronald D. Witherup, P.S.S.

For the past ten years, the Task Force on God in Paul's Letters has explored this neglected theme and thereby helped to fill a lacuna in Pauline scholarship. The study of themes in biblical literature is a time-honored way to do exegesis of the Scriptures in both Old and New Testaments. Our choice to trace the diverse ways the theme of "God" appears in Paul's undisputed letters, whether explicitly or implicitly, has only confirmed the utility of this approach. In the course of our discussions, however, various topics arose that piqued the participants' interest for future study. The purpose of this brief summary is to identify what avenues have opened up for further exploration in light of our research.

One obvious area stood out, namely, the need to apply the same kind of study to the six disputed letters that bear Paul's name. Is there any discernible difference of approach to the issue of God in these letters as compared to the undisputed ones? Could such a study contribute to resolving the question of authorship of these letters? Is it possible to see any growth or change in the understanding of God in these letters? In general, the Task Force thought it would be useful to pursue such a study.

Another area also seemed obvious. It would be worthwhile to explore the relationship between the diverse perspectives of Paul's individual letters concerning the image of God in order to compare and contrast them. Going beyond the Pauline corpus, Frank J. Matera has already done a similar exercise with regard to the soteriology of Romans and that of Hebrews.[1] He demonstrated how the diversity of theme and approach in these two letters was distinct but complementary. A similar comparison

---

1. Frank J. Matera, "A Study of Two Soteriologies: Romans and Hebrews," *Estudios Bíblicos* 76 (2018) 33–53.

of the diverse images of God in Paul's undisputed letters would also be worthwhile. Is there a singular theological outlook that appears and that can be found in all of Paul's undisputed letters? For example, if one were to compare Paul's view of God in Galatians (e.g., Witherup) with his view of God in Romans (e.g., Milinovich), are there areas of overlap? Is the outlook the same in both of these letters, which clearly relate thematically on another level regarding vital topics like freedom, justification, and faith? Or are there differences apparent that might be due to the unique situations of each of these letters? Another example could be the Corinthian correspondence (cf. the articles by Gillman and Pascuzzi). Is there a difference in the presentation of "God" in the two letters written to the same community on separate (and maybe multiple) occasions? Or is the approach uniform? This same question could be asked of 1 and 2 Thessalonians, as well. Even the short and very personal letter to Philemon was seen to have a discernible, coherent view of God that had implications for the relationship between Philemon and his slave Onesimus, as well as for the entire Christian community (Okorie). To add another level of complexity to this task, it would be helpful to examine the theme of God in all of Paul's letters, regardless of authorship, with a view to identifying the common threads or the diverse emphases that emerge.

A third area concerns the ongoing and varied attempts to summarize Paul's theology *in toto*. Some scholars still seek the elusive Holy Grail of the "center" of Paul's theology. Many have offered their own rich and sophisticated summaries of Paul's "theology" and from a multiplicity of methodological and thematic approaches. One area that has generally been overlooked, however, is Paul's image of God as expressed in the thirteen letters that bear his name. Now that this CBA Task Force has attempted to fill this lacuna, at least in part, the time is ripe to consider reexamining ways to interrelate the multiple aspects of Paul's overarching theological outlook. Thus, how does his *theology*—often expressed distinctly in different letters—relate to his christology, pneumatology, eschatology, anthropology, soteriology, and the like? This would obviously be a more synthetic and challenging task but one worth pursuing with the nuances of Paul's theological vision expressed in the essays in this collection.

A fourth area that opened up as a result of our investigations is the relationship between Paul's intense christological orientation and his *theo*logical outlook. Matera's introduction to this book already highlighted this concern; he drew attention to the ways numerous scholars have attempted to address this topic. Two areas stand out in this respect. One is what to make of Paul's rather amorphous understanding of what is usually called "participation," which some scholars discuss in terms of "Christ mysticism," "theosis," or "divinization."[2] Goodwin's article asserts that 1 Thessalonians shows that participation in the life of Christ also brings the believer into contact with God the Father. Can the notion of "participation" be understood more precisely? Is there equally participation in the life of Christ, by means of the Holy Spirit, and also in God's existence evident in all Paul's letters? Are there nuances to be discerned between the undisputed letters and the disputed ones?

An area that all agreed was wide open but which we had deliberately put in the background was a fifth concern—methodology. Readers will note that there is no uniform approach taken by the members of the Task Force. This was by design. The Task Force explicitly preferred not to make methodological issues our main focus; nor did we desire to innovate by applying new or multidisciplinary methods to the text. These were not off-limits, so to speak, but simply left to the side. Each individual was left to his or her own devices to choose how to approach the question. Brien's article, for example, broaches the question of God in Romans by a study of rhetorical questions in the letter. Milinovich, on the other hand, placed Paul's teaching in context by giving attention to its narrative background and structure. Indeed, the question of the "narrative" of Paul's theology, since there is a diversity of scholarly opinion on the shape and extent of this narrative, offers another possible field of exploration. From a different vantage point, Ayeni and Milinovich's approach focused on the language of prayer and liturgy in Philippians, as well as the titles of Father-Son-Lord in relation to one another. Haddad addressed the theme of "new creation" across the Pauline corpus and in its Old Testament context, while Maloney offered an in-depth analysis of the notion of "knowledge of God" in Paul.

In short, while methodology was left open-ended, it was understood that our focus was strictly oriented to the Pauline text itself. One could say that all the members of the Task Force attempted a "close reading" of the biblical text rather than applying any specific

---

2. The bibliography on this topic is extensive, but some recent important contributions include Michael Gorman, *Inhabiting the Cruciform God: Kenosis, Justification, and Theosis in Paul's Narrative Soteriology* (Grand Rapids: Eerdmans, 2009); Ben C. Blackwell, *Christosis: Pauline Soteriology in Light of Deification in Irenaeus and Cyril of Alexandria:* (WUNT 2/314; Tübingen: Mohr Siebeck, 2010); Constantine Campbell, *Paul and Union with Christ: An Exegetical and Theological Study* (Grand Rapids: Zondervan, 2012); Grant Macaskill, *Union with Christ in the New Testament* (Oxford: Oxford University Press, 2013); and Mark Goodwin, *Paul and Participation: The Patristic Witness* (Lanham, MD: Lexington Books/Fortress Academic, 2021).

methodology. Moreover, rather than attempt a summary of theological insights across the letters of Paul, each of us concentrated on identifying the various aspects of Paul's *theo*logical perspective in the context of individual letters.

Recognizing a diversity of approaches, the Task Force recommended that a next step would be an examination of method in Pauline studies. We acknowledge that a whole host of new methods has been developing in biblical scholarship that might bear fruit, and we encourage consideration of an interdisciplinary and multifaceted methodological approach. This could likely open up even more avenues to pursue.

In conclusion, the participants of this Task Force consider it to have been a fruitful exercise that bodes well for the future. Paul's letters will continue to garner great interest, and our hope is that others will be inspired to participate in exploring Paul's complex and intriguing "good news" about what God has done in Christ Jesus.

Bibliography

Aageson, James W. "Typology, Correspondence and the Application of Scripture in Romans 9–11." *JSNT* 10 (1987) 51–72.

Aletti, Jean-Noël. "Interpreting Rom 11:14: What Is at Stake?" In *Celebrating Paul: Festschrift in Honor of Jerome Murphy-O'Connor, O.P., and Joseph A. Fitzmyer, S.J.*, edited by Peter Spitaler, 245–64. CBQMS 48. Washington, DC: Catholic Biblical Association, 2011.

———. *Justification by Faith in the Letters of Saint Paul: Keys to Interpretation.* Translated by P. Meyer. Rome: Gregorian & Biblical Press, 2015.

Anderson, Gary A. *Charity: The Place of the Poor in the Biblical Tradition.* New Haven: Yale University Press, 2013.

———. *Sacrifices and Offerings in Ancient Israel: Studies in Their Social and Political Importance.* Harvard Semitic Monographs 41. Leiden: Brill, 1987.

———. *Sin: A History.* New Haven: Yale University Press, 2009.

Ando, Clifford. *The Matter of the Gods: Religion and the Roman Empire.* Transformation of the Classical Heritage 44. Berkeley: University of California Press, 2008.

Aune, David E. "Romans as a *Logos Protreptikos*." In *The Romans Debate*, edited by Karl P. Donfried, 278–96. 1977. Reprint, Grand Rapids: Baker Academic, 1991.

Barclay, John M. G. *Pauline Churches and Diaspora Jews.* 2011. Reprint, Grand Rapids: Eerdmans, 2016.

Barrett, C. K. *A Commentary on the Epistle to the Romans.* HNTC. New York: Harper & Row, 1957.

———. *The First Epistle to the Corinthians.* HNTC. New York: Harper & Row, 1968.

Barth, Karl. *The Epistle to the Romans.* Translated by Edwyn C. Hoskyns. Oxford: Oxford University Press, 1968. German original, 1919.

———. *The Resurrection of the Dead.* Translated by H. J. Stenning. Eugene, OR: Wipf & Stock, 2003. German original, 1924.

Bauckham, Richard. *God Crucified: Monotheism and Christology in the New Testament.* Grand Rapids: Eerdmans, 1999.

————. *Jesus and the God of Israel: God Crucified and Other Studies on the New Testament's Christology of Divine Identity*. Grand Rapids: Eerdmans, 2008.

Beavis, Mary Ann. *The First Christian Slave: Onesimus in Context*. Eugene, OR: Cascade, 2021.

Bell, Richard H. *Provoked to Jealousy: The Origin and Purpose of the Jealousy Motif in Romans 9–11*. WUNT 2/63. Tübingen: Mohr Siebeck, 1994.

Belli, Filippo. *Argumentation and Use of Scripture in Romans 9–11*. AnBib 183. Rome: Gregorian & Biblical Press, 2010.

Berg, Shane. "Sin's Corruption of the Knowledge of God and the Law in Romans 1–4." In *The Unrelenting God: God's Action in Scripture; Essays in Honor of Beverly Roberts Gaventa*, edited by David J. Downs and Matthew L. Skinner, 119–38. Grand Rapids: Eerdmans, 2013.

Best, Ernest. *The First and Second Epistles to the Thessalonians*. BNTC. London: A & C Black, 1972. Reprint, New York: Continuum, 1986.

Betz, Hans Dieter. *Galatians: A Commentary on Paul's Letter to the Churches in Galatia*. Hermeneia. Philadelphia: Fortress, 1979.

Binz, Antony. "'He Who Supplies Seed to the Sower and Bread for Food': The Pauline Characterization of God in 2 Corinthians 8–9." In *Theologizing in the Corinthian Conflict: Studies in the Exegesis and Theology of 2 Corinthians*, edited by Dominika Kurek-Chomycz, Ma. Marilou S. Ibita, Reimund Bieringer, and Thomas A. Vollmer, 305–17. Biblical Tools and Studies 16. Leuven: Peeters, 2013.

Bird, Graham. "Relevance Theory and Speech Acts." In *Foundations of Speech-Act Theory: Philosophical and Linguistic Perspectives*, edited by S. Tsohatzidis, 292–311. London: Routledge, 1994.

Blakemore, Diane. "Echo Questions: A Pragmatic Account." *Lingua* 4 (1994) 197–211.

Boakye, Andrew. *Death and Life: Resurrection, Restoration, and Rectification in Paul's Letter to the Galatians*. Eugene, OR: Pickwick, 2017.

Boer, Martinus C. de. *Galatians: A Commentary*. NTL. Louisville: Westminster John Knox, 2011.

Bolt, John. "The Relation between Creation and Redemption in Romans 8:8–27." *Calvin Theological Journal* 30 (1995) 34–51.

Bonneau, Normand. "Stages of Salvation History in Rom 1:16–3:26." *Église et Theologie* 23 (1992) 177–94.

Bookidis, Nancy. "Religion in Corinth: 146 BCE to 100 CE." In *Urban Religion in Roman Corinth: Interdisciplinary Approaches*, edited by Daniel N. Schowalter and Steven J. Friesen, 141–64. Cambridge: Cambridge University Press, 2005.

Boring, M. Eugene. *I & II Thessalonians: A Commentary*. NTL. Louisville: Westminster John Knox, 2015.

———. "Philippians and Philemon: Date and Provenance." *CBQ* 81 (2019) 470–94.

Bowens, Lisa M. "Divine Desire: Paul's Apocalyptic God of Rescue." *Theology Today* 75 (2018) 9–21.

Brown, Raymond E., and John P. Meier. *Antioch and Rome: New Testament Cradles of Catholic Christianity*. 1983. Reprint, Mahwah, NJ: Paulist, 2004.

Bultmann, Rudolf. *Theology of the New Testament*. 2 vols. New York: Charles Scribner's Sons, 1951–1955. Reprint, Waco, TX: Baylor University Press, 2007.

Burnish, Raymond E. G. "The Doctrine of Grace from Paul to Irenaeus." Dissertation, University of Glasgow, 1971.

Byrne, Brendan. *Paul and the Economy of Salvation: Reading from the Perspective of the Last Judgment*. Grand Rapids: Baker Academic, 2021.

———. *Romans*. SacPag 6. Collegeville, MN: Liturgical Press, 2007.

Campbell, Constantine R. *Paul and the Hope of Glory: An Exegetical and Theological Study*. Grand Rapids: Zondervan, 2020.

———. *Paul and Union with Christ: An Exegetical and Theological Study*. Grand Rapids: Zondervan, 2012.

Campbell, Douglas A. *Framing Paul: An Epistolary Biography*. Grand Rapids: Eerdmans, 2014.

———. *Pauline Dogmatics: The Triumph of God's Love*. Grand Rapids: Eerdmans, 2020.

Capes, David B. *The Divine Christ: Paul, the Lord Jesus, and the Scriptures of Israel*. Grand Rapids: Baker Academic, 2018.

Carr, Frederick D. "Beginning at the End: The Kingdom of God in 1 Corinthians," *CBQ* 81 (2019) 449–69.

Casson, Sarah H. *Textual Signposts in the Argument of Romans: A Relevance-Theory Approach*. Early Christian and Its Literature 25. Atlanta: SBL Press, 2019.

Chevallier, Max-Alain. "La construction de la communauté de la fondement du Christ (1 Co 3,5–17)." In *Paolo a una chiesa divisa, 1 Co 1–4*, edited by Lorenzo De Lorenzi, 109–36. Rome: Abbazia di S. Paolo, 1980.

Collins, Raymond F. *First Corinthians*. SacPag 7. Collegeville, MN: Liturgical Press, 1999.

———. "The Theology of Paul's First Letter to the Thessalonians." *Louvain Studies* 6 (1977) 315–37. Reprinted in Raymond F. Collins, *Studies on the First Letter to the Thessalonians*, 230–54. BETL 66. Leuven: Leuven University Press, 1984.

Conzelmann, Hans. *1 Corinthians: A Commentary on the First Epistle to the Corinthians.* Hermeneia. Philadelphia: Fortress, 1975.

Cranfield, C. E. B. *A Critical and Exegetical Commentary on the Epistle to the Romans.* 2 vols. 6th ed. ICC. Edinburgh: T & T Clark. 1975–1979.

Das, A. Andrew, and Frank J. Matera, eds. *The Forgotten God: Perspectives in Biblical Theology; Essays in Honor of Paul J. Achtemeier on the Occasion of His Seventy-Fifth Birthday.* Louisville: Westminster John Knox, 2002.

Davies, Jamie. "Why Paul Doesn't Mention the 'Age to Come.'" *SJT* 74 (2021) 199–208.

Deissmann, Adolf. *Paul: A Study in Social and Religious History.* 2nd ed. Translated by William E. Wilson. London: Hodder & Stoughton, 1926.

DelRio, Delio. *Paul and the Synagogue: Romans and the Isaiah Targum.* Eugene, OR: Pickwick, 2013.

Deppe, Dean B. *All Roads Lead to the Text: Eight Methods of Inquiry into the Bible; A Template for Model Exegesis with Exegetical Examples Employing Logos Bible Software.* Grand Rapids: Eerdmans, 2011.

De Villiers, Pieter G. R. "Love in the Letter to Philemon." In *Philemon in Perspective: Interpreting a Pauline Letter*, edited by D. Francois Tolmie, 181–203. BZNW 169. Berlin: de Gruyter, 2010.

Dodd, C. H. *The Epistle to the Romans.* MNTC. London: Hodder & Stoughton, 1932.

Donfried, Karl P., ed. *The Romans Debate.* 1977. Reprint, Grand Rapids: Baker Academic, 1991.

Dunn, James D. G. *Christology in the Making: A New Testament Inquiry into the Origins of the Doctrine of the Incarnation.* 2nd ed. Grand Rapids: Eerdmans, 1989.

——. *Did the First Christians Worship Jesus? The New Testament Evidence.* Louisville: Westminster John Knox, 2010.

——. *Romans 1–8.* WBC 38A. Waco, TX: Word, 1988.

——. *Romans 9–16.* WBC 38B. Waco, TX: Word, 1988.

——. *Theology of Paul the Apostle.* Grand Rapids: Eerdmans, 1998.

——. *Theology of the Letter to the Galatians.* Cambridge: Cambridge University Press, 1993.

Eastman, Susan Grove. "Israel and the Mercy of God: A Re-reading of Galatians 6.6 and Romans 9–11." *NTS* 56 (2010) 367–95.

Fee, Gordon D. *The First Epistle to the Corinthians.* NICNT. Grand Rapids: Eerdmans, 1987.

——. *God's Empowering Presence: The Holy Spirit in the Letters of Paul.* Peabody, MA: Hendrickson, 1994. Reprint, Grand Rapids: Baker Academic, 2012.

————. *Jesus the Lord according to Paul the Apostle: A Concise Introduction*. Grand Rapids: Baker, 2018.

————. *Pauline Christology: An Exegetical-Theological Study*. Peabody, MA: Hendrickson, 2007.

————. "Toward a Theology of 1 Corinthians." In *Pauline Theology*, vol. 2, *1 & 2 Corinthians*, edited by David M. Hay, 37–58. Minneapolis: Fortress, 1993.

Fitzgerald, John T. "Paul and Paradigm Shifts: Reconciliation and Its Linkage Group." In *Paul beyond the Judaism/Hellenism Divide*, edited by Troels Engberg-Pedersen, 241–62. Louisville: Westminster John Knox, 2001.

Fitzmyer, Jospeh A. *First Corinthians: A New Translation with Introduction and Commentary*. AYB 32. New Haven: Yale University Press, 2008.

————. *II Corinthians*. AB 32A. New York, Doubleday, 1995.

————. "Justification by Faith in Pauline Thought: A Catholic Perspective." In *Rereading Paul Together*, edited by Davie E. Aune, 77–94. Grand Rapids: Baker Academic, 2006.

————. "Letter to the Romans." In *The New Jerome Biblical Commentary*, edited by Raymond E. Brown, S.S., Joseph A. Fitzmyer, S.J., and Roland E. Murphy, O.Carm., 830–68. Englewood Cliffs, NJ: Prentice Hall, 1990.

————. *Romans: A New Translation with Introduction and Commentary*. AB 33. New York: Doubleday, 1993.

Furnish, Victor Paul. *1 Thessalonians, 2 Thessalonians*. ANTC. Nashville: Abingdon, 2007.

Gager, John G. *Reinventing Paul*. Oxford: Oxford University Press, 2002.

Gaventa, Beverly Roberts. "Apostle and Church in 2 Corinthians." In *Pauline Theology*, vol. 2, *1 & 2 Corinthians*, edited by David M. Hay, 182–99. Minneapolis: Fortress, 1993.

————. *When in Romans: An Invitation to Linger with the Gospel according to Paul*. Theological Explorations for the Church Catholic. Grand Rapids: Baker Academic, 2016.

Gieniusz, Andrzej. *Romans 8:18–30: "Suffering Does Not Thwart the Future Glory."* University of South Florida International Studies in Formative Christianity and Judaism 9. Atlanta: Scholars Press, 1999.

Goodwin, Mark. *Paul, Apostle of the Living God: Kerygma and Conversion in 2 Corinthians*. Harrisburg, PA: Trinity Press International, 2001.

Gorman, Michael J. *Inhabiting the Cruciform God: Kenosis, Justification, and Theosis in Paul's Narrative Soteriology*. Grand Rapids: Eerdmans, 2009.

————. "Paul and the Cruciform Way of God in Christ." *JMT* 2 (2013) 64–83.

Grieb, A. Katherine. *The Story of Romans: A Narrative Defense of God's Righteousness.* Louisville: Westminster John Knox, 2002.

Guthrie, Donald, and Ralph P. Martin. "God." In *Dictionary of Paul and His Letters*, edited by Gerald F. Hawthorne, Ralph P. Martin, and Daniel G. Reid, 354–69. Black Dictionaries on the Bible. Downers Grove, IL: InterVarsity, 1993.

Hahne, Harry. *The Corruption and Redemption of Creation: Nature in Romans 8.19–22 and Jewish Apocalyptic Literature.* LNTS 336. New York: T&T Clark, 2006.

Harris, Murray J. *The Second Epistle to the Corinthians: A Commentary on the Greek Text.* NIGTC. Grand Rapids: Eerdmans, 2005.

Harrison, James R. *Paul and the Imperial Authorities at Thessalonika and Rome: A Study in the Conflict of Ideology.* WUNT 273. Tübingen: Mohr Siebeck, 2011.

Hawthorne, Gerald F. *Philippians.* WBC 43. Waco, TX: Word, 1983.

Hay, David M. "The Shaping of Theology in 2 Corinthians: Convictions, Doubts, and Warrants." In *Pauline Theology*, vol. 2, *1 & 2 Corinthians*, edited by David J. Hay, 135–55. Minneapolis: Fortress, 1993.

Hays, Richard B. *First Corinthians.* Interpretation. Louisville: Westminster John Knox, 1997.

————. "The God of Mercy Who Rescues Us from the Present Evil Age: Romans and Galatians." In *The Forgotten God: Perspectives in Biblical Theology; Essays in Honor of Paul J. Achtemeier on His Seventy-Fifth Birthday*, edited by A. Andrew Das and Frank J. Matera, 123–43. Louisville: Westminster John Knox, 2002.

————. "Is Paul's Gospel Narratable?" *JSNT* 27 (2004) 217–39.

————. *The Moral Vision of the New Testament: Community, Cross, New Creation; A Contemporary Introduction to New Testament Ethics.* New York: HarperCollins, 1996.

Heil, John Paul. "Christ, the Termination of the Law (Rom 9:30–10:8)." *CBQ* 63 (2001) 484–98.

————. *The Letters of Paul as Rituals of Worship.* Eugene, OR: Cascade, 2011.

————. *Philippians: Let Us Rejoice in Being Conformed to Christ.* Early Christianity and Its Literature 3. Atlanta: Society of Biblical Literature, 2010.

Hill, Wesley. *Paul and the Trinity: Persons, Relations, and the Pauline Letters.* Grand Rapids: Eerdmans, 2015.

Holloway, Paul A. *Philippians: A Commentary.* Hermeneia. Minneapolis: Fortress, 2018.

Hooker, Morna D. *From Adam to Christ: Essays on Paul.* Cambridge: Cambridge University Press, 1990.

———. *Paul: A Short Introduction.* Oxford: Oneworld, 2003.

Horsley, Richard A. *1 Corinthians.* ANTC. Nashville: Abingdon, 1998.

Hubbard, Moyer V. *New Creation in Paul's Letters and Thought.* SNTSMS 119. Cambridge: Cambridge University Press, 2004.

Hubing, Jeff. *Crucifixion and the New Creation: The Strategic Purpose of Galatians 6.11–17.* LNTS 508. London: Bloomsbury T&T Clark, 2015.

Hurtado, Larry W. "'Ancient Jewish Monotheism' in the Hellenistic and Roman Periods." *Journal of Ancient Judaism* 4 (2013) 379–400.

———. "The Binitarian Pattern of Earliest Christian Devotion and Early Doctrinal Development." In *The Place of Christ in Liturgical Prayer: Trinity, Christology, and Liturgical Theology,* edited by Bryan D. Spinks, 23–50. Collegeville, MN: Liturgical Press, 2008.

———. *God in New Testament Theology.* Library of Biblical Theology. Nashville: Abingdon, 2010.

———. *Honoring the Son: Jesus in Earliest Christian Devotional Practice.* Snapshots. Bellingham, WA: Lexham, 2018.

———. *How on Earth Did Jesus Become a God? Historical Questions about Earliest Devotion to Jesus.* Grand Rapids: Eerdmans, 2005.

———. *Lord Jesus Christ: Devotion to Jesus in Earliest Christianity.* Grand Rapids: Eerdmans, 2003.

———. *One God, One Lord: Early Christian Devotion and Ancient Jewish Monotheism.* Philadelphia: Fortress, 1988.

Jeremias, Joachim. *New Testament Theology: The Proclamation of Jesus.* New York: Scribner, 1971.

Jewett, Robert. *Romans: A Commentary on the Letter to the Romans.* Hermeneia. Minneapolis: Fortress, 2007.

Johnson, Elizabeth A. *She Who Is: The Mystery of God in Feminist Theological Discourse.* New York: Crossroad, 1992.

Johnson, Luke T. "'God Was in Christ': 2 Corinthians 5:19 and Mythic Language." In *Myth and Scripture: Contemporary Perspectives on Religion, Language, and Imagination,* edited by Dexter E. Callender, 201–11. RBS 78. Atlanta: SBL Press, 2014.

Keener, Craig S. *1–2 Corinthians.* NCBC. Cambridge: Cambridge University Press, 2005.

Kirk, J. R. Daniel. *Unlocking Romans: Resurrection and the Justification of God.* Grand Rapids: Eerdmans, 2008.

Kujanpää, Katja. "From Eloquence to Evading Responsibility: The Rhetorical Functions of Quotations in Paul's Argumentation." *JBL* 136 (2017) 185–202.

Lambrecht, Jan. *Second Corinthians.* SacPag 8. Collegeville, MN: Liturgical Press, 1999.

Lee, Dorothy. "The Symbol of Divine Fatherhood." *Semeia* 85 (1999) 177–87.

Legarreta-Castillo, Felipe de Jesús. *The Figure of Adam in Romans 5 and 1 Corinthians 15: The New Creation and Its Ethical and Social Reconfiguration.* Emerging Scholars. Minneapolis: Fortress, 2014.

Levison, John R. "The Spirit and the Temple in Paul's Letters to the Corinthians." In *Paul and His Theology,* edited by Stanley E. Porter, 189–215. Leiden: Brill, 2006.

Lincicum, David. "Philo of Alexandria and Romans 9:30–10:21: The Commandment and the Quest for the Good Life." In *Reading Romans in Context: Paul and Second Temple Judaism,* edited by Ben C. Blackwell, John K. Goodrich, and Jason Maston, 122–28. Downers Grove, IL: Zondervan, 2015.

Lincoln, Andrew T. "'Stand Therefore': Ephesians 6:10–20 as Peroration." *BibInt* 3 (1985) 99–114.

Long, Frederick J. "'The God of This Age' (2 Cor 4:4) and Paul's Empire-Resisting Gospel at Corinth." In *The First Urban Churches 2: Roman Corinth,* edited by James R. Harrison and L. L. Welborn, 219–69. Writings from the Greco-Roman World Supplement Series 8. Atlanta: SBL Press, 2016.

Longenecker, Richard N. *The Epistle to the Romans: A Commentary on the Greek Text.* NIGNT. Grand Rapids: Eerdmans, 2016.

———. *Galatians.* WBC 41. Waco, TX: Word, 1990.

Malherbe, Abraham J. *The Letters to the Thessalonians: A New Translation with Introduction and Commentary.* AB 32B. New York: Doubleday, 2000.

———. *Paul and the Thessalonians: The Philosophic Tradition of Pastoral Care.* Philadelphia: Fortress, 1987.

Malina, Bruce J., and John J. Pilch. *Social-Science Commentary on the Letters of Paul.* Minneapolis: Fortress, 2006.

Maloney, Elliott C. *Saint Paul: Master of the Spiritual Life "in Christ."* Collegeville, MN: Liturgical Press, 2014.

Martin, Dale B. *Slavery as Salvation: The Metaphor of Slavery in Pauline Christianity.* New Haven: Yale University Press, 1990.

Martin, Ralph P. *Philippians.* NCB. London: Oliphants, 1976.

Martin, Troy W. "Perceived Reality and the Tenses of the Greek Verb." Paper presented at the Annual Meeting of the Midwest Region of the Society of Biblical Literature, South Bend, Indiana, February 10, 2019.

Martyn, J. Louis. "Epistemology at the Turn of the Ages." In idem, *Theological Issues in the Letters of Paul,* 89–110. London: T&T Clark, 1997.

———. *Galatians: A New Translation with Introduction and Commentary.* AB 33A. New York: Doubleday, 1997.

Matera, Frank J. *Galatians.* SacPag 9. Collegeville, MN: Liturgical Press, 1992.

———. *God's Saving Grace: A Pauline Theology.* Grand Rapids: Eerdmans, 2012.

———. *Romans.* Paideia. Grand Rapids: Baker Academic, 2010.

McCaulley, Esau. *Reading while Black: African American Biblical Interpretation as an Exercise in Hope.* Downers Grove, IL: IVP Academic, 2020.

McKnight, Scot. *The Letter to Philemon.* NICNT. Grand Rapids: Eerdmans, 2017.

Meeks, Wayne A. *The First Urban Christians: The Social World of the Apostle Paul.* New Haven: Yale University Press, 1983.

Mell, Ulrich. *Neue Schöpfung: Eine traditionsgeschichtliche und exegetische Studie zu einem soteriologischen Grundsatz paulinischer Theologie.* BZNW 56. Berlin: de Gruyter, 1989.

Milinovich, Timothy. "Once More, with Feeling: Romans 8,31–39 as Rhetorical *Peroratio.*" *Bib* 99 (2018) 525–43.

Moo, Douglas J. *The Epistle to the Romans.* NICNT. Grand Rapids: Eerdmans, 1996. 2nd ed., 2018, entitled *The Letter to the Romans.*

———. *Galatians.* BECNT. Grand Rapids: Baker Academic, 2013.

Moo, Jonathan. "Romans 8.19–22 and Isaiah's Cosmic Covenant." *NTS* 54 (2008) 74–89.

Morales, Rodrigo J. *The Spirit and the Restoration of Israel: New Exodus and New Creation Motifs in Galatians.* WUNT 2/282. Tübingen: Mohr Siebeck, 2010.

Morgan, Teresa. *Being "in Christ" in the Letters of Paul: Saved through Christ and in His Hand.* WUNT 449. Tübingen: Mohr Siebeck, 2020.

———. *Roman Faith and Christian Faith: Pistis and Fides in the Early Roman Empire and Early Churches.* Oxford: Oxford University Press, 2015.

Morris, Leon. "The Theme of Romans." In *Apostolic History and the Gospel: Biblical and Historical Essays Presented to F. F. Bruce on His 60th Birthday,* edited by Ralph P. Martin and W. Ward Gasque, 249–63. Exeter: Paternoster, 1970.

Murphy-O'Connor, Jerome. *Paul: A Critical Life.* Oxford: Oxford University Press, 1996.

———. *Paul: His Story.* Oxford: Oxford University Press, 2004.

Nicholson, Suzanne. *Dynamic Oneness: The Significance and Flexibility of Paul's One-God Language.* Eugene, OR: Pickwick, 2010.

Nygren, Anders. *Agape and Eros.* Translated by Philip S. Watson. Philadelphia: Westminster, 1953.

O'Brien, Peter T. *The Epistle to the Philippians: A Commentary on the Greek Text.* NIGTC. Grand Rapids: Eerdmans, 1991.

Okorie, Ferdinand. *Favor and Gratitude: Reading Galatians in Its Greco-Roman Context.* Lanham, MD: Lexington Books/Fortress Academic, 2021.

Osborne, Grant R. "Hermeneutics/Interpreting Paul." In *Dictionary of Paul and His Letters*, edited by Gerald F. Hawthorne, Ralph P. Martin, and Daniel G. Reid, 388–97. Black Dictionaries on the Bible. Downers Grove, IL: InterVarsity, 1993.

Osiek, Carolyn. *Philippians, Philemon.* ANTC. Nashville: Abingdon, 2000.

Perkins, Pheme. "Adam and Christ in the Pauline Epistles." In *Celebrating Paul: Festschrift in Honor of Jerome Murphy-O'Connor, O.P., and Joseph A. Fitzmyer, S.J.*, edited by Peter Spitaler, 128–51. CBQMS 48. Washington, DC: Catholic Biblical Association, 2011.

———. *First Corinthians.* Paideia. Grand Rapids: Baker, 2012.

———. "God's Power in Human Weakness: Paul Teaches the Corinthians about God." In *The Forgotten God: Perspectives in Biblical Theology: Essays in Honor of Paul J. Achtemeier on the Occasion of His Seventy-Fifth Birthday*, edited by A. Andrew Das and Frank J. Matera, 145–62. Louisville: Westminster John Knox, 2002.

Perkinson, James W. "Enslaved by the Text: The Uses of Philemon," in *Onesimus Our Brother: Reading Religion, Race, and Culture in Philemon*, edited by Matthew V. Johnson, James A. Noel, and Demetrius K. Williams, 121–41. Paul in Critical Contexts. Minneapolis: Fortress, 2012.

Pitre, Brandt, Michael P. Barber, and John A. Kincaid. *Paul, A New Covenant Jew: Rethinking Pauline Theology.* Grand Rapids: Eerdmans, 2019.

Porter, Stanley E. *The Apostle Paul: His Life, Thought, and Letters.* Grand Rapids: Eerdmans, 2016.

———. "Paul's Concept of Reconciliation, Twice More." In *Paul and His Theology*, edited by Stanley E. Porter, 131–52. Pauline Studies 3. Leiden: Brill, 2006.

———. "Reconciliation and 2 Cor 5,18–21." In *The Corinthian Correspondence*, edited by Reimund Bieringer, 693–705. BETL 125. Leuven: Leuven University Press, 1996.

Powery, Emerson B., and Rodney S. Sadler Jr. *The Generis of Liberation: Biblical Interpretation in the Antebellum Narratives of the Enslaved.* Louisville: Westminster John Knox, 2016.

Prothro, James. "Who Is 'of Christ'? A Grammatical and Theological Reconsideration of 1 Cor 1.12." *NTS* 60 (2014) 250–65.

Raboteau, Albert J. *Slave Religion: The "Invisible Institution" in the Antebellum South.* Oxford: Oxford University Press, 2004.

Reasoner, Mark. "Rome and Roman Christianity." In *Dictionary of Paul and His Letters*, edited by Gerald F. Hawthorne, Ralph P. Martin, and Daniel G. Reid, 850–55. Black Dictionaries on the Bible. Downers Grove, IL: InterVarsity, 1993.

Reumann, John. *Philippians: A New Translation with Introduction and Commentary*. AYB 33B. New Haven: Yale University Press, 2008.

Richardson, Neil. *Paul's Language about God*. JSNTSup 99. Sheffield: Sheffield Academic Press, 1994.

Rodriguez, Rafael. *If You Call Yourself a Jew: Reappraising Paul's Letter to the Romans*. Eugene, OR: Cascade, 2014.

Roetzel, Calvin. *Paul: The Man and the Myth*. Minneapolis: Fortress, 1999.

Rohde, Hannah. "Rhetorical Questions as Redundant Interrogatives." *San Diego Linguistic Papers* 2 (2006) 134–68.

Rooy, Robert van. "Negative Polarity Items in Questions: Strength as Relevance." *Journal of Semantics* 20 (2003) 239–73.

Rulmu, Callia. "The Use of Psalm 69:9 in Romans 15:3: Shame as Sacrifice." *BTB* 40.4 (2010) 227–33.

Sanders, E. P. *Paul and Palestinian Judaism: A Comparison of Patterns of Religion*. Philadelphia: Fortress, 1977.

Sasse, Herman. "αἰών, αἰώνιος," *TDNT* 1:197–209.

Schnelle, Udo. *Apostle Paul: His Life and Theology*. Translated by M. Eugene Boring. Grand Rapids: Baker Academic, 2003.

Schreiner, Thomas R. *Paul, Apostle of God's Glory: A Pauline Theology*. Downers Grove, IL: InterVarsity, 2001.

———. *Romans*. BECNT. Grand Rapids: Baker, 1998. 2nd ed., 2018.

Schroter, Jens. *Der versöhnte Versöhner: Paulus als unentbehrlicher Mittler im Heilsvorgang zwischen Gott und Gemeinde nach 2 Kor 2,14–7,14*. TANZ 10. Tübingen: Francke, 1993.

Scott, Ian W. *Paul's Way of Knowing: Story, Experience, and the Spirit*. Grand Rapids: Baker Academic, 2006.

Scott, James M. "The Use of Scripture in 2 Corinthians 6:16c–18 and Paul's Restoration Theology." *JSNT* 17 (1995) 73–99.

Seifrid, Mark A. *The Second Letter to the Corinthians*. Pillar New Testament Commentary. Grand Rapids: Eerdmans, 2014.

Sidebottom, E. M. "The So-Called Divine Passive in the Gospel Tradition." *ExpT* 87 (1976) 200–204.

Smith, Brandon R. "What Christ Does, God Does: Surveying Recent Scholarship on Christological Monotheism." *CurBR* 17 (2019) 184–208.

Smith, Murray J. "The Thessalonian Correspondence." In *All Things to All Cultures: Paul among Jews, Greeks, and Romans*, edited by Mark Harding and Alanna Nobbs, 269–301. Grand Rapids: Eerdmans, 2013.

Smyth, Herbert Weir. *Greek Grammar*. Revised by Gordon M. Messing. Cambridge, MA: Harvard University Press, 1980.

Snyman, A. H. "Style and the Rhetorical Situation of Romans 8:31–39." *NTS* 34 (1988) 218–31.

Soards, Marion L. "Some Neglected Theological Dimensions of Paul's Letters to Philemon." *Perspectives in Religious Studies* 17 (1990) 209–20.

Sprinkle, Preston M. "The Afterlife in Romans: Understanding Paul's Glory Motif in the Apocalypse of Moses and 2 Baruch." In *Lebendige Hoffnung, ewiger Tod?!: Jenseitsvorstellungen im Hellenismus, Judentum und Christentum*, edited by Michael Labahn and Manfred Lang, 201–33. Arbeiten zur Bibel und ihrer Geschichte 24. Leipzig: Evangelische Verlagsantalt, 2007.

Stalnaker, Robert. "Common Ground." *Linguistics and Philosophy* 25.5–6 (2002) 701–21.

Stegman, Thomas D. "Paul's Use of *DIKAIO*- Terminology: Moving beyond N. T. Wright's Forensic Interpretation." *TS* 72 (2011) 496–524.

Still, Todd. "Philemon among the Letters of Paul: Theological and Canonical Considerations." *ResQ* 47 (2005) 133–42.

Stirewalt, M. L. *Paul, the Letter Writer*. Grand Rapids: Eerdmans, 2003.

Stuhlmacher, Peter. *Paul's Letter to the Romans*. Translated by Scott J. Hafemann. Louisville: Westminster John Knox, 1994.

Tamez, Elsa, Cynthia Briggs Kittredge, Claire Miller Colombo, and Alicia J. Batten. *Philippians, Colossians, Philemon*. Wisdom 51. Collegeville, MN: Liturgical Press, 2017.

Tan, Randall K. J. "Color outside the Lines: Rethinking How to Interpret Paul's Letters." In *Paul and His Theology*, edited by Stanley E. Porter, 153–87. Pauline Studies 3. Leiden: Brill, 2006.

Thiselton, Anthony C. *Discovering Romans*. Grand Rapids: Eerdmans, 2016.

———. *The First Epistle to the Corinthians: A Commentary on the Greek Text*. NIGTC. Grand Rapids: Eerdmans, 2000.

Thompson, James W. *The Church according to Paul: Rediscovering the Community Conformed to Christ*. Grand Rapids: Baker Academic, 2014.

Thompson, James W., and Bruce W. Longenecker. *Philippians and Philemon*. Paideia. Grand Rapids: Baker Academic, 2016.

Thompson, Marianne Meye. *The Promise of the Father: Jesus and God in the New Testament*. Louisville: Westminster John Knox, 2000.

Thurston, Bonnie. "The New Testament in Christian Spirituality." In *The Blackwell Companion to Christian Spirituality*, edited by Arthur Holder, 55–70. Oxford: Blackwell, 2008.

Thurston, Bonnie B., and Judith M. Ryan. *Philippians and Philemon*. SacPag 10. Collegeville, MN: Liturgical Press, 2005.

Tilling, Chris. *Paul's Divine Christology*. Grand Rapids: Eerdmans, 2015.

Tobin, Thomas H. *Paul's Rhetoric in Its Contexts: The Argument of Romans*. Peabody, MA: Hendrickson, 2004.

Turner, Max. "The Spirit of Christ and 'Divine' Christology." In *Jesus of Nazareth: Lord and Christ: Essays on the Historical Jesus and New Tes-*

tament Christology, edited by Joel B. Green and Max Turner, 413–36. Grand Rapids: Eerdmans, 1994.

Vanhoye, Albert. *Lettera Ai Galati: Nuova versione introduzione e commento*. 2nd ed. Libri Biblici NT 8. Milan: Paoline, 2008.

Vincent, Marvin R. *Philippians and Philemon: A Critical and Exegetical Commentary on the Epistles to the Philippians and Philemon*. ICC. Edinburgh: T&T Clark, 1985.

Warrior, Valerie M. *Roman Religion*. Cambridge Introduction to Roman Civilization. Cambridge: Cambridge University Press, 2006.

Watson, Francis. "The Triune Divine Identity: Reflections on Pauline God-Language, in Disagreement with J. D. G. Dunn." *JSNT* 80 (2000) 99–124.

Whittle, Sarah. "Jubilees and Romans 2:6–29: Circumcision, Law Observance, and Ethnicity." In *Reading Romans in Context: Paul and Second Temple Judaism*, edited by Ben C. Blackwell, John K. Goodrich, and Jason Maston, 46–51. Grand Rapids: Zondervan, 2015.

Wilckens, Ulrich. *Der Brief an die Römer*. 3 vols. EKKNT 6. Zurich: Benziger, 1978–1982.

Williams, Demetrius K. "'No Longer as a Slave': Reading the Interpretation History of Paul's Epistle to Philemon." In *Onesimus Our Brother: Reading Religion, Race, and Culture in Philemon*, edited by Matthew V. Johnson, James A. Noel, and Demetrius K. Williams, 11–46. Paul in Critical Contexts. Minneapolis: Fortress, 2012.

Witherington, Ben. *Paul's Letter to the Romans: A Socio-Rhetorical Commentary*. Grand Rapids: Eerdmans, 2004.

Witherup, Ronald D. *Galatians: Life in the New Creation: A Spiritual-Pastoral Reading*. New York: Paulist, 2020.

———. *Mercy and the Bible: Why It Matters*. New York: Paulist, 2018.

———. *Scripture and Tradition in the Letters of Paul*. BSCBAA 4. New York: Paulist, 2021.

Wolter, Michael. "The Letter to Philemon as Ethical Counterpart of Paul's Doctrine of Justification." In *Philemon in Perspective: Interpreting a Pauline Letter*, edited by D. Francois Tolmie, 169–79. BZNW 169. Berlin: de Gruyter, 2010.

Wright, N. Thomas. *Galatians*. Commentaries for Christian Formation. Grand Rapids: Eerdmans, 2021.

———. *Paul and the Faithfulness of God*. Christian Origins and the Question of God 4. Minneapolis: Fortress, 2013.

Index of Ancient Sources

Index of Authors

Smith, Brandon, 39, 40
Smith, Murray J., 53
Snyman, A. H., 23
Soards, Marion L., 117, 123
Sprinkle, Preston M., 139
Stalnaker, Robert, 147
Stegman, Thomas D., 67
Still, Todd, 115
Stirewalt, Martin, 145

Tamez, Elsa, 80, 82
Tan, Randall K. J., 45
Thiselton, Anthony C., 35, 36, 38, 148
Thompson, James W., 77, 78, 79, 81, 87,
    93, 94, 103, 104
Thompson, Marianne Meye, 61, 62
Thurston, Bonnie B., 77, 78, 79, 85, 86,
    114, 126

Tobin, Thomas H., 15, 23, 132, 136, 147,
    162

Vahoye, Albert, 59
Villiers, Pieter G. R. De, 123
Vincent, Marvin R., 77, 80

Warrior, Valerie M., 15
Watson, Francis, 40, 63, 98, 161
Whittle, Sarah, 22
Wilckens, Ulrich, 138
Williams, Demetrius K., 122
Witherup, Ronald D., 37, 69, 71
Witherington, Ben, III, 23, 138
Wolter, Michael, 127
Wright, N. T., 2, 42, 56, 59, 65, 67